The Life and Death of Gus Reed

Ohio University Press Series on Law, Society, and Politics in the Midwest

SERIES EDITORS: PAUL FINKELMAN AND L. DIANE BARNES

The History of Ohio Law, edited by Michael Les Benedict and John F. Winkler

Frontiers of Freedom: Cincinnati's Black Community, 1802–1868, by Nikki M. Taylor

A Place of Recourse: A History of the U.S. District Court for the Southern District of Ohio, 1803–2003, by Roberta Sue Alexander

The Black Laws: Race and the Legal Process in Early Ohio, by Stephen Middleton

The History of Indiana Law, edited by David J. Bodenhamer and Hon. Randall T. Shepard

The History of Michigan Law, edited by Paul Finkelman and Martin J. Hershock

The Fairer Death: Executing Women in Ohio, by Victor L. Streib

The Rescue of Joshua Glover: A Fugitive Slave, the Constitution, and the Coming of the Civil War, by H. Robert Baker

The History of Nebraska Law, edited by Alan G. Gless

American Pogrom: The East St. Louis Race Riot and Black Politics, by Charles L. Lumpkins

No Winners Here Tonight: Race, Politics, and Geography in One of the Country's Busiest Death Penalty States, by Andrew Welsh-Huggins

Democracy in Session: A History of the Ohio General Assembly, by David M. Gold

The Dred Scott *Case: Historical and Contemporary Perspectives on Race and Law,* edited by David Thomas Konig, Paul Finkelman, and Christopher Alan Bracey

The Jury in Lincoln's America, by Stacy Pratt McDermott

Degrees of Allegiance: Harassment and Loyalty in Missouri's German-American Community during World War I, by Petra DeWitt

Justice and Legal Change on the Shores of Lake Erie: A History of the United States District Court for the Northern District of Ohio, edited by Paul Finkelman and Roberta Sue Alexander

The Life and Death of Gus Reed: A Story of Race and Justice in Illinois during the Civil War and Reconstruction, by Thomas Bahde

Surveillance and Spies in the Civil War: Exposing Confederate Conspiracies in America's Heartland, by Stephen E. Towne

THOMAS BAHDE

The Life and Death of Gus Reed

A STORY OF RACE AND JUSTICE IN ILLINOIS
DURING THE CIVIL WAR AND RECONSTRUCTION

Ohio University Press ~ Athens

Ohio University Press, Athens, Ohio 45701
ohioswallow.com
© 2014 by Ohio University Press
All rights reserved

To obtain permission to quote, reprint, or otherwise reproduce or distribute material from Ohio University Press publications, please contact our rights and permissions department at (740) 593-1154 or (740) 593-4536 (fax).

Printed in the United States of America
Ohio University Press books are printed on acid-free paper ∞ ™

24 23 22 21 20 19 18 17 16 15 14   5 4 3 2 1

Library of Congress Cataloging-in-Publication Data
Bahde, Thomas William.
 The life and death of Gus Reed : a story of race and justice in Illinois during the Civil War and Reconstruction / Thomas Bahde.
   pages cm — (Ohio University Press series on law, society, and politics in the Midwest)
 Includes bibliographical references and index.
 ISBN 978-0-8214-2104-8 (hardback : acid-free paper) — ISBN 978-0-8214-2105-5 (paperback : acid-free paper) — ISBN 978-0-8214-4494-8 (pdf)
 1. Reed, Augustus, 1846?–1878. 2. African Americans—Illinois—Springfield—Biography. 3. Freedmen—Illinois—Springfield—Biography. 4. Springfield (Ill.)—Race relations—History—19th century. 5. African American prisoners—Crimes against—Illinois—History—19th century. 6. African Americans—Legal status, laws, etc.—Illinois—19th century. 7. Discrimination in criminal justice administration—Illinois—History—19th century. 8. Racism—Illinois—History—19th century. 9. Illinois—History—Civil War, 1861–1865. 10. Reconstruction (U.S. history, 1865–1877)—Illinois. I. Title.
 F549.S7B34 2014
 305.896'073077309034—dc23

2014020211

The lives of individuals of the human race form a constant plot, in which every attempt to isolate one piece of living that has a meaning separate from the rest—for example, the meeting of two people, which will become decisive for both—must bear in mind that each of the two brings with himself a texture of events, environments, other people, and that from the meeting, in turn, other stories will be derived which will break off from their common story.

—*Italo Calvino,* If on a winter's night a traveler

CONTENTS

List of Illustrations ix
Acknowledgments xi

Introduction 1

ONE   Georgia Roots 8
TWO   Illinois in Wartime 18
THREE Black Springfield 45
FOUR A White Man's Country 69
FIVE The Underworld 97
SIX   The Penitentiary 122
EPILOGUE Springfield, 1908 154

APPENDIX A Timeline of Known Dates in the Life of Augustus "Gus" Reed 161
APPENDIX B Nativity of Springfield's Black Population, 1860, 1870, 1880 163
APPENDIX C Sangamon County Convicts Sent to Illinois State Penitentiary by Year and Race, 1860–80 164
APPENDIX D Criminal Cases in Sangamon County Circuit Court, 1870–80 165
APPENDIX E Disposition of Criminal Cases (Continuance and Appearance) in Sangamon County Circuit Court, 1870–80 166

Notes 167
Selected Bibliography 207
Index 223

ILLUSTRATIONS

FIGURE 1. Hallway of solitary confinement cells, Illinois State Penitentiary at Joliet, ca. 1890   123

FIGURE 2. A prisoner handcuffed to a cell door in solitary confinement, Illinois State Penitentiary at Joliet, ca. 1890   127

FIGURE 3. Robert W. McClaughry, at the time of his appointment to warden of the Illinois State Penitentiary at Joliet, ca. 1874   140

ACKNOWLEDGMENTS

Giving shape to the world of Gus Reed has been a long and rewarding task. If there is value in the story, it is because friends, colleagues, and mentors have pushed me to find it. At the University of Chicago, Kathleen Conzen was a supportive and inspiring mentor, and her early and unflagging faith in this project was more valuable than she knows. Julie Saville and Jim Grossman often asked questions for which I had no ready answers but trusted also that I would find them. Jonathan Levy, Roman Hoyos, and Gautham Rao all read parts of this work when it was very young, and I am grateful to them for their insights. Alison Lefkovitz and Timothy Stewart-Winter asked questions in workshops, talked with me in hallways, and most importantly, seemed glad to do it. Later, as the book manuscript plodded toward completion, Alison Efford, Daniel Herman, and Stacey Smith all read and provided valuable insight on several chapters in the late stages. Useful correspondence and encouragement were also received along the way from Susan Sessions Rugh, who met Robert McClaughry before I did, and with Roberta Senechal de la Roche. Karen Blair and Daniel Herman provided a forum to discuss my work with the faculty and graduate students of the History Department at Central Washington University; they also gave me their friendship and support. At Oregon State University, I am grateful to Ben Mutschler in the School of History, Philosophy, and Religion and Toni Doolen in the University Honors College for welcoming me so warmly.

I was blessed with outstanding archives in Springfield, Illinois, and equally outstanding archivists and librarians. At the Abraham Lincoln Presidential Library, Glenna Schroeder-Lein, Debbie Hamm, and Cheryl Schnirring always made me feel welcome, and once even shared a slice of cherry pie with me. At the Illinois State Archives, John Reinhard helped me locate records in the Joliet penitentiary files and many other collections, and fielded many long-distance queries. At the University of Illinois at Springfield, archivist John Wood and his staff of graduate students provided me with many heavy carts of court records, and their excellent assistance with remote reference queries saved me a great deal of time and travel. I also owe tremendous thanks to Gillian Berchowitz at Ohio University Press, as well as series editors Paul Finkelman and Diane Barnes, who helped me finish the book with something like sanity and peace of mind.

This work received assistance from a Littleton-Griswold Research Grant from the American Historical Association, a research fellowship from Chicago's Black Metropolis Research Consortium, the King V. Hostick Prize from the Illinois Historic Preservation Agency, and the Martin Dissertation Research Award from Chicago's Union League Civic and Arts Foundation. I am extraordinarily grateful to those organizations for the assistance they provided this project.

Friends and family provided more support than they are likely to know. My father, Bill, and my wife, Anne, made suggestions that materially benefited the manuscript, but their limitless love and support were their most enduring contributions. In fulfillment of a promise made long ago, this work is dedicated to my mother, Barbara, and my grandmother Sara, both of whom were gone long before I began it, but without them it would never have been possible.

Introduction

> Bits of wreckage. Some bones. The words of
> the dead. How make a world of this? How live
> in that world once made?
>
> —*Cormac McCarthy*, The Crossing

AUGUSTUS "GUS" REED died early in the evening of May 7, 1878, his final screams still echoing through the solitary confinement block of the Illinois State Penitentiary. His wrists were shackled to the iron door of his cell and a wooden gag was buckled tightly to his head with leather straps. He had been cuffed to his cell door for two days, shouting as loudly as he could with the gag between his teeth. In an effort to silence him, one of the guards had whipped him with a leather strap, but to no avail. The night he died, Gus Reed screamed so hard and long with the gag in his mouth that his lungs began to hemorrhage, and within a few minutes he drowned in his own blood. The night guards unshackled his body and the next day took it to a makeshift morgue on the prison grounds. After an autopsy was performed, the coroner's jury determined that "persistent yelling with a gag in his mouth" had caused the prisoner's death. The penitentiary's board of commissioners ordered an investigation and listened to two days of testimony from guards, administrators, and doctors. They eventually decided that two guards had been responsible for the prisoner's death. The guards were dismissed; the investigation was closed; and Gus Reed was forgotten.[1]

According to the information he gave most consistently, Gus Reed was born in Georgia and came to Illinois during the Civil War at just eighteen years old.

Penitentiary records described him as "mulatto," but all other sources referred to him simply as "negro," "black," or "colored."[2] He spent most of his twelve years in Illinois in county jails and the state penitentiary, first appearing in the criminal records of Springfield in 1866 for stealing flour from a mill with two other men. In the years before he died, he was in and out of the city's police courts for fighting, and appeared regularly in the circuit court for burglary and larceny. He was sentenced to the state penitentiary three times, and during his relatively brief periods of freedom, may have been the leader of a gang of thieves that roamed central Illinois. When he died in his solitary cell in the spring of 1878, Gus Reed was just thirty-two years old, but his short, hard life spanned some of the most significant events in nineteenth-century America, from the final years of the slave system and the war that brought it to an end, to the flawed reconstruction that shaped the contours of national race relations for more than a century to come. With Gus Reed's unique history to give it shape, this book considers the consequences of the Civil War, emancipation, and Reconstruction in the nation's heartland, and traces the changing influence of race in politics, culture, and criminal justice during the latter half of the nineteenth century.

Taking cues from both biography and social history, this book uses Gus Reed's life as a framework on which to hang a larger story of the evolving relationship between race and justice. This is not biography in a traditional sense, for whereas biography often seeks to paint a portrait of the individual, the task in this book is similar to painting the individual within a landscape—or perhaps, painting a landscape within the individual. Organizing this book around Gus Reed's life and death poses challenges because he left so few historical traces, but it also provides opportunities to connect people, places, and events. Each chapter focuses on topics and themes from Gus Reed's life, but he does not always play a prominent role. We begin, as he did, in antebellum Georgia and then move to wartime Illinois; we make our way to the black community of Springfield and confront, as he did, white resistance to emancipation, civil rights, and black citizenship; we follow him into the criminal underworld and then to the state penitentiary. Through all of this, people and events about which he knew little if anything shaped his world, and so they also shape this narrative.[3]

Gus Reed's encounters, or near-encounters, with two individuals in Illinois were particularly significant in shaping what we know of his life and death. In the autumn of 1877 he stole some meat from the house of a well-known Springfield attorney named Elliott Herndon, brother of William Herndon, last law partner of Abraham Lincoln. For this, he was sent to the penitentiary for the third and final time in the spring of 1878. Elliott Herndon, unlike his brother, was a staunch Democrat who advocated the preservation of slavery where it existed and appealed to the white citizens of Illinois to keep their civil and political institutions free from the contagion of black citizenship and suffrage. Elliott Herndon and his fellow Democrats strove to exclude southern blacks like Gus Reed, rootless young men set loose from the restraining bonds of slavery that now threatened the stability and integrity of a state founded by and for white men. Concerns about black criminality were especially effective in stirring the prejudices of white voters during the decade after emancipation because crime seemed to have become a national epidemic. Penitentiary officials and criminologists developed new ways to track, profile, and reform criminals as public demand for more effective incarceration intensified. At the forefront of this work was Robert Wilson McClaughry, warden of the Illinois State Penitentiary when Gus Reed died.

Robert McClaughry had been the editor of a Democratic newspaper in Hancock County until he joined the army in 1862 and became major of the 118th Illinois Infantry, later serving as an army paymaster in Springfield. Like many Democrats who volunteered, McClaughry's wartime service led him to join the Republican Party before the war's end. His new political affiliation probably helped him gain an appointment to the wardenship at Joliet and later to the post of police commissioner in Chicago during the World's Columbian Exposition. McClaughry was part of a new generation of penologists and criminologists in the vanguard of reforming the criminal justice system. He introduced the first English translation of French criminologist Alphonse Bertillon's system of anthropometry—body measurement—to identify repeat offenders. As criminal anthropology gained followers in the 1890s, Bertillon and other anthropometric systems were used to identify known criminals and to classify the physical traits of certain criminal types in order to establish physiological criteria by which varieties of criminal could be distinguished. Racial theorists found support in this data for their own ideas about the inherent criminality of certain races. By the turn of the century, a broad consensus had developed that blacks were both biologically and culturally doomed to an unavoidable descent into vice and criminality. The science of criminology thus seemed to validate the popular suspicions and prejudices that had motivated Illinoisans and other Americans to resist emancipation, citizenship, suffrage, and civil rights for African Americans during the Civil War and Reconstruction. Gus Reed's crimes, convictions, and multiple incarcerations led to his connection with Elliott Herndon and Robert McClaughry. Herndon and McClaughry were linked to each other through their participation in Democratic politics in Illinois, and all three men experienced and helped shape the legal, political, and cultural consequences of the Civil War in the latter half of the nineteenth century.

The year Gus Reed left Georgia for Illinois, Union general William Tecumseh Sherman marched his army from Atlanta to the sea, leaving the wreckage of the state's slave economy in his wake, and amassing a following of freed people. Whether it was Sherman's march, or another experience with the dissolution of the slave system, something set Gus Reed in motion toward the Midwest. Although Illinois was not a theater of the war, it was nevertheless contested terrain in the ongoing national struggle over emancipation, black rights, and the future of US citizenship. Some believed that a vast conspiracy threatened to throw the state into open warfare, while others feared the wartime expansion of federal authority and the nullification or circumvention of state laws that restricted black residence and citizenship. Throughout the war, the question of whether to strengthen or abolish the state's Black Laws kept the conflict's racial undercurrent foremost in the minds of the people. By entering Illinois when he did, Gus Reed carried the consequences of emancipation into a state struggling mightily with its own racial demons.

Reconstruction was a long national process that took unique shapes depending on time and place. In Illinois, as in many other places throughout the Midwest, it meant a vigorous contest over the nature of citizenship and civil rights in a society that had ostensibly been shaped by and for white men. Many of the legal, political, and cultural assumptions regarding race in Illinois before 1865 seemed to collapse, and it was not clear what would take their place. The Reconstruction era in Illinois was characterized by attempts to make sense of the changes wrought by the Civil War and face the dissolution of foundational assumptions that had guided much of the state's lawmaking for the preceding half-century. Most significant, the war set the context in which Illinoisans encountered the consequences of emancipation and black citizenship. They had already endured decades of debate, controversy, and even violence and bloodshed as they tried to work out who belonged, who did not, and how best to define and enforce those boundaries.[4] The end of the war made these questions as central for Illinoisans as for Southerners. As Abraham Lincoln observed in 1864, the Reconstruction government in Louisiana had already produced a new constitution that was "better for the poor black man than we have in Illinois."[5] The Black Laws were not repealed until 1865, and it was not until 1870 that a new constitution finally struck the last of the old racial exclusions from the state's organic law. It was no coincidence that these dates corresponded with the first and last of the Reconstruction amendments, for Illinois in its way was as badly in need of reconstruction as the Southern states.

Much of this book centers on the city of Springfield in Sangamon County, and also on Hancock County in western Illinois. The latter was the home of Robert McClaughry, and it was also one of the state's Democratic strongholds. Like every other county in the state, Hancock County was ideologically divided by the Civil War, even as its soldiers fought and died for the Union. But the divisions were not clean or immutable; the war and its immediate aftermath brought deeply confusing and unsettling changes to local politics, community identity, and popular notions of law and order. Springfield was also divided by the war and, of course, was home to Abraham and Mary Todd Lincoln before they departed for Washington, DC, in February 1861. Shortly after his assassination, it became the final resting place of the Great Emancipator. No other city in the nation experienced the war and its aftermath in quite the same way, but Lincoln's presence was not the only thing that gave Springfield a unique place in Reconstruction America. As the capital, the city was at the center of the state's contentious politics and was frequently in the national spotlight even before the presidential election of 1860. Because politicians and political contingents from all over the state flocked to Springfield, the statehouse, the streets of the city, and the columns of the newspapers were stages on which legal, political, and cultural performances took place before a national audience. Springfield also sat geographically and ideologically on a broad line that divided Illinois into a traditionally antislavery north and proslavery south for much of the nineteenth century. The city was central in several significant respects to Illinois's struggle with race and the consequences of emancipation, and it was emblematic of broader experiences with these contentious issues.

Springfield is also where Gus Reed spent most of his time as a free man and a thief after his arrival in Illinois. He may have had family there, part of the diasporic community of southern blacks who arrived during and after the Civil War. Gus Reed's story is thus interwoven with the history of the postemancipation black migration into the Midwest. Tens of thousands of southern blacks moved north in the years following emancipation, the largest such migration to date. Illinois's black population more than tripled between 1860 and 1870, just as the Black Laws were repealed and the question of blacks' legal status remained uncertain. As historian Leslie Schwalm has noted: "For Midwesterners whose understanding of white supremacy had been premised on the right and ability to exclude first Indian people and then African Americans from the region, the physical mobility of former slaves suggested an unwelcome change in racial boundaries and practices in a post-slavery nation."[6] This mobility revitalized both the existing black communities in the Midwest and the race prejudice of many whites. The new arrivals forced the issue of black citizenship, not only politically, but also socially and culturally within communities such as Springfield that saw local black populations increase rapidly. The reaction to black migration and the growth of black communities in the postbellum decade did much to shape the national response to race for more than a century to come.

Placing Illinois and the Midwest at the center of a story about the Civil War and Reconstruction situates this work within a historiographical shift that is moving west from Appomattox and toward a "Greater Reconstruction" that extends beyond familiar geographical and historical boundaries. Like Elliott West's examination of the Nez Perce War of 1877, this book finds that the issues that characterized the Reconstruction of the states of the former Confederacy also shaped nationwide concerns and debates about federal authority, citizenship, and race. Although historians continue to examine the national repercussions of Reconstruction, other states and regions are often positioned as reacting to policies and politics that were primarily oriented toward the South. But Americans everywhere participated in their own unique reconstructions that refigured and reconfigured many of their antebellum legal, political, and cultural norms, especially concerning race and the role of African Americans in the nation. An examination of Gus Reed's world allows us to consider the problems of race and justice within the national heartland, where legal, political, and cultural influences from both North and South shaped a region that came to stand for mainstream America. Gus Reed's is one of many stories about one of the many reconstructions that took place here. It suggests a way of understanding the intertwined regional and national impacts of the Civil War and emancipation, as well as the beginnings of a widespread retrenchment against African American citizenship and civil rights in the decades that followed.[7]

White midwesterners who were uncomfortable with free blacks before and during the Civil War remained so in its wake.[8] For many, emancipation and the gradual advance of civil and suffrage rights deepened old animosities and raised new concerns. The postwar resistance to black citizenship grew especially out of wartime critiques made by Democrats, who advanced white supremacist rhetoric to defend bastions of white privilege and exclusivity.[9] Although these critiques did not gain lasting electoral traction in national politics after the Civil War, they nevertheless shaped attitudes toward race for the next century. The political calculations of Republicans and Democrats produced electoral consequences, but they also shaped and were shaped by popular notions of democracy, community, and justice. For most Americans, the politics of race was inseparable from, even inconceivable without, the real and significant repercussions on the streets of their cities and towns.

The durability of antebellum concepts of blackness, conceits of citizenship, and tactics of political rhetoric was part of the midwestern story, and the broader American story, of the late nineteenth century. Understanding how this troubling legacy gave shape and precedent to a nationwide epidemic of racial violence at the turn of the century helps us understand why race persisted throughout twentieth-century thinking about crime and why it continues to be part of an ongoing national conversation about crime and justice. Discussions and debates regarding black criminality circulated within legal, political, social, and cultural spaces. The race problem was linked to the crime problem, as well as to deeper concerns about the nature of the body politic. With the rise of professional criminology and the apparent confirmation of black criminality, popular feeling on race and crime joined with the authority of professional judgment, and the decades after the Civil War laid the ideological groundwork that led many white midwesterners and other Americans to turn violently against their black neighbors around the turn of the century.[10]

The night he died, Gus Reed uttered his only recorded words. With a wooden gag between his teeth and his wrists chained to his cell door, he shouted his own name—wildly, urgently, loudly—over and over, until his lungs hemorrhaged from the effort and he slumped against the cold iron bars and bare stones of his solitary cell. Whether it was a mad, desperate assertion of identity and agency in his last few moments, or a final cry for help, it echoes still in what follows. Gus Reed's life and death were not quiet, but their sound died against the greater roar of history. This book proposes that Gus Reed need not remain imprisoned by the silences that surround him in the historical record and that even a life like his can help us see the history with which it was interwoven with fresh perspective and new insight. With his final breath and his only recorded words, Gus Reed reminds us how acutely opaque any long-dead historical subject must remain. Bits and pieces are all that remain to suggest who Gus Reed may have been and why he lived as he did, but we can hang stories on his bones and gather around him the wreckage of the past and the words of the dead, and from it all we can make a history that tells something about the world as it was and the world as it is.

ONE

Georgia Roots

> Learned us to steal, that's what they done.
>
> —*Robert Falls, former slave*

BEFORE GUS REED was first incarcerated in 1869, little information about him is available. He was illiterate for most of his life, although he could apparently "read a little" by 1878. Beyond his final words, nothing he said was ever verifiably recorded, and he neither wrote his signature nor made an "X" on any known court or prison documents. When he was received at the Joliet penitentiary for the last time in March 1878, the admitting clerk completed a form that provides the most detailed information we have about him, and a few other details about his physical appearance were revealed after his death. At five feet six inches, he was of average height. His hair was black, and his eyes were dark brown. Several prominent scars on his body told of a rough life: on his left hand, a scar ran from the first joint of his little finger into his palm, another ran down from his third finger; on his right hand, there was a small scar near the end of his index finger. On his head, there was a scar above his left ear and "a very plain scar" on the back of his head. The doctors who performed his autopsy remarked that he had otherwise been in good health except for the injuries sustained at the penitentiary, and one newspaper called him "strong and muscular." After his death, in a graphic imagining of his last desperate moments, the *Chicago Tribune* believed that the wooden gag forced into his mouth had done greater harm because he had only a few teeth and could not prevent the gag from slipping farther into his mouth.[1]

The only other thing we know with any certainty about Gus Reed is where he was born. When he was first processed at the Illinois State Penitentiary in 1869, he told the clerk that he had been born in Georgia. At that time, he said he had already been in Illinois for five years. The age he most often gave would have meant that he was probably born in 1846. Beyond that, we know nothing certain about what his life was like as a child and adolescent. We do not know the names of his parents or any other family members by which to trace him. We do not know exactly where he was born, or whether he was free or enslaved. Records about him, if any were made, would have been sparse or ambiguous in either case. There were few chances for him to be verifiably recorded as a child, especially if he was enslaved, since slaves' surnames were seldom acknowledged. If he were free, he would have held no property as a child, and even if he had committed petty crimes, he would likely have been punished outside the formal channels of the criminal justice system. Because he left Georgia before the end of the Civil War, he is also absent from the records created by the Freedmen's Bureau and other federal agencies, and he does not appear in the military or pension records of the Union army. In some respect, he enters the historical record only once he enters Illinois. But although we do not know precisely how and where he lived, an inquiry into his Georgia roots opens an exploration into black childhood and adolescence in the slave South, and the experiences and possibilities that confronted him suggest the frames of reference that guided him as he undertook the momentous and life-changing journey out of the state.[2]

Gus Reed may have grown up in any number of places and circumstances, but chances are good that he was born into slavery. According to the 1850 census, slaves made up 42 percent of Georgia's total population, while free blacks made up less than one half of 1 percent. If he was indeed born a slave, it is likely that he grew up in the agricultural countryside.[3] He would have been put to work even before adolescence tending chickens, hogs, and gardens and toting water, firewood, victuals, and messages to masters and overseers. If he performed such work, he might have learned the relative value of the goods in the pantry and smokehouse. He may even have pilfered a piece of ham or a handful of meal on his trips to and from the larder.

Slave childhood was contentious terrain. As Marie Jenkins Schwartz observes of enslaved children: "Theirs was a world in which the lines of authority were murky.... Children under these circumstances could find themselves in a precarious position, needing to understand and to separate the requirements of owners and parents."[4] Enslaved children learned to value obedience but also developed an understanding of how and under what circumstances it was permissible to disobey. They quickly learned the nuances and boundaries of authority and, as they grew, undoubtedly discerned gaps that could be exploited to their advantage. Children learned to negotiate the complex roles expected of them from the adults in their lives, and they formed their own ideas of slavery and mastery, honor and authority. For Gus Reed's generation, the national crisis of the 1860s corresponded with their own coming of age, and had significant implications in their own lives that caused them to strike out and make their own way through the fraying edges of a system they had already learned to exploit.

Gus Reed was fifteen years old when he became a resident of the Confederate States of America in January 1861 and eighteen when he left the state. Whether he was enslaved or free, the already strict limits placed on him would have become more onerous, as laws restricting the activities of free blacks and prohibiting slave travel became harsher during the antebellum decade. Adolescence would likely have been a troubled time for him even if war had not already begun to destabilize the slave system. If he was a slave, the uncertainty of sale away from his home place and family, more demanding labor, and perhaps even his own personal yearnings for freedom coincided with the disruption of the first three years of the war. We do not know how long he bided his time before leaving Georgia, or what finally put him in motion, but when General William Tecumseh Sherman made his celebrated march across the state in 1864, he had apparently decided to move on.[5]

The war disrupted daily life in the coastal areas of Georgia from the beginning, as the federal blockade and the potential for further Union invasion kept the population on edge. The Union-held sea islands off the coast provided a tempting goal for slaves in the adjacent counties and cities, including Savannah, and Confederate troops along the coast became what historian Clarence L. Mohr has referred to as a "gigantic slave patrol . . . charged both with regulating black passage in and out of Savannah and, more important, with preventing black escapes."[6] The entire state underwent a sort of upheaval as white patrols organized to combat imagined slave rebellions and keep potential runaways on their plantations scoured the countryside. The activities of what slaves called "pater-rollers" in the antebellum era took on a more vital law-and-order function, as the slaveholders' social order came under siege. Mob action against alleged fugitives and black criminals in cities like Savannah increasingly raised the specter of a war at home while the Confederate armies fought the Yankees.[7]

When Union soldiers arrived with General Sherman in 1864, many slaves who encountered them readily put down their tools, packed up their belongings, and joined the marching columns. As they marched through Georgia, Sherman's soldiers continued a practice they had learned throughout their campaigns in the war's western theater, scouring the southern countryside for food and supplies. This meant stripping both slaves' garden patches and the masters' fields and orchards. To the soldiers, such was their due for the blood and treasure they had already sacrificed to put down the rebellion. Few probably realized that the rationale they used to excuse their own larceny was similar to that used by slaves to resist and subsist within the slave South.

It is probable that Gus Reed was exposed to some amount of theft as an adolescent. He would have been aware of how stolen goods circulated in the illicit economy of cooperation between enslaved blacks and poor whites, and he would have learned what was valuable, to whom, and how best to dispose of it. The historian Timothy Lockley has observed of slave theft in Georgia that "a significant part of the trade between rural bondspeople and white shopkeepers involved goods stolen from the plantation or the mansion house," and "the complicity and encouragement of white shopkeepers was of vital importance in enabling slaves to retail stolen goods."[8] Gus Reed might also have learned to value theft for more than its economic or subsistence benefits. The historian Jeff Forret has noted of the illegal commerce between whites and enslaved blacks that "slaves could enjoy a fleeting moment of empowerment as they transacted business. . . . The choices they made in the underground marketplace affected their own lives and inherently marked a denial of their enslaved condition."[9] By simply interacting with poor whites, he would have participated in a subversion of the racial order imposed by elite slaveholders. Black and white socialization among those near the bottom of the economic hierarchy imperiled the racially ordered society slaveholders wanted to create.

Slave theft was considered one of the antebellum South's most pernicious problems, so much so that one white visitor observed that "the fear of theft haunts the slave holder at all times and in all places."[10] Some whites believed that thievery was endemic to all blacks, enslaved or free, while others speculated that the conditions of slavery produced an altered morality peculiar to the enslaved. A North Carolina slaveholder expressed the widespread belief that "there is one fact incident to negro slaves—they *will steal.* . . . Stealing is common to all negro slaves."[11] Even an antislavery writer in distant Illinois observed matter-of-factly that "negroes are middling light fingered."[12] A former slave from Oglethorpe County, Georgia, observed simply: "A nigger is jus' bound to pick up chickens and eggs effen he kin. . . . He jus' can't help it."[13] Another former slave offered a similar opinion: "You know some Niggers gwine steal anyhow."[14]

In his *Notes on the State of Virginia*, Thomas Jefferson suggested that slave theft was a unique variety of larceny, noting: "That disposition to theft with which they have been branded, must be ascribed to their situation, and not to any depravity of the moral sense." Indeed, said Jefferson, "The man, in whose favor no laws of property exist, probably feels himself less bound to respect those made in favor of others." Observing the slaveholder's tendency to condemn slaves for stealing, Jefferson asked "whether the slave may not as justifiably take a little from one who has taken all from him, as he may slay one who would slay him?" Broadening the moral dimensions of the issue, Jefferson even noted: "That a change in the relations in which a man is placed should change his ideas of moral right and wrong, is neither new nor peculiar to the color of the blacks."[15] Similarly, placing the blame on the institution of slavery as a corrupter of the morals of enslaved people, a federal official in charge of the contraband camp in Mississippi during the Civil War observed that "many [former slaves] are dishonest—the result of a system which compels them to steal from their masters."[16] The notion that the conditions of slavery created an altered morality was most eloquently phrased by former Georgia slave John Brown, who recalled: "We felt we were living under a system of cheating, and lying, and deceit, and being taught no better, we grew up in it, and did not see the wrong of it."[17] In her antebellum plantation diary, Georgia resident Frances Kemble remarked similarly on the morality of slave theft: "After all, it is very natural these people should steal a little of our meat from us occasionally, who steal almost all their bread from them habitually."[18] Frederick Douglass stated flatly of his own experience with theft: "The morality of free society could have no application to slave society."[19]

Many former slaves characterized theft either as a necessity or as part of the complex slave/owner relationship. Some claimed that nothing was ever stolen, whereas others remembered stealing chickens, eggs, hogs, and vegetables, but only in order to supplement meager plantation diets. John Brown remembered, "If we did not steal, we could scarcely live."[20] Another former slave recalled simply: "Come down to chicken—if you got it you stole it."[21] Others remembered that their masters induced them to steal from other slaveholders. Isaiah Green claimed that "some of de white folks would learn you how to steal fum other folks. Sometimes ol' marster would say to one o' us: 'Blast you—you better go out an' hunt me a hog tonight an' put it in my smokehouse—dey can search you niggers' houses but dey can't search mine."[22] With this double standard in place, exhortations against slave theft rang hollow. Tom Hawkins recalled that the slaves on his plantation attended a church with "our white folks" where the preacher told them: "It's a sin to steal; don't steal Marster's and Mist'ess' chickens and hogs; 'an' sech lak." Hawkins reflected, "How could anybody be converted on dat kind of preachin'? And 'sides it never helped none . . . 'cause de stealin' kept goin' right on evvy night."[23]

Slaves employed a subversive logic regarding theft from their own masters that turned their enslavement into a sort of exculpatory advantage. John Brown "never considered it wicked to steal, because I looked upon what I took as part of what was due to me for my labour."[24] Shang Harris of Stephens County, Georgia, summarized the issue of slave theft more articulately than most when he observed: "Dey talks a heap 'bout de niggers stealin.' Well, you know what was de fust stealin' done? Hit was in Afriky, when de white folks stole de niggers."[25] Historians have referred to these justifications for theft as part of the "moral economy" of enslaved people. Slaves were aware that the social order in which they lived considered theft a crime; indeed, they did not steal *despite* knowing it was a crime, but *because* they knew it to be a crime. Theft thus operated in active opposition to a legal culture that sanctioned human bondage, yet condemned the theft of a chicken, a barrel of flour, or a few pounds of bacon.[26] It was both subversion and subsistence, weighted differently in different situations, and although it was acknowledged to be legally and perhaps even morally wrong, it was nevertheless also considered fair.

The complicated moral dimensions of the theft question were ably expressed by the distinction many former slaves described between "stealing" and "taking," the latter meaning theft from one's own master, the former implying larceny within the slave community. Recalling a long list of offenses for which slaves were beaten to death, the Reverend W. B. Allen of Columbus, Georgia, included "Taking things—the whites called it stealing."[27] John Brown recalled that theft was considered acceptable by slaves "so long as we were not acting against one another. . . . Any one of us who would have thought nothing of stealing a hog, or a sack of corn, from our master, would have allowed himself to be cut to pieces rather than betray the confidence of his fellow-slave." Brown was quick to add: "Perhaps, my mentioning this fact may be taken as a set-off against the systematic deception we practiced, in self-defence, on our master."[28] The sense of moral justice implied by the term "taking" indicates that slaves operated on the assumption that such activity served more as a kind of redistribution of rightly shared and much-needed resources rather than as an activity that materially damaged the owner. When a slave in Alabama confessed in 1855 to taking a turkey from his master, he described this redistributive concept simply: "When I tuk the turkey and eat it, it got to be part of me." One piece of his master's property was transfigured into another.²⁹ Slaves thus acknowledged varieties of theft, excusing those that damaged their masters as morally justified, while condemning those that damaged their own slave community.

The arrival of Yankee soldiers, plundering plantations in their march across the South, added a new dimension to these rationalizations. Former slaves recalled that blue-coated soldiers carried off everything they could from slave cabins and plantation houses, drove away livestock, and raided smokehouses and vegetable patches. "I 'members dem Yankees comin' down de big road a-stealin' as dey went 'long," recalled a former Georgia slave. "Dem Yankees stole all de meat, chickens, and good bedclothes and burnt down de houses."³⁰ Samuel Elliot testified after the war: "When they came there and began to take my things I asked them 'Massa' you going to take all, and leave me nothing to live on, and they said we are obliged to, we come to set you free, and we must have something to eat." According to Elliot, the Union soldiers even "took my pants and coat and all. They did not leave me a thing."³¹ Former slave Nancy Johnson likewise testified that Union soldiers took all of the property belonging to her and her husband and killed all of her chickens because "they wouldn't believe I could have such things." Johnson remembered that she could not believe "a Yankee person would be so mean."³² What they did not steal themselves, soldiers encouraged slaves to steal, as they were now entitled to the produce and prosperity they had helped create for their masters. "Dey said slaves was all freed from bondage and told us to jus' take anything and evvything us wanted from de big house and all 'round de plantation whar us lived," recalled Alice Green; "Dem thievin' sojers even picked up one of de babies and started off wid it."³³

For former slaves, the theft committed by Union soldiers seemed unambiguously wrong, even though it was carried out as part of the war that liberated them. Their notions of the value of theft cannot be wholly reduced to an alternate moral economy that functioned as a feeble corrective to wrongs perpetrated by the structures of a slaveholding society. They heard exhortations from white ministers and their own black lay preachers that stealing was wrong, and they were whipped and jailed for stealing; yet they were encouraged by their masters to steal from neighboring plantations, and they witnessed Yankee soldiers rifling through the master's house and the slave cabins with equal zeal, at one and the same moment appearing as liberators and looters. Theft thus accompanied and embodied both acts of virtue and of vice, acts of resistance and subsistence. When Gus Reed left Georgia, he brought with him this complicated set of beliefs regarding the utility, legality, and morality of theft.

Growing up in the slave South did not make him a thief, but it very likely gave him an understanding of theft that would set him at odds with those who viewed it with less ambiguity.[34]

Like many others, Gus Reed did not wait to find out what life would be like in postemancipation Georgia. He and thousands of others walked away from the homes they had known, hoping to reach a Union camp or patrol. As many as 19,000 black refugees followed General Sherman's army on its march to Savannah, and Gus Reed could very easily have been among these before he decided to turn north and west. Doing so might have meant abandoning his parents, friends, and other family members, but perhaps the attractions of freedom outweighed these considerations.[35] If he made a conscious decision to head for Illinois, he probably moved along river networks that connected larger cities and larger free black populations. He could have boarded with black families, or in lodging houses run by sympathetic whites, and he may have been quietly secreted in a porter's cart or aboard a riverboat. Even on the river, however, the way was not always clear. As nurse and relief worker Mary Livermore steamed up the Mississippi and Ohio rivers during the war, she witnessed "half-imbruted contrabands . . . under military *surveillance,* clad in the tattered gray and black 'nigger cloth,' and shod with the clouted brogans of the plantation." Livermore recalled between three and four hundred former slaves crowding into the middle deck of the riverboat, "going forth, like the Israelites, 'from the land of bondage to a land they knew not.'" Already full to capacity, Livermore's boat could not stop to pick up another large group of "negroes, of all sizes" that had gathered along the banks. When Livermore was asked to conduct a young black boy into Illinois to reunite with his mother in Chicago, she was warned by a member of the Illinois legislature, who cautioned, "You will run great risk in undertaking to carry a negro boy through Illinois." As Livermore explained, "The infamous 'Black Laws' of Illinois were then in force, and any one who took a negro into the state was liable . . . to heavy fine and imprisonment. Under the stimulus of a most senseless and rabid Negrophobia, then at fever heat, the provost-marshal at Cairo [Illinois] searched every Northern-bound train for negroes, as well as deserters. Whenever they were found, they were arrested; the former were sent to the contraband camp, an abandoned, comfortless, God-forsaken place."[36]

The Union army's decision to consider blacks as human contraband of war contributed substantially to the growth of Illinois's black population during the war. A nearly universal wartime term for black refugees from the South, the word "contraband" carried loaded meanings for both advocates and opponents of emancipation. The term could be used to refer to "menacing migrants, the butt of jokes, citizen-soldiers in the making, ideal free laborers, objects of pity and reform, or avatars of racial uplift," depending on the context.[37] The term signified a period of transition in the popular conception of black Americans. No longer clearly slaves but not yet entirely free, contraband blacks occupied an ambiguous status in the minds of Northern whites and free blacks alike. For the latter especially, the term came loaded with a mixture of both positive and negative connotations. While some used the term disparagingly to distinguish between themselves and unsophisticated former slaves, others took the term to signal a more hopeful postslavery future and readily took refugees into their homes and communities.

Some whites also welcomed refugee former slaves. Illinois soldiers serving in the South wrote to their families that runaway slaves were flocking to their camps and were eager to find new homes in the North. Francis Moore of Quincy, serving with the 2nd Illinois Cavalry across the Mississippi River from Cairo, wrote that runaway slaves "persist in thinking that we are their friends and have come to deliver them from bondage." Moore reported that his company regularly helped blacks escape across the river into Illinois under cover of night, and he even sent his black cook home to his family in direct violation of the Black Laws.[38] Albert Chipman of Kankakee County, serving in the 76th Illinois Infantry, likewise disregarded the laws when he advised his wife: "If you want a she contraband you must send with the others and get one. I have no chance to send one from here. You can see by the papers how they do it."[39] A farmer in Grundy County wrote to Governor Richard Yates to ask if he could obtain contrabands for farm labor: "I would like to get one female and two males," he wrote, and "there is a number of good farmers in this vicinity who wish to obtain some of both sex and would pay them liberally and treat them kindly."[40]

Other parts of Illinois dealt not with a shortage of black refugees, but an influx. In December 1863, a committee of women in Quincy formed an impromptu relief organization for the contraband refugees who were entering from Missouri in "great numbers entirely destitute of every thing." The committee informed Governor Yates that refugees were arriving in "such numbers that it will be difficult for the Ladies to keep them from dying from hunger and cold unless they receive some assistance."[41] Because of the Black Laws, Yates could offer no such assistance, nor could his successor Richard Oglesby, who wrote in 1865 that he could "only aid them by bringing to the notice of our people unofficially their circumstances of want and care." With benign indifference, Oglesby added, "I hope however they will soon be able and learn to rely upon their own efforts for support and maintenance."[42] Beyond necessities like food, clothing, and shelter, black migrants wanted little else other than to be allowed to rely upon themselves. For most, the opportunity to do so was among their primary reasons for landing on Illinois's shores or crossing its borders during the war.

Gus Reed probably entered Illinois at a larger town like Cairo in the south, or Quincy in the west, where he could have joined the growing camps of black refugees. We do not know his first destination once he stepped foot on free soil, and indeed, we do not know what he did or where he went for his first two years in the state. He is absent from the records of Springfield—where he would later make his home—until 1866, when he was first apprehended for stealing. He might have tried to earn a living by legal means in those first two years. He was a strong young man, and there was no shortage of either farm work or unskilled city work to be done, so long as he avoided attracting the wrong kind of attention. But because of the Black Laws, Gus Reed's mere presence made him an outlaw for the first year he lived in Illinois, and even after the laws were repealed in 1865, his status in the state was uncertain. He was no longer an illegal migrant, but neither was he a citizen. As Illinois struggled with the significant question of who belonged in the state and who did not, recent black migrants from the South found themselves in the midst of a contentious struggle for the future of the state. Had Gus Reed known the troubled history of race relations in his new home, he might have thought twice about staying.

TWO

Illinois in Wartime

> The indifference of many and hostility of some
> of my acquaintances made me apprehensive
> that, before the struggle would end, even
> Illinois might be the theater of civil conflict.
>
> —*John M. Palmer, governor of
> Illinois, 1869–73*

NEWS OF Abraham Lincoln's assassination reached Springfield in the early hours of April 15, 1865. Riders departed on every road to bear the sad news to the rural reaches of Sangamon County. Patriotic bunting had hung from the statehouse for only one week in celebration of the war's end, and was replaced now with somber black as Lincoln's hometown prepared to receive the body of an assassinated president, a friend, and a neighbor. Both the Democratic *Illinois State Register* and the Republican *Illinois State Journal* ran black-edged columns and enormous headlines of heavy black type to announce the assassination and mark the journey of the funeral train. When it arrived in Springfield, Lincoln's body was taken to the statehouse, where it lay until the funeral procession to Oak Ridge Cemetery on May 4. A Springfield resident wrote: "Springfield wears a mournful appearance since President Lincoln was shot. . . . The State-House was fixed up in Splendid stile [sic], it being draped in mourning clear to the top of the dome. A great many people were here Wednesday to see the funeral train come in and Thursday the city was crowded and jammed full to attend the funeral."[1] The *Journal* estimated that the city of 15,000 had swelled to over 150,000 by the time the train arrived. To meet the needs of the huge crowd, a committee that included Lincoln's former law partner William Herndon called on the farmers of Sangamon County "having provisions and edibles for sale" to bring "large quantities of the same, of every description, and also . . . quantities of good dry straw, for sale at the market house, and also . . . on the day of the funeral cooked provisions for sale in their wagons."[2] Local farmer Philemon Stout paid one dollar and fifty cents for mourning badges for his family and witnessed "the largest prosession [sic] and the most pomp and display I ever saw." Stout, a Democrat who had voted for Stephen Douglas in 1860, was disappointed that the speeches at the funeral were "very eloquent but ultra abolition."[3] The city's black residents, many of whom could not afford mourning attire or the memorial trinkets offered for sale, tied or pinned scraps of black cloth to their sleeves, hats, or breasts. At the rear of the funeral procession, Lincoln's longtime friend and barber William Florville led a delegation of local blacks, having declined a more prestigious place near the front of the procession. A correspondent from the *New York Daily Tribune* wrote of Lincoln: "With his companionable nature and open heart it follows that he was the personal acquaintance and friend of all the men, women, and children in the city, and in all the region round about."[4]

Among the crowd gathered for Lincoln's funeral procession were two men with quite different understandings of the assassinated president's significance. For Major Robert McClaughry, stationed in Springfield as an assistant paymaster, the sight of the city's black residents in deep mourning was emblematic of Lincoln's uncertain legacy: "They well knew that their greatest friend was passing to his rest, and the future seemed dark enough to their vision."[5] Local attorney and Democratic activist Elliott Herndon cared little about such things when he later wrote of Lincoln: "I believe myself wholly indifferent as to the future of his memory. . . . The adulation of base multitudes . . . and the pageantry and hypocarcy [sic] surrounding a dead President does not shake my well settled convictions of the mans [sic] mental caliber. . . . There may have been many now and forever resting in oblivion which might have confirmed my opinion."[6] The two men were emblematic of the range of reactions with which Illinoisans and other Americans confronted the challenge of emancipation and the possibility of black citizenship during Reconstruction. Both were Democrats in 1860, but McClaughry had turned Republican before war's end, while Herndon burrowed deeper into the racial and political principles that lay at the core of the Illinois Democratic Party. For McClaughry, sympathy and fellow feeling with blacks grew from his military service; while for Herndon, Lincoln's eventual embrace of emancipation consigned the president to a well-deserved infamy and the nation to an unhappy future of racial strife.

Gus Reed may also have been among the crowd in Springfield to witness Lincoln's funeral procession. He probably appreciated the gravity of the situation as much as anyone, but he likely did not see his future any differently with Abraham Lincoln dead or alive. We do not know for sure what drew him to Springfield, whether it was family, friends, opportunity, or chance. Freedom from slavery, or escape from the South, must have initially seemed a blessing, but once in Springfield, Reed likely realized that even the legacy of a man now celebrated as a martyr would make little real difference to the conditions of his own life in Illinois. The year Gus Reed arrived, the state's supreme court decided that laws passed in 1853 permitting the arrest and public sale of black migrants violated neither the state's prohibition on slavery nor the federal Fugitive Slave Act. Like many others, Gus Reed initially faced the threat of involuntary servitude and the assumption of criminality just for being black in Illinois. Even after the repeal of the Black Laws, there were many in Springfield who believed that the mere presence of blacks fundamentally damaged the social fabric of a free state founded by and for whites. Stephen Douglas spoke for many Illinoisans when he declared before Congress in 1856: "Our people are a white people. . . . Our State is a white state."[7] Douglas was dead before the end of the war, but the sentiment he expressed remained alive and well. Democrats combined the threat of black equality with allegations of a wartime Republican assault on civil liberties and states' rights. Federal policies that seemed to encourage black migration to Illinois in violation of the Black Laws allowed them to phrase their appeals in overtly racial tones. In Springfield, as with other places across the nation, the conflict that came to a head during the war years had been growing steadily toward a climax for over a decade.

Springfield in the 1850s presented an inauspicious profile for new arrivals. Although it grew from fewer than 5,000 people in 1850 to nearly 10,000 in 1860, it remained a town dominated by politics and agriculture. In 1860 young attorney John Hay, who would soon become Lincoln's personal secretary and later an influential statesman, complained about being "a second rate lawyer in a country town," and on another occasion said that he felt stranded "on the dreary wastes of Springfield—a city combining the meanness of the North with the barbarism of the South."[8] Hay likely referred to the same persistent race prejudice that led the *National Anti-Slavery Standard* to criticize Springfield as "a place after the heart of the slave-catchers," because of the frequency with which alleged fugitive slaves were captured there. The *Standard* even chided: "Illinois is usually reckoned a *Free* State, but occurrences like this would seem to indicate that she is on the other side of the line." In the opinion of the *Atlantic Monthly* in 1858, in Springfield and elsewhere, there was "still too large an infusion of the cruel slavery spirit in the laws of Illinois."[9]

Local Democrats such as Elliott Herndon were better pleased by Springfield's reputation. Elliott and his brother William were sons of Kentucky migrants Archer and Rebecca Herndon. Archer Herndon had served as a Democratic member of the state legislature in 1836, and he was active as one of the elders of the Springfield Democratic Party until he died in 1867. Springfield's *Illinois State Register* eulogized him as "an ardent and uncompromising [D]emocrat."[10] A later history of Sangamon County added that "an Abolitionist, in his eyes, was a man not to be trusted in any capacity."[11] William abandoned his father's Democratic partisanship when he went off to Illinois College, but Elliott remained steadfastly committed. Although younger than William by two years, Elliott was admitted to the state bar a year ahead of his brother and quickly rose among the ranks of Springfield's many lawyers, and among its many active Democrats. Before the Civil War, he served as both city and county attorney, and in 1860 was appointed federal attorney for the southern district of Illinois by President Buchanan.[12]

In August 1857, the Herndon brothers—by then both successful local attorneys—brought their competing partisanship to opposite sides of a fugitive slave case. Frederick Clements entered Illinois earlier that summer to visit his free wife in Logan County, north of Springfield. Clements was owned by Hiram McElroy, a prosperous small farmer from Union County, Kentucky. Clements claimed he had a pass to visit his wife, but McElroy alleged that he had run away. Clements was captured and brought before a federal commissioner in Springfield in accordance with the Fugitive Slave Act of 1850. McElroy hired Elliott Herndon to swear out the appropriate affidavits and present the case before the commissioner, while William Herndon volunteered to represent Clements. The Fugitive Slave Act was unclear as to whether accused fugitives had a right to legal representation, but Elliott argued that a slave was not a citizen and therefore could not be a defendant or retain counsel. William argued in response that he, at least, was a free citizen and had a right to appear in court on behalf of whomever he chose. Elliott retorted, "[William Herndon] appeals to his rights as a free citizen. He has such rights, but in regard to any right to appear here as the attorney for the negro, we deny it. Nobody has a right to appear for that negro."[13] Allowing Clements legal counsel, claimed Elliott, would give him a voice not permitted by law. The commissioner decided that since the hearing was not actually a trial, William was not formally engaged as legal counsel and could be permitted to remain as an adviser. Days later, William wrote to the abolitionist Theodore Parker: "I came near having my own dear rights stricken down in Court by my own brother." He lamented that "the poor negro was tried and sent south—could not prevent it. You cannot do any good when the iron-chain . . . is around the man and fetters are on his limbs."[14] The Democratic *Illinois State Register* lauded the outcome by bragging of the "superiority of the moral condition of Springfield" over that of Chicago, where fugitive slaves were regularly concealed and where "if a law is displeasing to a few of its leaders, it is set at open defiance."[15]

By the time the Clements case was heard, Democrats in Illinois faced an impending crisis. In 1857, Stephen Douglas, already thinking ahead to the elections of 1858 and 1860, came out strongly against Kansas's proslavery Lecompton Constitution. Douglas gambled that the majority of northern Democrats were more concerned about controlling the expansion of slavery than they were about defending Kansans' right to self-government. Douglas also hoped to win moderate and conservative Republicans by demonstrating that Democrats were not so rabidly in favor of states' rights that they were blind to the problem of slavery's expansion. But for Democrats like Elliott Herndon, Douglas's repudiation of the Lecompton Constitution and his apparent rejection of his own popular sovereignty doctrine amounted to party treason. Conservative Democrats formed their own splinter faction, which they called the National Democrats.[16] As the Lecompton controversy hit full steam in 1858, Springfield businessman James Clarkson started a campaign newspaper called the *Illinois State Democrat,* which became the voice of the National Democrats in Illinois. Clarkson enlisted Elliott Herndon as coeditor, and they set about decrying Stephen Douglas and his apparent concessions to the "Black Republicans." Herndon and Clarkson also railed against "Negro equality" and suffrage, running dozens of articles and vignettes culled from both Northern and Southern Democratic newspapers depicting black hardships in the North and the kind paternalism of the slave South. A piece reprinted from the *Detroit Herald* summarized the National Democratic stance: "We have stated that negro slavery, or negro subordination, was a natural relation, and that the negro was incapable of occupying any higher position than that of a subordinate to the white, or Anglo-Saxon race. This we have from time to time laid down as good sound democratic doctrine." The piece asserted: "We speak of the negro as a being just such as God has created him to be, and as occupying that natural relation to the superior white man which God intended he should."[17] Although split over Douglas's stance on Lecompton, Democrats of all stripes shared the conviction that the nation be safeguarded from the possibility of unruly free blacks and their influence on free white institutions.

National Democrats attempted to sway the 1860 Democratic convention in Charleston away from Stephen Douglas in favor of John C. Breckenridge, joining southern Democrats in withdrawing from the convention and holding their own meeting. Illinois's delegate Orlando Ficklin remained at the convention and drafted resolutions and minority reports that repudiated Douglas's nomination, but to no effect. Even in Springfield, where Elliott Herndon and James Clarkson expended so much effort in the columns of the *Democrat,* there were few who seriously considered the National Democratic platform or nominations, and enthusiasm for Douglas remained high. On July 25, farmer Philemon Stout recorded in his diary, "Went to Springfield . . . to ratify the nomination of Douglas for President. Saw the largest crowd I ever saw together. Much enthusiasm manifested." In October, Stout brought his wife and children into Springfield to hear Douglas speak, and reported "a very large crowd."[18] Sangamon County ended up giving Stephen Douglas forty-two more votes than hometown candidate Abraham Lincoln, and Breckenridge finished with only seventy-seven votes countywide. Governor Richard Yates, a Republican, defeated his Democratic challenger by just eight votes. The county remained divided, as it had for most of the previous decade, along familiar party lines.[19]

If the collapse of the National Democrats bothered Elliott Herndon, the election of Abraham Lincoln brought more immediate concerns. In June, Elliott had been appointed by President Buchanan to district attorney for the southern district of Illinois, but just five days after Lincoln's inaugural address in March 1861, his name disappeared from the federal docket books. The fugitive slave cases that had once made up a share of the local federal court's business also abruptly disappeared. Throughout 1860 and the first few months of 1861, the federal commissioner in Springfield heard seven fugitive slave cases, but with the coming of war in the spring of 1861, no further such cases were heard at the court. In February 1860, William Herndon had again volunteered on behalf of the alleged fugitive, and again lost. Two other cases resulted in the return of the fugitives to their claimants, including a family of five slaves from Saint Louis apprehended in Chicago, and a decision of "no warrant" was found in the other four. By the first week in April 1861, however, the federal commissioner in Springfield had heard his last fugitive slave case.[20]

Throughout the 1850s, Democrats like Elliott Herndon had argued forcefully in favor of enforcing the federal Fugitive Slave Act and against the laws passed by many midwestern states to protect fugitive slaves and free blacks from slave catchers and kidnappers.²¹ As the new Republican administration turned away from prosecuting fugitive slave cases, Democrats likewise turned away from the federal government, and toward a more rigorous application of states' rights principles. Especially in Illinois, which had never passed any personal liberty laws, Democrats now rejected the notion that the federal government had a right to intervene against the laws of the state. As the historian Mark Neely notes of this changing attitude: "The Democratic party, which had encouraged federal intrusions on the power of the state courts to issue binding writs [as to the enforcement of the Fugitive Slave Act] suddenly became the defender of the great writ [of habeas corpus]," against a federal government increasingly willing to imprison dissenting white citizens in the interest of national security. It was part of a great shift in national priorities that reached deeply into the structure of local life and the nature of politics in Springfield after 1860.²²

When Lincoln's election was announced, sixteen-year-old Anna Ridgely, daughter of a prominent Springfield Democratic family, confided her fears to her diary: "We hear of Mr. Lincoln's election. . . . I tremble for our country. . . . I hope he will keep the peace but I am afraid that our union has commenced to break and will soon fall to pieces."²³ The coming of war brought Democratic worries about civil liberties, federal power, and the possibility of emancipation into sharp relief. In 1862, Richard Merrick, speaking at the Chicago Young Men's Democratic Invincible Club, linked rabid negrophobia with the assault on white civil liberties he claimed the Lincoln administration was perpetrating, citing the federal establishment of a contraband camp for freed slaves in Cairo in violation of Illinois's prohibition on black immigration. Merrick's list of other violations included the imposition of martial law and military tribunals, which he claimed were "of the same class of Executive usurpations, aggrandizing the Federal authority at the expense of the rights of the States, and showing the progressive development of a centralized and despotic power."²⁴ Orlando Ficklin, Illinois's delegate to the 1860 Democratic convention, was even more explicit in denouncing the "attempt . . . to nullify the constitution and laws of our state not only in respect to the liberty of her citizenry, but also by flooding the state with a class of miserable, imbecile and wholly worthless *freed* negroes, than which a greater scourge and hellish curse could not be inflicted on the people of a free state."²⁵

Similar arguments appeared everywhere in the Democratic press. When Lincoln's Emancipation Proclamation was announced in 1862, Springfield's *Illinois State Register* criticized the president for "resolv[ing] that Illinois *shall* be an asylum for freed negroes from the south. . . . This is Lincoln's policy for his own state—his own county and town, both of which have received his first installment of negro pets." The *Register* warned against "the tide of negro pauperism" and the "negro invasion of Illinois," and asserted that although the government had "the bayonets to enforce its decrees . . . the people of Illinois have the votes, to protest against it." It was the white voters' responsibility to defend the state against federal intervention and the "pauper negro population" the government intended to force upon Illinois.[26] The *Chicago Post* imaginatively argued that allowing freed blacks to enter the state would encourage slaveholders from Kentucky and Missouri to free their slaves, then relocate them to Illinois, where they could legally indenture them, thus reestablishing slavery on Illinois soil, something that had not been openly tolerated since the 1820s. "The introduction of this cheap African labor," argued the *Post*, "is the inevitable forerunner of slavery as a permanent institution of the state." Not only was federal intervention through black resettlement circumventing the laws of a sovereign state, it was actually expanding the slave system it claimed to be destroying.[27]

As Illinois Democrats voiced their substantial fears of federal power run rampant and the consequences of emancipation, Republicans feared equally the specter of treason and violent insurrection instigated by Democrats. In 1862, when the Democratic-controlled constitutional convention considered a sweeping set of reforms to limit the power of the governor, Republican Governor Richard Yates and his agents encouraged rumors that a secret treasonable society known as the Knights of the Golden Circle had infiltrated and was controlling the Democratic Party, plotting an overthrow of the state in preparation for allegiance with the Confederacy. Springfield's Republican newspaper even referred to its Democratic rival as "the Copperhead K.G.C. organ."[28] Republicans claimed that these secret societies advocated desertion from the Union armies and armed resistance to recruitment and draft efforts, as well as distribution of treasonous peace literature and proposed allegiance with the Confederacy.[29]

As political rhetoric became increasingly polarized, Illinois seemed to have become a theater of the war in miniature. Republicans exaggerated the threat posed by antiwar and anti-Union activity, but many Illinoisans believed the threats were real. The isolated nature of many rural communities encouraged an independent streak among local political factions, which were often ruled as strongly by local issues and relationships as by national partisan discourse, encouraging locals to engage in open and willful resistance to state and federal authority. In the rural counties of Illinois, the conspiracy theories that circulated at the capital seemed all too real as political differences precipitated violence and crime. John M. Palmer, a Union general and later governor, recalled that at the beginning of the war, "I did not myself feel the greatest confidence in the ultimate success of our intended efforts to suppress the rebellion. The indifference of many and hostility of some of my acquaintances made me apprehensive that, before the struggle would end, even Illinois might be the theater of civil conflict."[30] In 1863, Anna Ridgely feared that encroachments on civil liberties would lead to open rebellion in Illinois: "The people are beginning to be aroused," she wrote, and "they will not much longer submit to this reign of terror. They will rise in rebellion, and what then—God knows, no one else."[31]

Others across the state echoed these fears that Illinois was dividing against itself. From rural Fancy Creek Township, north of Springfield, Currency Van Nattan wrote to her husband and son in the 73rd Illinois Infantry: "Old Illinois is not like it was when you left home you can not find t[w]o of one Opinion," and "some thinks that we will have fighting wright here and that before long."[32] Other concerned Unionists wrote to Governors Richard Yates and Richard Oglesby asking for government support and soldiers "in the suppression of Rebellion in Ills."[33] In March 1863, James Brewster from Montgomery County warned Yates that "everything indicates that civil war is almost upon us."[34] In Saline County to the south, John Stucker of Mitchellsville reported that, "The secesh or, southern sympathizers are getting very bold in our town and section of county," and "they are threatening to hang some Union men, shoot some, and rob others." Although this might have been bad enough, Stucker added: "Also, they have appointed the 4th of April next to meet at Harrisburg, our County seat, to resist the [Emancipation] proclamation, etc., or properly speaking to secede, and invite Gurilas [sic] into our midst."[35] A similar situation prevailed in Monroe County on the border with Missouri in 1863, when a group of citizens wrote to inform the governor that "numbers of our people sufficiently large to entitle their actions to consideration seem to be almost frenzied in opposition to the war" and "publicly proclaim their purpose to resist the laws should their enforcement be insisted upon."[36] From Macon County, east of Springfield, Elizabeth Howell wrote to Yates that "wretched home Traittors" had murdered a local man for refusing to take an oath against the Union. A mob had entered his house in the night armed with knives and although his wife had shot one of the intruders, the others "split her husband's head open" and then killed her. The only survivor was the couple's eight-year-old daughter, who escaped and related the story to a neighbor. Howell named the local Copperhead leaders and reported on their meetings, urging the governor not to reveal her name, "or myself and husband will severly [sic] suffer, perhaps with our lives."[37] In Coles County, to the east of Springfield, Cyrus Gifford wrote to warn the governor that "it is a common thing in some places hereabouts for men to hurrah for Jeff Davis," and "Copperheads stalk abroad at noon day."[38]

Cyrus Gifford's warning was a portent of Illinois's bloodiest clash one year later. In March 1864, a squad of Union soldiers was among the crowd on the opening day of the circuit court in Charleston, the seat of Coles County. The soldiers had been sent from their garrison in Springfield several days earlier to quell a supposed uprising, but the alarm had apparently been false and the troops were waiting to catch a train to rendezvous with the rest of their force. The court session had just begun when a man in the crowd pulled a revolver from his coat and fired into a group of soldiers, striking Private Oliver Sallee in the chest. Sallee fired back and killed his assailant. Colonel G. M. Mitchell recalled that "immediately firing became general." The county sheriff rushed out from the courthouse, but instead of calming the crowd, he reportedly "marshaled the insurgents, put himself at their head, and directed all their subsequent movements."[39] When the fray was over, six federal soldiers and three civilians were dead, and five soldiers and seven civilians were wounded. The military later captured several of the alleged assailants, but the others escaped into the countryside. Military officials blamed the Knights of the Golden Circle for inciting "a deliberate plot . . . to murder the soldiers of the United States," and they believed that "an extensive and formidable conspiracy is being formed against the Government."[40] United States Representative John T. Stuart echoed the fears of residents across the state when he wrote to his wife after the incident: "So many conflicts and rows occurring between soldiers and citizens if not stopped will lead to a general fight and then all will be lost."[41]

In June 1864, with the dust of the Charleston affair barely settled, a federal agent named William Taylor arrived in Springfield to infiltrate the local chapter of the Order of American Knights, another organization his superiors believed was plotting to overthrow the federal government. Taylor reported that he attended a meeting of the order in "a temple about three miles from Springfield," where a new member was initiated and speeches were made. From the meeting that night, and from his further observations, Taylor concluded: "In Illinois the organization, though as strictly military in its nature and purposes as anywhere, partakes more of a political character than in Missouri," but he observed that "they are all armed." Taylor made note of the attendees at the meeting and observed the activity at the "copperhead hotel"—the Owen House—in order to come up with a list of the principal members of the secret order in Springfield and Sangamon County, including Elliott Herndon, Mayor John S. Vredenburg, and the county sheriff.[42] If Taylor's report is to be believed, these men belonged to the most organized and most dangerous treasonous organization in the nation. Government agent Edward F. Hoffman (apparently an alias), who delighted in representing himself as a cloak-and-dagger secret agent, agreed with Taylor. He reported that Springfield and Chicago were the centers of treason in the state, and concluded, "Illinois, believe me, is the great focus of this organization."[43] Others also named Springfield as a focal point for disloyal activity. Greenberry Wright of Fayette County wrote to warn Governor Yates in 1863 that a relative of his had heard some men talking about a rebellion that would begin in the capital and spread across the state: "One was telling the other that he had good news from Springfield they had one thousand minie [sic] rifle and was distributing a rifle and revolver to every man that would agree to use them and says he will hear from them in less than thirty days Dick Yates will be hung and Springfield laid in ashes and then says he the work commences." The writer failed to consider what would motivate the traitors to destroy their own city but thought it advisable to warn the governor, for "it can do no harm if it does no good."[44]

Despite these grim predictions, however, Springfield was hardly a town on the verge of rebellion. With Camp Butler located just a few miles away, any armed uprising in the city would have been certain folly. Although many of the town's leading citizens were Democrats, they insisted on time-honored principles of due process and civic order in confronting the challenges posed by the war. In 1862, the *Register* demanded "in the name of Illinois sovereignty, that her citizens, dragged to the prisons of the federal government, shall be released, and given speedy hearing before the courts of their state."[45] For those accused of treason, the federal district courts would have to suffice.

The sorts of cases handled by the federal district court for southern Illinois during the war ranged from its one and only indictment for treason in June 1861, to habeas corpus petitions from the victims of overzealous federal marshals, and frequently, confiscation of alleged contraband goods. The most numerous cases before the court were charges of enticing soldiers to desert, harboring deserters, or resisting the draft, hundreds of which were heard between 1861 and 1865. In just two months in 1864, thirty cases were brought before either the federal circuit or district courts for harboring, concealing, or employing a deserter, or helping a deserter escape. For at least two of these cases, Elliott Herndon and his partner, Isaac Keyes, were retained for the defense, which put them in a precarious professional position. In late 1862 and early 1863, several prominent Democratic lawyers were arrested by federal authorities on spurious charges of disloyalty, and although they were ultimately vindicated, their arrests made it clear to Democratic attorneys that defending their political principles in the courtroom might bring them unwelcome scrutiny from federal officials. Fortunately for Herndon and Keyes, the federal district judge for southern Illinois was Samuel Treat, a sympathetic Democrat who had also been identified by federal agents as a member of the treasonous Order of American Knights.[46]

In 1864, Herndon and Keyes defended Ethan Brewster, a schoolteacher from Logan County, against charges that he had enticed a soldier from the 11th Iowa Cavalry to desert while the regiment passed through the town of Lincoln. Brewster claimed that he was the victim of the drunken antics of two local men who were overheard scheming to frame him after the soldiers had departed. The soldier he was supposed to have enticed to desert was already in Saint Louis with his regiment by the time the charges were brought before the federal grand jury. Nevertheless, the federal jury returned a true bill against Brewster, and the case was continued on the docket until June 1866, when it was finally dropped. Elliott Herndon and Isaac Keyes also defended a man named William Dial against charges that he had harbored deserters. Dial was charged in June 1864, but it took one year before a verdict was rendered. The details of this case have not survived in the records, but Dial was eventually found guilty and sentenced to six months in the county jail and a fine of fifty dollars. By the time he was sentenced in June 1865, the war was over.[47]

While Elliott Herndon and his fellow Democratic stalwarts fought their own war on the home front against federal encroachment on their state's sovereignty and the freedom of its white citizenry, others joined the army, following Stephen Douglas's 1861 deathbed admonition: "A man cannot be a true Democrat unless he is a loyal patriot."[48] By the end of the war, many of these volunteers had departed the Democratic Party entirely, condemning those who remained as traitors and Copperheads. Among them was Robert McClaughry, then a young newspaper editor from Hancock County, who responded to Abraham Lincoln's call for volunteers in the summer of 1862 by organizing a company of infantry in the town of Carthage. Robert was the son of Matthew and Mary McClaughry, who came to Illinois from New York in 1837, part of the Northern counterpart to the migration of Southern families like the Herndons. Robert grew up in the rural township of Fountain Green, where he worked the family farm in the summer and attended school in the fall and winter. When he graduated from Monmouth College in 1860, he was appointed instructor of Latin at the college. But Robert was apparently not satisfied with the life of a small-town college instructor, and in 1861 he took a position as coeditor, with his brother-in-law Dr. A. J. Griffith, of the *Carthage Republican,* which, despite its name, was the leading Democratic newspaper of Hancock County. Under McClaughry and Griffith, the *Carthage Republican* became a voice for Douglas Democrats and was decidedly pro-Union and promilitary. Although Hancock County Democrats rejected the usurpation of state autonomy by the federal government, they nevertheless vowed to support the Union, the duly elected administration, and the soldiers in the field.[49]

In September 1862, McClaughry's company of ninety-seven enlisted men and three elected officers departed for training at Camp Butler. With the editor of the *Republican* at their head, many of the Carthage volunteers who marched off to war in September 1862 believed that they did so first and foremost to preserve their own state's freedom, a cause that went hand in hand with preserving the integrity of the Union. Throughout September and October, the companies that would form the 118th Illinois Infantry Regiment, including McClaughry's, drilled six hours a day, until, as one volunteer complained, "It seems as though I was more of a machine than a man."[50] Elections for regimental officers were held in early October, and McClaughry was elected major, third in the chain of command. The 118th Illinois was officially mustered in to federal service on November 7, 1862, for three years' service with 820 enlisted men and officers. They were already at Camp Butler when they learned of President Lincoln's intention to issue the Emancipation Proclamation. For many Democrats, resistance to the proclamation was a rallying point and increased the tenor of their political resistance to the Republican administrations in Springfield and Washington, DC. Illinois Democrats had long warned of the dangers of increased black migration from the South, and this new federal policy that seemed to encourage Southern slaves to leave their plantations made the threat even more imminent. Many of the young men in McClaughry's regiment would have been dismayed to read the announcement in the newspapers they received at Camp Butler. The status of Southern slaves likely played little or no role in their decision to volunteer. Indeed, many believed they were fighting for their state's right to exclude black migrants from the South. But the army they had just joined now seemed part of a Republican mission to free the slaves and, if newspapers like the *Carthage Republican* were to be believed, set them loose upon the white populace of the Midwest. With Copperheads at home resisting the war and the federal government now enforcing emancipation, Democratic soldiers felt betrayed both by their party back home and by the government they had recently enlisted to defend.

As their duty to defend the Union came increasingly into conflict with their Democratic politics, Robert McClaughry and many of his men underwent a political transformation. The army was a sort of crucible for many volunteer soldiers in which divergent political opinions fused into shared notions of duty to protect and sustain the nation. This powerful ideological bond often led soldiers to accept emancipation as a war measure and to soften their racial opinions. But the fact that Lincoln received almost 80 percent of the soldier vote in 1864 is not necessarily indicative of a dramatic refiguring of racial opinion among those in the military. Their support for Lincoln, the Union, and eventually for emancipation, was an affirmation of the Union and a rejection of Copperheadism, but it did not signal unambiguous acceptance of the policies of the Lincoln administration or the Republican Party, nor did it indicate soldiers' support for black rights or eventual citizenship.[51]

Through their military service, Robert McClaughry and the men of the 118th Illinois confronted slavery and larger black populations than they had known in western Illinois. There were only 20 free blacks living in Hancock County in 1860, alongside a white population of nearly 30,000. Neighboring Adams County had almost 200 free blacks, but a white population of more than 41,000. In all of Hancock and the surrounding counties in 1860 there were only 352 blacks, compared with 169,809 whites, meaning that blacks represented less than 1 percent of the population. For soldiers from western Illinois, the South must have seemed like a world apart. The 1860 census listed more than 1,000,000 slaves and more than 25,000 free blacks in the four states through which the 118th Illinois campaigned.[52] Private Sidney Little of McClaughry's Company B wrote to his mother about "niggers by the carloads" in Memphis in 1862, a sight that clearly impressed him.[53] As they marched through Tennessee, Mississippi, Arkansas, and Louisiana, McClaughry and his men saw opulent plantation houses abandoned by their owners, and slave quarters standing empty. On other plantations, former slaves remained, living still in their tiny cabins, even though their masters had departed. As the regiment moved, many former slaves followed, forming a vast refugee train. These experiences affected the Illinoisans in different ways. Some found themselves tentatively questioning the prejudicial racial assumptions they had grown up with, whereas others believed their assumptions fully confirmed.[54]

As the regiment cruised past Helena, Arkansas, in late December 1862 on the steamboat *Northerner,* Private Samuel Gordon wrote to his wife: On "every plantation we pass by the negroes are singing and dancing they appear to be overjoyed at the prospect of freedom," and each plantation seemed to Gordon to have, "the appearance of a small village" where "there is but few

Illinois in Wartime — 31

of the white population to be seen."⁵⁵ Gordon was one of the few men in the 118th Illinois who seemed to grow more sympathetic toward emancipation as he encountered slaves who considered themselves freed by the arrival of Union soldiers. In Mississippi the next spring, Gordon again noted: "The inhabitants mostly black were out in force and gave us a hearty greeting as we marched along when asked where massa and missus was their answer was that they had run off."⁵⁶ In Louisiana in the fall of 1863, Gordon observed: "The darkies . . . represented the very picture of good nature with a broad grin upon their faces showing their ivory to good advantage they would implore a Gods blessing upon as we passed by."⁵⁷ The fact that Gordon so frequently mentioned these happy scenes in his letters home suggests that he felt some pride to be part of the army that brought the hope of freedom. But Gordon was not always able to put aside the racial assumptions he had grown up with. When he wrote to his wife in January 1863, Gordon mentioned another group of former slaves that "were overjoyed to see the Yankees as they called us," but the scene he described was full of racial stereotypes: "The Capt inquired if they had any sweet potatoes. Yes Massa we have lots of them. . . . Some of the boys went into the negroes quarters and ordered some breakfast. The negro women flew around lively and soon had breakfast on the table smoking hot. . . . The negroes appeared much pleased with the attention paid them and invited the boys to come again. . . . The Capt also confiscated two negroes for the benefit of the Company to do washing carrying water, etc., etc."⁵⁸

Although Gordon's use of the word "confiscated" may be his way of playing on the idea of slaves as property, more likely he saw nothing problematic about slaves becoming Union property in much the same way as confiscated cattle or horses. The expectation that blacks would perform as servants to Union soldiers was widespread wherever slaves were "confiscated." Gordon's conclusion that "the negroes appeared much pleased with the attention paid them" evoked stereotypes of childlike blacks and also probably misapprehended the real cause of their evident pleasure at encountering federal soldiers. For Gordon, the nonthreatening images of childish or buffoonish slaves predominated in his characterization of the blacks he encountered. In Louisiana in the summer of 1864, Gordon observed that "the majority of the inhabitants are of African descent or as they call themselves *Smoked Yankees*," and told his wife, "The negro women are very fond of making a great display of fine clothes."⁵⁹ Two months later, Gordon described "a group of Ladies of *African* descent belonging to the tribe of cotton pickers" who passed his picket line on their way to the fields. As Gordon described them, "They were rigged out in full bloomer costume omitting the trousers they appeared quite happy and content laughing and joking one another as they went." For Gordon, the idea of the merry slave translated easily into an understanding of freed blacks as happy, simple, and content to remain among "the tribe of cotton pickers."[60] When a brigade of black soldiers was organized in the summer of 1863, Gordon noted that several of his comrades had taken commissions as officers in the new regiments. Although he believed that "the negroes . . . will make first rate soldiers," Gordon was not willing to join his friends, although it would have meant a promotion. "I had the offer of a place in the new brigade if I desired it," Gordon wrote to his wife, but explained that he had declined because "the servise had to run five years unless sooner discharged and other conciderations I thought it best not to accept a commission in the first Mississippi African briggade."[61] The other considerations to which Gordon referred were probably similar to the reasons his comrade George Safford urged his sister that she "must not lisp" the news that some members of the regiment were going to become officers in a black unit, "for I don't send it to have the neighborhood know it."[62] As much as Gordon and some other members of his regiment might have supported freedom, there were limits to their relatively benign opinions of blacks as well as limits on what communities back home would tolerate. An apparent commitment to black rights while in the army might imperil the interests of loved ones back home and sour a soldier's triumphant return at war's end.

Other soldiers in the 118th Illinois wrote of their wholly negative impressions of the former slaves they encountered. Like many of his comrades, Sidney Little was a dedicated Democrat who imbibed the party's ideology straight from the *Carthage Republican,* which he received in camp at Memphis, and which made him feel "more at home." Little reported that former slaves followed the regiment wherever it went and were willing to perform menial camp duties rather than face continued slavery. "They all have a nig that are allowed to have one," Little complained of his fellow soldiers, and "some regiments have twenty of them, and they get as saucy as they can be."[63] Little was referring to soldiers like Thomas Mix of his own company, who wrote in his diary in May 1863: "We went to a plantation to shell corn and started the mill and ground corn and made the negroes bake us corn bread."[64] In April 1863, Little wrote with even greater bile: "The [Emancipation] Proclamation is one thing which I disdain and abhor. If Abe will withdraw that, he will gain friends. We don't want their nigs anyway, for they are a burden to any regiment. They become trifling and lie around the camp just like dogs."[65] In a letter to his brother in June 1863, Little wrote: "[The Rebels] did come in here, or above here, the other day, last Sunday, and had a very hard fight, killing about seventy-five niggers and wounding about the same; but the nigs killed about the same of them. . . . The nigs make a good soldier, but don't put them by white men. They are very good to have about camp to haul water and wood and do the dirty work. They have to do it when they come around where I am, and I have anything I want done."[66] In a few sentences, Little expressed his grudging admiration for black soldiers and relegated them to his personal servants. His admonition "don't put them by white men" can be read either as a boast that black soldiers could not compare with white soldiers, or a warning that proximity bred animosity. No matter how well blacks served as soldiers, Little's opinion that they were best suited for hauling water and wood and other dirty work reflected the opinions of many Democrats that, even with freedom, blacks belonged at the bottom of the social hierarchy, forever subordinate to whites. Many of Sidney Little's comrades in the 118th Illinois expressed similar opinions. George Safford of Company C wrote to a friend: "You speak of the darkies. Mark my word those that have them will soon find to their sorrow that they are the greatest curse that they ever meddled with and they and those that are innocent will have to suffer from their influence. I say try and elevate them but not to the utter ruin of three fourths of the whites at the North. I am here among them all the time in short I see more of them than I do of the whites and do not think them fit subjects to enter the northern states."[67]

As clear and passionate as these antiblack sentiments were, the increasingly poor reputation of the Democratic Party complicated soldiers' reactions to the politics of emancipation. When it left home, the 118th Illinois was known as the "Democratic regiment," owing in large part to prominent Democratic officers such as Robert McClaughry. But as the war progressed and Democrats at home were vilified as Copperheads and traitors, Democratic soldiers suffered a political identity crisis. In 1864, McClaughry ran for Hancock County clerk on the Union Party ticket, while serving in Springfield as an army paymaster. Elliott Herndon and other stalwart Democrats characterized men like McClaughry as party traitors, frightened away from their Democratic principles by accusations of treason and Copperheadism. But McClaughry's political conversion was due to more than just the increasingly poor reputation of Democrats back home. As the historian Adam I. P. Smith has noted of wartime partisanship among Northern soldiers, being part of the military was itself a kind of political activity that "utterly transformed the context in which electoral competition happened."[68] This altered partisan terrain left soldiers like Sidney Little, who was as devoted to his Democratic identity as he was to his racial prejudices, with substantial political doubts. Little wrote to his mother in 1863 to assure her: "I am still a Democrat but not a Copperhead.

I am one who will fight to the last for the old Stars and Stripes and more, if they up home do keep their mouth still."⁶⁹ Likewise, even as George Safford was writing that blacks should be wholly excluded from the North, he also expressed his support for Major McClaughry's Union Party bid for Hancock County clerk in 1864. Safford was willing to overlook the strong Republican element of the Union Party in favor of a loyal candidate and fellow soldier. William Rand of McClaughry's company expressed his complex political and racial opinions more directly. Rand was a proud Democrat, but found the antiwar actions of members of his party indefensible. When his father wrote him in February 1863 that opinions on the war were divided at home, Rand replied: "You have some men in Hancock Co. who need to have some hemp and cold lead applied to them if they do not behave themselves."⁷⁰ A few days later Rand added: "You have got a lot of men about Hancock Co. that need to have their necks stretched a mile who would have though of horrid rebel meetings in Carthage I would rather help hang B. T. Schofield and other of his *black hearted traitorous* crew than to help hang old Jeff [Davis] himself."⁷¹

By October 1864, with the election looming, Rand wrote to his father that Major McClaughry had sent some pamphlets to the regiment about the Democratic convention in Chicago. The pamphlet was printed by the Republican/Union *Chicago Tribune* as a "campaign document" and consisted of denunciations of the "Copperhead" platform and the antiwar goals of the Democratic Party. Rand told his father that "after a careful perusal . . . I have come to the conclusion that the Platform is too rotten and corrupt and the party will sink into oblivion."⁷² Later that month, Rand was even more direct in his disillusionment with the Democrats and his support for the Union Party: "I hope . . . that Hancock County has elected a union ticket nothing would please me better than to have the 'copps' cleaned out of the 'old Hancock' but I am like you, I think the so called Democratic ticket will win this fall but it would not if the soldiers could have voted; our Regt. took a vote and 'Mac' got 106 votes to 'Uncle Abe' 257. McClaughry 311 to Carey 31. So you can see that the old "*Democratic*" Regt is *all right*."⁷³ Despite his growing antagonism toward the actions of antiwar Democrats back home, Rand still clung tightly to the racial doctrine of the Democratic Party. Referring to a Hancock County farmer arrested for harboring fugitive slaves (the case is discussed below), Rand wrote: "I am glad that they arrested O. K. Hawly I want them to keep the niggers out of the state. I do not want them to get a foot hold in Ills. We see so many darkies down here that we are sick of them."⁷⁴

Like his comrades George Safford and Sidney Little, Rand believed strongly in the continued enforcement of the Black Laws on the grounds that formerly enslaved blacks would damage and degrade the free white institutions and values he cherished, even as he voted for a party that seemed to subvert those values. Support for the Union and for emancipation existed in uneasy tension for Democrats in the army, who retained their anti-black stance even as they turned their political allegiance away from the party that had nurtured their racism.[75] George Safford endorsed McClaughry's departure from the Democratic fold because "I think him a sound union man," a characteristic that he placed temporarily ahead of his own resistance to emancipation and rejection of black citizenship.[76] William Rand explained his support of the Union ticket as a means to end the war: "I wish that the north was not divided as much . . . if it was united as the south the war would end soon."[77] Sidney Little said similarly in 1863: "If the Copperheads as well as the Abolitionists would hold their tongue, it would have a tendency to close this war a great deal sooner."[78] Soldiers on the front lines developed a direct personal investment in crushing the rebellion and a sense of camaraderie that tended, at least temporarily, to smooth over partisan differences by linking their own fate with the fate of the Union.

Back home in Illinois, this uncoupling of political and racial opinions did not occur so easily. Political campaigns and elections still dominated the home front, and for many at home, partisan lines were still the battle lines that mattered most. Democratic rallies across the state raised issues that still resonated with many Illinoisans. A broadside advertising a Democratic rally in McDonough County on the eve of the 1864 election called on "White men of McDonough . . . brave men, who hate the rebellion of Abraham Lincoln, and are determined to destroy it [and] noble Women, who do not want their husbands and sons dragged to the valley of DEATH by a remorseless Tyrant" to use their "strength and numbers" to fight the war at home.[79] As Susan Sessions Rugh has noted of politics in Hancock County, and particularly in Robert McClaughry's home community of Fountain Green: "Rather than being united by the war, adherence to party loyalties rent the fabric of community in a contest of wills. . . . The loyalty of the soldiers to Lincoln seems to have had little immediate effect on elections at home. . . . Party feeling was alive and well in western Illinois, a contested terrain where Democrats struggled to hold onto local offices."[80] Civilians in Hancock County read letters from their loved ones serving in the South warning of the curse of freed slaves while also reading in the pages of the *Carthage Republican* and other Democratic newspapers that blacks were streaming across the border from Missouri into western Illinois, welcomed by antislavery Republicans. In 1862, the people of Hancock County, together with a majority of Illinois voters, overwhelmingly supported a separate article of the otherwise defeated "Copperhead Constitution" that would have provided for even more restrictive anti-immigration measures.[81] As the political rhetoric became more heated, support for the Black Laws signaled Illinoisans' opposition to black immigration and demonstrated their state's autonomy from a Republican-dominated federal government bent on emancipation. Although the Black Laws were inconsistently enforced before their repeal in 1865, they were symbolic expressions of antiblack sentiment and provided a legal structure for excluding and punishing black residents whenever local jurisdictions chose to do so.

As a border county, the problem of black immigration seemed particularly acute in Hancock County, despite the fact that it was relatively rare. Slavery existed legally just across the Mississippi River, and many whites feared that the war and emancipation would open the floodgates for former slaves. To prevent this, Hancock County determined to enforce the Black Laws, and in early 1863, found a case to affirm black exclusion. On Christmas Day 1862, "a tall slim mulatto, about 55 years old" arrived at the home of a local Republican named Orestes Hawley. The man, known only as Nelson, came with his wife at Hawley's invitation to work on his farm for ten dollars a month plus board. Nelson and his wife had crossed into Illinois from Saint Louis several days earlier, believing that the Emancipation Proclamation had freed them. A few months before Nelson and his wife entered Illinois, the *Republican* warned: "Negroes are swarming upon our borders by thousands . . . and are welcomed to homes of abolitionists with enthusiastic demonstrations of delight." If this state of affairs continued, the *Republican* asked its readers, "Are you willing to be reduced to penury in order to furnish a home to indolent, ignorant negroes?"[82] Another headline shouted, "FREE NEGROES IN ILLINOIS. They are brought here to Compete with White Men."[83] Orestes Hawley, although operating out of benevolent motives when he offered Nelson work, must have underestimated the impact of such rhetoric. Nelson's arrangement with Hawley was soon brought before the county sheriff. Although the antiblack amendments to the proposed 1862 constitution had not been adopted because the proposed constitution failed, older laws still stood, including an 1853 law that stated clearly: "If any negro, or mulatto, *bond or free,* shall hereafter come into this State and remain ten days, with the evident intention of residing in the same, every such negro or mulatto shall be deemed guilty of a high misdemeanor" (emphasis added). Orestes Hawley and Nelson, along with five other blacks, were arrested in early February 1863 and charged with violating the 1853 statute. In the formal cadence of their sworn testimony, witnesses averred: "Said mulatto person was not born in said state of Illinois nor was a resident thereof at any time on or before the 12th day of February

A.D. 1853," and the "defendant had been in this state more than ten days, with the evident intention of residing here, at the time of his arrest, and is still in this state residing at Mr. Hawley's."[84]

Nelson was brought before Carthage justice of the peace George M. Child, a lifelong Democrat who had preceded Robert McClaughry as editor of the *Carthage Republican,* and under whose editorship the newspaper was described as "an intensely Democratic sheet."[85] In 1860, Child attacked Republican gubernatorial candidate Richard Yates for being soft on black immigration and supporting repeal of the Black Laws, and in 1861 reported under the headline "Negro Equality" that sixteen Republicans in the state assembly had voted in favor of a law that would "repeal the black laws and . . . bestow on Cuffy all the rights and privileges of a white man."[86] In the wake of the Emancipation Proclamation, Child saw an opportunity to assert Illinois's and Hancock County's judicial independence from the Republican administrations both in Washington, DC, and in Springfield. In January 1863, Child issued subpoenas to three witnesses who could prove that Nelson was a recent migrant to the state and that he had come with the intention of settling in Hancock County. Two witnesses, Metgar Couchman, who was another prominent local Democrat, and William Hamilton, the county sheriff, were white; the third was a black man named John, one of the five other defendants charged with entering the state at the same time as Nelson. Nelson's attorney objected to the inclusion of John's testimony because, under Illinois law, "a negro cannot be a witness for either party." Child overruled the objection on the grounds that the law only specified that blacks could not appear in court against whites; allowing a black man to testify was acceptable when it helped to prosecute another. On February 6, a white jury heard the case and delivered a guilty verdict. Nelson was fined fifty dollars and fees, and Child ordered the sheriff to "take possession of the person of said mulatto . . . until said fine and costs are paid, or he be otherwise disposed of according to law." Fifty dollars was an impossible sum for most recent black migrants, especially if they were fleeing slavery. When the fine could not be paid, to be "otherwise disposed of" meant mounting an auction block. Child set the public auction of Nelson and five other black defendants for the afternoon of February 19 at the west door of the courthouse. It was not the first time during the war that Illinois judges ordered the auction of black immigrants. In December 1862, a justice in tiny Marcelline, Adams County, consigned several blacks to the auction block. Only one of the defendants drew a bidder, and a farmer named R. H. Brooks reportedly purchased George Prise for a term of ninety-nine years and six months. In August 1863, a black woman named Annie Long was similarly fined and sentenced in Edgar County but was saved by sympathetic Republicans who raised funds to purchase her from the auction block.[87]

Unlike George Prise and Annie Long, Nelson and the five others avoided mounting an auction block in a free state. On February 11, a deputy sheriff served Child with an injunction to stay the auction while Nelson and the other defendants appealed to the Hancock County circuit court. On March 6, a jury was impaneled and more witnesses were called, including Orestes Hawley. The prosecuting attorney made a brief statement of the facts, aware that he needed no elaborate argument to persuade the jury, while the defense argued that the law restricting black migration into Illinois was unconstitutional, immoral, and unjust. Whether or not the jury believed that Nelson had entered the state with the intention of residing there, the state of Illinois had no jurisdiction under the Fugitive Slave Act, and the state law under which the entire proceeding had taken place should be judged "null, void, and inoperative." The prosecution objected to this argument (there is no mention of why), the judge instructed the jury to disregard the defense arguments, and the jury quickly affirmed the lower court's guilty verdict. The next day, Nelson's lawyers requested a change of venue to Adams County, which was granted. After a brief review of the evidence, the Adams County court again affirmed the decision, and Nelson was ordered to pay the fifty-dollar fine plus all of the accrued court fees, or again face public auction. This time, Nelson's attorney appealed the case to the Illinois Supreme Court, where it took almost a year to receive a hearing.[88]

The case *Nelson v. The People* was decided during the January 1864 term. The case gave the Illinois Supreme Court an opportunity to decriminalize black immigration and thereby nullify an important portion of the Black Laws. Nelson's attorneys argued that the 1853 state laws punishing black immigration exceeded the state's authority by providing for the punishment of fugitive slaves and that the laws practically established slavery in the state through public auction and servitude. They also argued that the laws violated article 4, section 2 of the United States Constitution: "The citizens of each State shall be entitled to all privileges and immunities of citizens of the several States." The last argument drew on a recent wartime precedent and would have meant a radical redefinition of the rights of Illinois blacks to citizenship. Nelson's attorneys asked the court to consider the consequences of the 1853 law for free blacks. If Nelson had been free, "while he was no voting citizen" and "was under many other proper disqualifications which prevented his being placed on equality with white people," his attorneys argued that he could still be considered "a citizen for many purposes." They cited the recent opinion of Attorney General Edward Bates that under the revenue laws of the United States, a black person was a citizen of the United States such that they could command a coasting vessel; broadening the notion of who could be considered a citizen and for what purposes. Nelson's attorneys asked that the court consider citizenship in this broader—but still strictly limited—sense to extend to free blacks constitutional protections. Free black citizens, they argued, must be protected against a law that "creates slavery instead of repressing negro immigration."[89]

In its decision on *Nelson*, the Illinois Supreme Court refrained from assessing the potential citizenship of free blacks, instead remaining true to precedents established during previous decades of wrangling over the nature of servitude in Illinois and the rights of slaveholders to their property. On the question of whether the state had a right to punish fugitive slaves through public auction, the court turned to a case that had been decided in 1843 and involved the use of the state's criminal code to punish whites who harbored black fugitives. In *Eells v. The People*, the court had admitted: "It may be an act of humanity, in many cases, to afford shelter and succor to a slave, while knowing him to be a slave, and the property of another," but "the essence of the offense consists in the attempt to defraud the owner of his property."[90] The issue at hand was the slaveholder's right to property, a right the court held dear. The *Eells* decision was based on a long line of precedent that both upheld the rights of the slaveholder to his property and affirmed the right of the state to punish black immigration. In 1828, in *Nance v. Howard*, the court ruled that colored slaves and servants were legally considered chattel property under state law, and although the court determined that same year in *Phoebe v. Jay* that "it would be an insult to common sense to contend, that the negro, under circumstances in which he was placed, had any free agency" in the formation of indenture contracts, the state constitution of 1818, which permitted such indentures, had been approved by Congress, thus permitting a modification of article 6 of the Ordinance of 1787. The court acknowledged that practical conditions of slavery existed within the state but that the indenture contracts that permitted such bondage were sanctioned by the people and thus completely legal.[91]

The presumption of servitude marked all Illinois blacks as potential bondsmen, and also suggested that all were potential outlaws. As Justice Lockwood noted in his dissenting opinion in *Chambers v. The People* (1843), in which the court upheld the conviction of a white man punished for harboring runaway slaves and black indentured servants: "If the offense . . . is to be considered as . . . harboring or secreting any . . . colored person, who turns out to be a slave or servant, it will be dangerous for the people of this State to extend the most common offices of humanity to that unfortunate class of mankind, to whom God has given a skin colored differently from ours. It would be illegal to receive such persons into our houses, although they were perishing in the streets, with hunger, cold, or sickness."[92] Lockwood's concern was primarily for white citizens who might be unfairly tried for unknowingly harboring fugitive slaves, but he rightly observed that white Illinoisans might consequently look upon all blacks in the state as potential fugitives. For Lockwood, blacks were "unfortunate" to have "a skin colored differently from ours" because that inescapable difference inevitably rendered them a suspect population.

The same year, the court affirmed another conviction against a white man for "knowingly secreting" a mulatto girl owned by a Louisiana slaveholder traveling through Illinois. In *Willard v. The People,* the arguments before the court concerned the constitutionality of allowing slaveholders to retain the rights to their slaves when they entered Illinois. But the court took up a different issue in its judgment, stating that the issue at hand was not in fact slavery, but whether the state had a right to enforce its own criminal statutes. The people had deemed it illegal to harbor or secret fugitives from labor, and the state had a right to punish its citizens who violated the law. In his majority opinion in *Willard,* Justice Scates noted that the state laws were intended "to protect us from vagabond, or pauper slaves; to punish or prevent them from entering our territory, if we think proper; to forbid it, or punish those who may encourage them to come, or harbor or secret[e] them." With borders abutting both Missouri and Kentucky, Illinois was "exposed irremediably, for hundreds of miles of contiguous boundary . . . to heartburnings, criminations, and recriminations, quarrels, brawls, excitements, affrays, and breaches of the peace, arising from the influx of that unwelcome population, and the disturbances to which it may and does give rise."[93] The threat came equally from "that unwelcome population" of southern blacks, as well as from white Illinoisans who might harbor them. Scates argued that the issue of slavery had no bearing on the function of the criminal laws; the real crux of the case was whether Illinois had a right to defend its borders against the potentially criminal population of southern blacks that seemed to press from all sides. The court's ruling reflected the assumption that blacks would prove a destabilizing and dangerous element if they were allowed into the state. Justice Lockwood agreed with the majority in *Willard,* and added his opinion that if slaveholders were denied the right to safely cross Illinois with their slaves, there would be "danger that such refusal would engender feelings on their part not favorable to a continuance of our happy Union."[94] The court thus sought to appease both antiblack Illinoisans and proslavery Southerners, a stance that was reflected in the *Eells* decision that same year. The court again affirmed in *Eells*: "If a State can use precautionary measures against the introduction of paupers, convicts, or negro slaves, it can undoubtedly punish those of its citizens who endeavor to introduce them." Once more, the court suggested imputations of criminality or degeneracy by linking black slaves with paupers and convicts, citing the state laws as bastions against the disorder that would follow if these undesirable populations were allowed to enter the state.[95]

In *Thornton's Case* (1849), the court added considerable nuance to the question of whether state or federal law had authority in fugitive slave cases. As had become its custom, the court made a distinction between protecting its citizens from freed or fugitive slaves and actually acting to punish fugitives and those who harbored them. The case involved the attempt of a constable from Sangamon County to capture and hold an alleged fugitive. Although this was allowed under Illinois law, the fact that "Congress . . . by the act of the 12th of February, 1793 [the first Fugitive Slave Act], prescribed the mode by which the master may retake . . . his slave found in another state," together with the US Supreme Court's affirmation of federal authority in fugitive slave cases in *Prigg v. Pennsylvania* (1842), made void the state law under which the fugitive was arrested.[96] Instead of resolving the question of federal versus state authority, *Thorton's Case* forced the court to circumvent it. By the mid-1850s the court had parsed the difference between state and federal citizenship in a way prescient of later federal Supreme Court rulings on the Fourteenth Amendment. Nine years after *Eells,* on the question of whether state or federal law applied to prosecution of fugitive slave cases, the US Supreme Court decided in *Moore, Executor of Eells v. The People* (1852) that "every citizen of the United States is also a citizen of a State or territory" and "the same act may be an offense or transgression of the laws of both." Although the dissenting opinion delivered by Justice McLean argued that it was "contrary to the . . . genius of our government, to punish an individual twice for the same offense," the majority opinion affirmed that the state and federal laws, and thus the crimes committed, were of an entirely distinct nature. The federal law was intended to facilitate the return of fugitives to their masters, whereas the Illinois laws against harboring or concealing fugitive slaves were intended to "protect . . . against the influx either of liberated or fugitive slaves, and to repel from their soil a population likely to become burdensome or injurious, either as paupers or criminals." Because the offenses were different, the state laws remained in effect alongside the federal laws.[97] The Illinois court applied this reasoning in

Nelson; the proper functioning of the state law did not hinder or obstruct the Fugitive Slave Act, and so Nelson could properly be subject to both.

As for whether the 1853 law violated the state's constitutional prohibition on slavery, the court determined in *Nelson* that "the legislature has declared the immigration of persons of color to, and their settlement in, this State as an offense. . . . The punishment by involuntary servitude, provided by the act, is not unusual, but is one of the common means resorted to, to punish offenses, as the State penitentiary, and the various houses of correction in our State, fully attest. . . . This does not reduce the person convicted to slavery, but it is a mode of punishment not prohibited by the 16th section of article XIII of the Constitution." The distinction between involuntary servitude as punishment and chattel slavery allowed the court to sidestep the question of whether the punishment mandated by the Black Laws amounted to slavery, but it did not resolve the more fundamental issue of Nelson's citizenship status before the law. Indeed, punishment by imprisonment, to which the court likened being sold at a public auction, was presumably applicable only if the prisoner was considered a citizen of the state in which he was arrested, and if he could not be claimed by another jurisdiction—or, in Nelson's case, his Missouri owner. Despite the complexity of the citizenship question, the court's determination on Nelson's status was abrupt: "It is only necessary to say that this record contains no evidence that the plaintiff . . . is a citizen of any State. When that shall appear it will be time to discuss the question." Just what the criteria for citizenship were, the court did not say, only that a slave, as Nelson admitted to being, was not a citizen. The court conceded that the 1853 law violated the Fugitive Slave Act to the extent that it required a master claiming a fugitive punished by public auction to pay the original fifty-dollar fine imposed by the court, which "may obstruct or hinder the execution of the act of Congress." The court added that the state did not have the power to "prescribe a different tribunal for the purpose of ascertaining whether the fugitive is a slave from that created by congress." This was irrelevant to this particular case, however, since Nelson's master had not yet come forward to claim him. Even then, "if portions of an act are constitutional, and a portion is not, such parts as are free from the objection may be executed and enforced. . . . The provisions under which these proceedings were had, violate no provision of the State or national Constitutions, or any enactment of congress, and they warranted the judgment of the court below."[98] With that the court found that the Black Laws, although imperfect, were far from obsolete. However, just thirteen months after the *Nelson* decision, a recently elected Republican-dominated state assembly repealed the Black Laws in their entirety.

As the war ground to a close in the late winter and spring of 1865, Illinois had in many respects weathered its own internal conflict and, like the nation, emerged fundamentally altered. It is not clear what finally became of Nelson, his wife, and the other five black men that entered Hancock County. They may indeed have ended up on the auction block, or perhaps they somehow escaped. That Gus Reed was not also charged with entering the state "with evident intention to reside," was probably due simply to chance, for even with the Black Laws in place and validated by the courts, unprecedented numbers of migrants like Reed entered Illinois and settled in communities across the state. The new arrivals joined longtime residents in rapidly growing communities that for the first time began to look forward from the dark days of slavery. When Gus Reed arrived in Springfield between 1864 and 1866, the black community he found there was growing daily with other migrants. Like him, many of them were natives of the Deep South and by coming to Illinois they sought new opportunities in a free land.

THREE

Black Springfield

> We are disfranchised in the State of our
> residence, without the commission of any
> crime by ourselves, as a reason for our
> disfranchisement.
>
> —*Proceedings of the Illinois State
> Convention of Colored Men, 1866*

IN SEPTEMBER 1869, Illinois governor John Palmer addressed the black population of Springfield on the seventh anniversary of the Emancipation Proclamation. A former Democrat and Union general, Palmer had made a name for himself among Republican converts by bringing a former slave into the state in open violation of the Black Laws in 1864, and by preemptively declaring all of Kentucky's slaves free a year later. After the war, he became one of the most vocal white advocates on behalf of Illinois's black citizens. Palmer told Springfield's black residents that "officers rule over you now that you did not select," but he assured them that they would soon be able to vote and thus attain a significant hallmark of citizenship. "Suffrage is the most powerful and most valuable weapon of defense," Palmer noted, and "the rights that belong to other citizens [cannot] be much longer withheld from you. . . . Hereafter the inquiry will not be, what is the color of the voter, but what are his duties?"[1] For Palmer, these duties were joined tightly with the other responsibilities that came with freedom and citizenship: to work and be industrious, to raise and educate children, and to safeguard the best interests of the community.

Between the repeal of the Black Laws in 1865 and the ratification of the Fifteenth Amendment in 1870, Springfield's black population, like others around the state, existed in a sort of limbo under Illinois law; blacks no longer risked imprisonment, auction, and involuntary servitude for residing in the state, but they could not vote and were still excluded from many areas of public life. The Fourteenth Amendment labeled all native-born and naturalized residents "citizens of the United States and of the State wherein they reside," but the Illinois constitution specified suffrage only for white male inhabitants, and state law still excluded blacks from most public schools. The question that dominated discussion among the black community, and among Democrats and Republicans, was whether black citizenship under the Fourteenth Amendment was really citizenship when state laws continued to discriminate.

When Governor Palmer gave his speech, Gus Reed was 160 miles away, hauling rock in the quarry at the Joliet penitentiary. In March, he had been arrested as the alleged ringleader of a small band of thieves, and in June was sentenced to the penitentiary for five years. We know that Reed arrived in Springfield between 1864 and 1866, but we do not know with certainty what brought him. He may have had family in the city. One of the accomplices with whom he was arrested in 1869 was a black woman named Eliza Lewis, who was charged (but not convicted) along with Gus Reed and two others. When Gus was processed at the penitentiary in 1878 he gave his only relation as Robert Lewis, living in Springfield.[2] Neither Robert nor Eliza could be located in extant records, but their shared surname suggests that they may have been married, which could mean that Gus and Eliza were siblings, and that Robert was Gus's brother-in-law. This possible family connection suggests why Gus Reed went to Springfield in the first place and why he returned there after each incarceration rather than moving somewhere he was less notorious. If it was indeed family that brought him to Springfield, he was not alone in seeking to reestablish some of the bonds severed by the war and emancipation. Black migrants who arrived and settled in Springfield in the 1860s and 1870s were part of the largest migration that had yet occurred out of the South and into the Midwest. Later migrations would center on big cities like Chicago, but as former slaves and other black Southerners moved into the Midwest during and after the Civil War, they often settled in smaller cities, towns, and rural counties. The communities they created began to voice claims on suffrage, citizenship, and civil rights through rallies, conventions, parades, demonstrations, and participation in the hallmarks of middle-class public life and respectability.

Springfield's black community had its roots in the decades before the Civil War. Among the first free black migrants to the area was William Florville, a young Haitian who became a barber and a friend to Abraham Lincoln.

Florville arrived in the area in the early 1830s and married Phoebe Roundtree (daughter of Lucy Roundtree, sometimes also spelled "Rountree"), who lived in one of Sangamon County's few early free black households. The Florvilles raised a large family in Springfield during the antebellum decades, and William's successful barbershop, as well as several lucrative real estate ventures, placed him among Springfield's leading citizens.[3] Most in the antebellum black community were not as prosperous as the Florvilles nor so easily able to bridge the divide between white and black. They were laborers and artisans, single people and families, locals and migrants. Forty-five percent of Springfield's blacks in 1860 were born in slave states, particularly Kentucky, Virginia, Missouri, and Tennessee. Half were native to Illinois, although it is impossible to tell from census data how many of these were born in Springfield or Sangamon County. The rest hailed from places as diverse as Washington, DC, Indiana, New York, Ohio, Pennsylvania, and the West Indies. Out of this mélange, antebellum black Springfielders, like members of other free black communities, created "networks of family, friends, and coworkers cemented by bonds of obligation and shared disadvantage and were both based in and transcended geography."[4] Freeborn blacks mingled with former slaves, some of whom were fugitives, and as they shared experiences with mobility, related the status of distant family and friends, and discussed strategies for survival and prosperity, these bonds grew in breadth and depth.

The community's growth in the 1850s was primarily due to a large number of Illinois-born children. In 1850, there were 171 black residents, or about 4 percent of the town's population. By 1860, the population had grown to 272 black and mulatto men, women, and children, or about 3 percent of the total population. In 1860, nearly a third of the black population was under ten years old, and more than half were under twenty. Of the thirty-five families with children in 1860, twenty-seven had at least one child—often several— younger than ten years of age, and eleven families had a child less than one year old. John and Matilda Jackson, from Virginia and Kentucky, respectively, had four children born in Illinois between 1841 and 1850, and there were many families like theirs. Spencer Donegan and his wife Elizabeth came from Kentucky and North Carolina, and started their large family in Illinois in 1845 with the birth of their first daughter. The Donegans had six more children well spaced over the next fifteen years. Hiram and Julia Barger, from Kentucky and Virginia, started their family before arriving in Illinois and enlarged it after they arrived. Daughter Ema was born in Missouri in 1853, and four years later daughter Lucy was born in Illinois, followed by daughter Ella in 1859.[5]

There were relatively few single adults in antebellum Springfield, and most single men and women either boarded with black families or, in the case of many of the younger and older women, lived as domestic servants in the homes of their white employers. Boarding gave mobile young men and women a chance to familiarize themselves with a new community without becoming paupers, created ties of friendship that helped the community grow, and provided both financial and personal support. There was a roughly even mix of male and female boarders in Springfield's black households before the Civil War. Most were in their late teens or twenties, and most had been born in slave states. Many of the single boarders recorded in the 1850 and 1860 federal censuses had moved on or married by the time the next census was taken, and others had arrived to take their places.[6]

For blacks who lived as servants in white households, their condition was materially often little better than that of slaves. Most were young women like eighteen-year-old Rebecca Smith of Illinois, whose light complexion (she was listed in the census as mulatto) made her a desirable servant for local banker Jacob Bunn. Forty-year-old Charlotte Sims (also listed as mulatto), from Washington, DC, lived with prominent local attorney and Democratic activist John McClernand, and had likely been a domestic servant—either in or out of slavery—for most of her life. After a trip to Saint Louis in 1860, eighteen-year-old Anna Ridgely, daughter of a prominent local Democrat and banker, sounded more like a Southern belle than an Illinois girl when she referred to her servant Becky as "the same old faithful thing. She never expresses much but I think she was glad to have me return."[7] What the young Miss Ridgely accepted as dumb silence was more likely to have been quiet resentment from a woman kept in virtual bondage by her employer.

To live independently in one's own household was a significant improvement over living with a white employer, but it was not easy for black women and men who occupied marginal economic roles in the antebellum community. Beyond keeping house, women who lived with their own families also worked as servants and washerwomen in white households. Men worked as bill posters, cooks, draymen, hostlers, laborers, servants, shoemakers, and whitewashers. Eleven barbers and eight farmers were among the most prosperous, but the pursuit of a single career was a luxury not many could afford. Henry Vance, who was listed in the census simply as a "laborer," owned a mule and cart that he used to perform a variety of tasks for different employers throughout Springfield, including hauling firewood in the winter, and in better weather "tearing down old ramshacks and building new brick buildings, some three stories high." He also fished, hunted, and scavenged to provide for his family. His wife, Mariah, for whom no occupation was listed in the 1860 census, worked as a domestic servant in the homes of several white families, including that of Abraham and Mary Lincoln. The Vances supported a family of eight children with their two incomes, and by 1860 had amassed a respectable sum of 850 dollars, putting them just under the average wealth for black Springfield. Of forty-three individuals for whom the value of estates (real and/or personal) was listed on the 1860 census, the average value of real estate was $886.67 and the average value of personal estate was just $209.87. Among those listed as mulatto, average wealth was about fifty dollars greater than for those listed as black, suggesting the greater earning potential of those with lighter skin. Altogether, black Springfield was worth $34,785, with a family average of $808.95. The wealthiest among Springfield's blacks, with combined estates of $1,000 or more, included five of the eleven barbers (William Florville among them), four farmers, one shoemaker, one laborer, and two whose occupation was not listed. Compared to their white neighbors, however, the total value of real and personal property among Springfield's blacks amounted to less than 1 percent of the aggregate wealth for Sangamon County.[8]

Springfield's antebellum black community participated in a variety of events and institutions that drew them together. Segregated Baptist and Methodist churches served their spiritual needs since they were not allowed to attend church with whites, and their children were taught in independent schools organized through the churches and funded by donations. In 1846, a group placed an advertisement in the *Sangamo Journal* for a schoolmaster "to teach a School of colored children in Springfield."[9] Four years later, another advertisement announced a public supper at the Colored Baptist Church to raise funds for the school. Pride in their own schools even led some community members to oppose propositions for a publicly funded black school. The signers of a petition published in the *Sangamo Journal* in 1852 asserted: "We . . . feel a deep, very deep interest, in our schools, and think it the only sure way to redeem ourselves from the bondage we are now in . . . , and will do everything that is in our power to educate our children . . . without the boldness to ask aid from the people of the State."[10]

The public school system in Springfield was formed in 1854, "to furnish gratuitously, to all white children and youth, resident of the city, between the ages of five and twenty-one, a free course of instruction; the cost of which to be defrayed by public taxation."[11] This initiated a debate within the black community regarding public funding for their schools. Some wanted the formation of public schools for black children, since black residents paid school taxes, but their children were not allowed to attend with white students.

Others worried that public schools would undermine the existing independent schools and erode their community support. In 1858, the school board decided to "organize a school for the Colored children within the City, by procuring a competent teacher, subject to the approval of the Board, and [select] a room suitable for school purposes."[12] There was apparently no discussion at the time that in so doing, the board would be violating their own provision to admit only white students, adopted just four years earlier. As long as the black students were segregated, the board was willing to provide them with a school. A teacher was appointed at only $500 per year, several hundred dollars less than teachers at the other public schools, and for a "suitable" room, the board selected a shanty behind Saint Paul's African Methodist Episcopal Church. Classes were regularly attended beginning in 1859, even by students who lived outside the city limits.[13]

Regular events cemented ties of family and friendship, and addressed political concerns of interest to the black community. Local residents participated in the pan-American holiday known as Emancipation Day on August 1st, celebrating the abolition of slavery in the British West Indies. Emancipation Day festivities typically included a parade, speeches, preaching, and picnicking in a local grove. These celebrations were important social occasions, as well as political and cultural events that connected small black communities like Springfield's to a nationwide tradition of black celebration. During the 1850s these events increasingly occupied public spaces, where black celebrants demonstrated orderly public celebration and voiced an activist, secularized opposition to slavery. Emancipation Day celebrations brought black residents and their white friends together and provided a forum in which to discuss abolition, assistance for fugitive slaves, and anti–Black Laws activism. Especially in the Midwest, where fugitive slaves often fled and where the proximity of the Kansas-Nebraska controversy lent urgency to the issues, Emancipation Day celebrations became increasingly political events. As historian J. R. Kerr-Ritchie has observed, by the 1850s the festivities had "shifted from being commemorative to being *demonstrative,* and were concerned with the self-defense of black people and war on slavery."[14] Springfield's black population was smaller and less overtly activist than larger black communities in Chicago, Indianapolis, or Cincinnati, but the local celebrations adopted a common vocabulary and created a space in which topics such as freedom, citizenship, and civil rights could be discussed openly.[15]

Springfield's blacks could not mobilize as a voting bloc to influence elections or legislation, but they could show themselves as organized and aware political actors in other ways. When the statewide Convention of Colored

Citizens was held in Alton in November 1856, Sangamon County did not send any delegates, but word of the proceedings would have spread from the delegates of neighboring counties and towns. Writing in the early 1870s, the Reverend J. H. Magee remembered a large extended antebellum community of black friends and family in central Illinois. Magee recalled attending prayer meetings that brought "a large number of our people" from around Macoupin, Madison, and Sangamon counties.[16] These meetings also spread political information; the 1856 convention was convened in Alton's Colored Baptist Church, where over three days, the attendees heard speeches and drafted resolutions calling for the abolition of the Black Laws, the end of taxation without representation, admission of black children to public schools, and the opening of the judicial system. The convention resolved: "The thorough organization and united effort of the colored people is absolutely essential to the successful termination of the great struggle in which we are now engaged for the attainment of our rights."[17] Even without a formal representative at the proceedings, Springfield's blacks would certainly have discussed and debated such resolutions among themselves.

A growing sense of engagement with nonelectoral political action was also manifested during the winter of 1860, when an alleged fugitive slave from Missouri named Edward Canter was captured and brought before the federal commissioner in Springfield. As he had done in 1857, William Herndon volunteered to represent the alleged fugitive in court, writing to a friend in Quincy to send him some papers that Canter said would prove his freedom. Herndon concluding his letter by asking, "If any white man knows [Canter] send him here and our black population will foot the bill—pay his expenses. If the white man knows that he is *free*."[18] Although Canter eventually lost his bid for freedom, the willingness of Springfield's black population to involve themselves in such a case was itself a political statement.[19]

Black Springfield in 1860 was certainly a politically aware community, but most in the community were likely more concerned with the daily struggle to earn a living than with taking direct action to address the challenges posed by discriminatory laws and popular prejudice. Indeed, black Springfielders knew that many white Illinoisans were already suspicious of their presence, and most probably assumed that the best way to survive was simply to work hard and demonstrate that they presented no particular threat. Black Springfielders understood the gravity of the national situation in 1861 as well as their white neighbors, but there was considerably less they could do about it. When Camp Butler was established a few miles northeast of the city, only white volunteers were accepted as soldiers for the army. By the time black regiments

were organized locally in 1864, only nine blacks from Sangamon County—
and only one from Springfield—volunteered for service.²⁰

The most significant consequence of the war was the rapid increase in
the size of the black community. By 1865, when the state census was taken,
the black population of Springfield had almost doubled in just five years to
nearly five hundred. A postwar history of the city's black population noted:
"It was not until and after the war that the race made their advent here in
large numbers," and "the first installment of 'contraband' that arrived while
the war was in progress were almost as much objects of curiosity as the first
[blacks] that came."²¹ In 1864, the *Illinois State Register* remarked on the arrival
of "hundreds of negroes, amongst us contrary to law, and earning their living
nobody can tell how." The *Register* distinguished between the "old colored
residents" who owned property and engaged in business, and "the horde of
late importations—great, muscular, stalwart fellows, who came from no one
knows whither, who do not work for their living, and are liable to punishment
for being here contrary to law."²²

Despite their prejudicial view of the "horde," the *Register* rightly perceived
the wartime growth of the city's black population, and their suspicions as to
the cause of this growth—the phrase "from no one knows whither" referred to
the South—were generally accurate. Histories of postemancipation black migration have emphasized the control that Southern whites quickly reasserted
over freed people and how little the racial demography of the South changed
during the postemancipation decades to conclude that there was only a trickle
of postemancipation black migration out of the South. But although Southern black migrants after emancipation did not move in easily recognizable
streams, this migration was so significant that, as historian Michael P. Johnson
has observed, "These refugees from Dixie comprised the largest voluntary interstate migration of African Americans in the first century of the nation's history."²³ A conservative estimate suggests that at least 60,000 Southern blacks
moved into the Midwest after emancipation, and the number was probably
closer to 80,000. Indiana's black population more than doubled between 1860
and 1870, and Illinois' more than tripled. Ohio, which already had a much
higher number of blacks in 1860 than any other midwestern state, added more
than 26,000 black residents by 1870. Even Michigan and Wisconsin, more
geographically distant, and less economically appealing, came close to doubling their black populations during the 1860s.²⁴

The most dramatic growth occurred in towns and cities like Springfield
where the antebellum black populations had been small.²⁵ In Evansville, Indiana, the black population jumped from 127 in 1860 to over 1,400 in 1870,

a growth rate of more than 1,000 percent. In Muncie, Indiana, the antebellum black population was only 16, but by 1870, there were 48 blacks, and by 1880, nearly 200. In 1860, blacks made up less than 1 percent of Muncie's total population, but by 1880 they were nearly 4 percent of the city's residents.[26] The growth occurred in rural areas as well. In Pulaski County, in southern Illinois, the black population grew from just 40 in 1860 to 1,487 in 1865, and to 2,394 in 1870. Countywide, between 1860 and 1870, blacks in Pulaski went from 1 percent of the population to more 25 percent of all residents.[27] In Minnesota and Wisconsin, sympathetic local religious leaders arranged to bring hundreds of former slaves into their communities to settle and fill the wartime labor shortage. The black population in small towns such as Racine, Wisconsin, and Saint Paul, Minnesota, literally grew overnight with the arrival of hundreds of blacks by steamboat.[28]

Between the federal census of 1860 and the Illinois state census of 1865, Springfield's black population nearly doubled from 272 to 497. Although the state census did not list black individuals by name, making it impossible to determine the nativity of the newcomers, it is likely that the majority of this new group arrived from the South.[29] This is supported by the growth that occurred between 1865 and 1870, when another 260 blacks came to settle in Springfield. Of Springfield's 757 black residents in 1870, 64 percent were born in slave states, compared with only 45 percent a decade earlier. The number born in free states did not quite double between 1860 and 1870, but the number born in slave states nearly quadrupled. Most of the Southern-born black adults in antebellum Springfield were born in Missouri, Kentucky, Tennessee, or Virginia, but in 1870 a greater number of them came from states farther south: Mississippi, Louisiana, Georgia, and Alabama.[30]

Black Springfield after the war was a more mature and more male-dominated community than it had been in 1860. Whereas only 42 percent of the population was male in 1860, men constituted 52 percent of the black community by 1870. The single largest age group in 1870 was men in their twenties, reflecting single men's greater opportunities for mobility following emancipation. Young men who had seen some form of military service were a particularly remarkable subset of this group, and tended to become prosperous long-term residents. Of twenty-five prominent local blacks whose biographies were included in a history of Sangamon County compiled in 1881, nine saw some form of Civil War service before settling in Springfield. Noah Thomas, a blacksmith in 1870, was born in Hinds County, Missouri in 1842. In 1863, he was employed by Captain Franklin Fisk of the 4th Illinois Cavalry as a hostler. When Fisk mustered out a year later in Springfield, Thomas remained to establish his own business. Similarly, Robert Gorum, born in North Carolina, arrived in Springfield in 1865 as a waiter for Chaplin Mathew Bigger of the 50th Illinois Infantry. After his employer was discharged, Gorum worked in hotels in Springfield, was listed by 1870 as a "coachman" in the household of Springfield attorney John Rosette, opened his own restaurant, and worked in the governor's office, among other jobs. By 1881, he owned "a nice residence on the southwest corner of Scarret and Passfield streets." Others, like Madison Veal of Wilkinson County, Mississippi, enlisted as soldiers in Illinois regiments and were discharged at Camp Butler. Veal moved around Illinois for a few years after his discharge and even returned home to Mississippi to visit his family, but ultimately settled back in Springfield where he married, joined the Methodist church, and worked as a farmer. George Stevens ran away from his owner in Missouri to join General John M. Schofield's Army of the Ohio, and served until the close of the war, when he was discharged in Springfield and took a job in a lumberyard. William Holt took a more circuitous route from a plantation in North Carolina to General William T. Sherman's headquarters (where he served as a cook), to Saint Louis, Pine Bluff, Arkansas, Little Rock, Cairo, Chicago, and finally Springfield by 1870. By 1881, the former slave, army cook, waiter, and traveler owned a home in Springfield where he lived with his wife and daughter.[31]

Black Springfield remained a relatively young community after the war, with 25 percent of the population under ten years of age, and 44 percent under twenty. Twenty-seven percent of women and 34 percent of men were in their twenties. This new demographic changed, among other things, the residence patterns of the community. Although many single young women still lived with their white employers as domestic servants, fewer overall lived in white households by 1870. Single people now often roomed together, rather than with families. Forty-year-old farmer James Lee shared his house with Ephraim Allen, a twenty-six-year-old laborer from South Carolina, fifteen-year-old Willis Robinson from Missouri, and twenty-three-year-old laborer John Watts from Alabama; and Narcisa Donegan, thirty-six, and Margret Lee, twenty-five, both from Kentucky, roomed with seventy-year-old Leanna Knox.[32]

Despite the new arrangements brought about by a larger proportion of younger single people, families continued to form the backbone of black Springfield. One hundred and seven families in 1870 had children at home, compared with only thirty-five families in 1860. Of these families, eighty-seven had children under ten years of age, and twenty-three families had a child under one year. Of the 294 individuals under twenty years of age in 1870, 62 percent were born in Illinois, with Kentucky and Missouri providing most of the remaining 38 percent. Although most of the children were born in Illinois, the postbellum population growth also owed much to the arrival of whole families set in motion by the war. Tennessee-born Oliver and Martha Craven had four children together in their home state before the war. By 1866, they were living in Kentucky, where a fifth child was born, and by 1868, had moved to Illinois for the birth of their sixth child. In some cases, couples from different states started their families on the move, landing in Springfield after a lengthy series of migrations. John and Mary Perkins, from Kentucky and Virginia, respectively, had migrated to Missouri by 1858, when their first son James was born. Seven years later, perhaps seeking a new start in the North, they were in Pennsylvania for the birth of son John in 1865. They remained there only three years at the most, moving to Illinois by 1868 when their third son George was born; by 1870, they lived in Springfield. Other families moved during the chaos of the war, traveling across war-torn regions to reach Illinois. Virginia-born William and Maryland-born Madeline Morgan probably met and married in the Chesapeake region in the early 1850s, perhaps as slaves. Their first son, Webster, was born in Virginia in 1853, but the family (or Madeline, at least) soon moved to Louisiana, a relocation so dramatic that it may have been the result of a slave sale. Somehow at least part of the family stayed together, and son Charles and daughter Julia were born in Louisiana in 1856 and 1861. The Morgans may then have taken advantage of the tumult of the war years to move northward. By 1865, they had reached Illinois in time to receive daughter Lucinda, and had two more children over the next five years. Others waited until the war had ended to move their families to Illinois, like Edward and Ellen Henson, who brought their four Maryland-born children to Illinois between 1866 and 1870, toting baby Cornelia all the way.[33]

The aftermath of the war also brought new types of family arrangement that had not been common before the war. Of the families with children, fifteen were headed by single women who lived with relatives or friends; or, like Martha Smith and her five-month-old son, Commodore, in the homes of their white employers. Two families were headed by single men: Isaac Wright, a thirty-five-year-old brick mason, had two sons at home; and six-year-old Willie Sappington lived with his father and uncle. Adoption or foster care also became much more common. Several local families took in young orphans, the children of other family members, or the children of friends. Abraham and Caladonia Galdin took in four Illinois-born siblings surnamed Allen, all of whom were ten years of age or under, in addition to their own two-month-old daughter; and sixty-five-year-old Aaron and fifty-six-year-old Louisa Yarbor took three siblings between the ages of nine and sixteen into their household.³⁴ These new family bonds could become just as significant as those of traditional families. William Florville's adopted son Samuel was allowed to "have an equal share, the same as my own children" when William made out his last will and testament in 1868.³⁵

As families of all sorts put down roots in Springfield, they were drawn into existing networks of kinship, friendship, and faith. A stable core of families had remained throughout the 1850s, 1860s, and 1870s, forming the heart of the black community. Using census or city directory information to determine persistence can be difficult as daughters marry and change names, grown children make temporary moves outside of the community, spouses die and widows remarry, and census takers err. However, comparing the 1850, 1860, and 1870 federal census for Springfield reveals the stabilizing role played by long-term families, including the William Florville family, Jameson Jenkins family, John Jackson family, Aaron Dyer family, and Henry Vance family, all of which remained throughout those decades. Using 176 individuals from the 1850 census as an original population, 57 (32 percent) recur in the 1860 census, and 13 (7 percent) in the 1870 census. As new families arrived, and were created or patched together with adopted children, marriage and the creation of nuclear families were important stabilizing factors, connecting families to one another and to community institutions. The Florville family alone was directly linked to at least a dozen different families by the mid-1870s. When Clark Duncan, a native Kentuckian and veteran of the 115th U.S. Colored Infantry, landed in Springfield in the late 1860s, he met and married Julia Chavious, daughter of Alseen Florville (herself the daughter of William and Phoebe Florville) and Mahlon Chavious. Mahlon had died some years previous and Alseen was remarried to farmer Richard Wright. Alseen and Richard had three children of their own by the mid-1870s, much younger stepbrothers to Julia. Clark and Julia Duncan's own three children likely grew up and played with Alseen and Richard's children, probably considering them more like siblings than uncles. The net effect was to cement several generations and several nuclear families tightly in Springfield by tying them into a broad web of extended familial connections. Even the restless Clark Duncan, who had roamed the Midwest and upper South for the better part of five years after his war service, secured a good job as a porter at the Leland Hotel and became a member of the Methodist Church, a Knight Templar, and a Mason. By 1875, the Duncans owned a "nice residence at 312 North Thirteenth Street," and Clark had brought his elderly mother Louisa from Kentucky to live with his new Illinois family. There were dozens of other stories like Clark Duncan's, and hundreds of family connections that bound black Springfield into a community.³⁶

When Governor Palmer spoke before the black citizens of Springfield in September 1869, he advised them that, "The family is the foundation of society, and homes are essential to the existence of an intelligent, virtuous, well ordered family." Palmer continued, "you must have homes, where you can shelter those you love, and where you may teach your children to love the father's house—homes, forever humble, but your own homes, that you may improve and adorn them . . . Go forth, then, and get homes, for a homeless race cannot progress in civilization or refinement."[37] But Palmer's audience hardly needed to be told about the importance of home life and family bonds. The black Springfielders who listened to him were already husbands, wives, children, brothers, sisters, aunts, uncles, cousins, grandparents, stepparents, and foster parents; and they knew already the need to stitch families back together, to welcome orphans into new homes, to celebrate life by bringing another son or daughter into a growing household. Already, the "homes, forever humble" of Springfield's black families were filled with husbands and fathers who worked as barbers, brickmasons, carpenters, blacksmiths, and other skilled tradesmen; mothers who took in laundry, sewing, and piecework to help ends meet; children who carried their lessons home from the Colored School to teach their siblings and parents.

Not all of black Springfield in 1869 was, as Governor Palmer suggested, a population newly sprung from the soil of slavery, ignorant of their rights and responsibilities, but a sizeable portion of the community had arrived from the Southern states within the last decade. These new arrivals transformed the demography of black Springfield, but they also shared common goals and priorities with the antebellum black population: family, security, prosperity, education, and ultimately, citizenship. By the census of 1880, black Springfield reflected the demographic changes that had occurred over the preceding two decades. A large migration from the South had initially swelled the black population, and over the next decade, as families settled in Springfield, the population began to sustain its own natural growth. After the arrival of so many Southern-born migrants in the 1860s, only about 33 percent of Springfield's blacks were Illinois natives in 1870, down from nearly 50 percent a decade earlier. By 1880, however, the percentage of Illinois-born black residents was back up to 47 percent. In fact, there were as many Illinois-born blacks in 1880 as the total number who claimed nativity in former slave states.[38]

A broader range of employment opportunities helped postbellum black Springfielders feel as though they had a greater stake in the larger community. Although many continued to work as unskilled laborers or servants, many now worked at skilled, semiskilled, and even professional positions, and others ran their own businesses. Women's opportunities outside of the ubiquitous category "keeping house" were still limited primarily to working as laundresses or servants, but by the 1870s, two women were listed in the census as dressmakers or seamstresses, and one was listed as a cook. In the 1880 census, several women were also listed as carpet weavers and schoolteachers. By far the most exotic occupation belonged to sixty-year-old Mary Trouble, who was described in the census as a fortuneteller. The range of men's occupations expanded more dramatically. The Leland Hotel, which opened in 1867, was the single largest employer of Springfield's young black men, twenty-two of whom worked there as porters and waiters in 1870. Men also commonly worked as brickmasons, cooks, paper hangers, carpenters, painters, teamsters, miners, grocers, hostlers, millers, plasterers, private watchmen, and ministers. There were several clerks, a number of confectioners, farmers, engineers, preachers, a shoemaker, whitewashers, a butcher, and even a police officer. The largest single category for men was still "laborer" or "help," but by the mid-1870s, a large proportion of men were listed in the city directory as miners, illustrating the growth of the central Illinois coal industry and the new options it presented for Springfield's laboring population. By the mid-1870s, a significant number of Springfield's blacks were also employed as rolling mill operators by the Springfield Iron Company, which opened in 1871.[39]

With public schooling open to them, black children in Springfield during the late 1860s and 1870s also had greater opportunities than ever before. The location of what became known as the "Colored School" changed several times throughout the 1860s. The superintendent recommended to the board that the facilities be upgraded but noted that the students were making excellent progress despite the poor conditions. In 1862, a report to the school board noted, "The house at present occupied by the Colored School is unsuitable for the purpose for which it is used, being old, dilapidated, unventilated, leaky, and otherwise in bad repair . . . too warm in summer, and too cold in winter, injurious to the health of the children, and thus greatly impairing the usefulness of the School."[40] It was five years before another building was chosen to house the school, but despite the poor facilities, Springfield's black residents eagerly took advantage of the opportunity to send their children. In 1863, forty-seven pupils were enrolled, forty-four of whom attended regularly.[41] By 1866, there were sixty children attending on a regular basis, and another sixty-one listed as registered but not attending, probably because there was no room for them. So many students were enrolled in the Colored School that the board asked its committee on teachers to hire an assistant for the school's only teacher. The next year, a motion was adopted by the board restricting the age of students at the Colored School to eighteen years, evidently to curb enrollment by older students, but the rule was suspended two months later.[42] In 1867, a new location was finally chosen that was well heated and ventilated, and had larger rooms than many of the other city schools. Two teachers now taught four grades, and the superintendent noted that "the present condition of the school is a great improvement over the former state of things, when all the pupils were crowded into one small room. The future is looked for with interest, since now, for the first time, this school is to be opened with advantages that will bear some comparison with those long enjoyed by a more favored race."[43]

By the late 1860s it was apparent that a single school was inadequate for Springfield's growing black population. In June 1870, 120 students were enrolled with just two teachers, and 20 more students were added by December. Another 40 students were added a year later without hiring more teachers.[44] In addition to being overcrowded, the single schoolhouse was too far away for some of the children to attend regularly. Springfield's white children could attend schools close to their homes in each of the city's wards, but not all of the city's black children could easily reach the single Colored School. In July 1872, the school board heard a "petition of Colored Citizens for redress of grievances etc.," which probably included the problems of accessibility and overcrowding. The next month, the board ordered the Committee on School Houses and Furniture to "ascertain the present residences as near as may be of the Colored population of this City or the majority of the same with the view of determining a suitable place to open another school for the colored children for their better accommodations, and also that they ascertain how many rooms are requisite for such purpose, and also where the same can be procured, and upon what terms."[45] By the next year, the need was so great that the assistant teacher petitioned the board to hold extra classes during the summer in order to accommodate the number of eager students who could not attend during the rest of the year.

By the early 1870s, two apparently contradictory trends had emerged in the city's prioritization of the Colored School. The overworked white principal and teachers were paid less than their counterparts in the all-white ward schools, and despite the complaints of black citizens, and offers of vacant buildings from concerned citizens and churches, the school board acted only reluctantly on the need for more space. However, the very existence of the school indicated that the board believed its own rules unfairly excluded the city's black children from a public education, and although the needs of the school were not always addressed in a timely manner, the Colored School was a regular part of the board's agenda every year. From buying clocks and curtains to hiring teachers, supervising annual exams, and disciplining unruly pupils, the board regularly involved itself in the affairs of the school and took a positive, if tentative, stand on behalf of the city's black residents.[46] By 1880, there were many black children attending school, including forty-six girls between the ages of seven and fifteen, or about 44 percent of school-age girls. Forty-four boys between the ages of seven and eighteen attended school, or about 29 percent, and twenty-year-old Henry Brown was listed in the census as a law student, indicating that there was even some chance for black students to move beyond a secondary education.

As the black population took advantage of improved employment and educational opportunities, they also asserted a greater sense of participation in the community and its institutions, and entered social and political life in more diverse ways. The Reconstruction amendments, together with federal civil rights legislation and new state laws, gave them new opportunities to involve themselves as citizens in legal, political, and social issues. There were also new annual celebrations commemorating the anniversary of the Emancipation Proclamation and the ratification of the Thirteenth, Fourteenth, and Fifteenth Amendments, which helped create a new sense of community identity. There were also rallies, public meetings, and debates on subjects ranging from education to suffrage. These events reinforced bonds of thought and action that connected the community to activists across the state and the nation, providing a sense of shared identity that was periodically reinforced by visiting speakers. In January 1865, a mass meeting of black citizens convened at the Colored Baptist Church to draft a petition to the state legislature to repeal the Black Laws. The meeting was attended by anti–Black Laws activists from across the state, including John Jones from Chicago. Local barber Spencer Donnegan, one of Springfield's most active community organizers, chaired the meeting. When the Black Laws were repealed one month later, Springfield's blacks advanced toward citizenship and gained a sense of what could be accomplished by common action.[47]

With the repeal of Illinois's Black Laws, a larger black population, and Republican support, community leaders gained a stronger voice. In November 1865, when the 29th United States Colored Infantry was mustered out at Camp Butler, Springfield's black community raised funds and organized a public dinner and reception for the troops. Thomas Killion, an Illinois-born barber with a Virginia-born wife and three Illinois-born children, chaired the meeting and introduced the distinguished white speakers, including William Herndon and Governor Richard Oglesby. For such dignitaries to address a primarily black audience, most of whom were still in uniform, must have seemed a surreal proceeding for both white and black participants. Even the sympathetic Republican *Illinois State Journal,* which ran a laudatory story on the event, commented, "It was an unusual scene for the State of Illinois."[48]

After Abraham Lincoln's burial in Springfield, prominent speakers were drawn to the city, including Frederick Douglass, who gave two lectures in April 1866. Although both were addressed to distinguished white audiences, his remarks would certainly have circulated through the black community. The first lecture on Lincoln's assassination contained few mentions of blacks beyond "a well deserved meed of praise to the colored race" and an assertion of their "fidelity to freedom now in the days of peace."[49] The second lecture focused on the conservatism of the Johnson administration and the political allegiance of "defeated rebels with the Copperheads of the North." Douglass observed, "Slavery is dead, but the sentiments it created still live." Despite this, Douglass was certain that a civil rights bill would soon be passed and that blacks would attain equal rights before the law. "We are betrayed," he claimed, "but are not ruined."[50] Although not addressed specifically to the black community, these words from a black celebrity of the abolition movement would have energized and inspired locals to work for change within their community and beyond.

Frederick Douglass visited the city again in 1868 for a celebration on the anniversary of the Emancipation Proclamation, and this time he attended a meeting of black citizens, although his formal remarks, if any, were apparently not recorded. The day began with the firing of cannon, followed by a parade, and speeches that lasted well into the night. Beginning at the African (or Colored) Methodist Church, the celebratory procession was led by the local Rogers Cornet Band, composed entirely of black musicians, representatives from the Young Men's Aid Society, the black pupils of the Sunday schools, and finally, as the *Journal* noted, a large number of "colored citizens." The procession marched to Lincoln's house, then to the skating rink, where speakers addressed a large rally. The officials and marshals included Landon Coleman, a shoemaker; John Jackson, a laborer; Thomas Killion, a barber; Primus Chase, a laborer; John Oglesby, a teamster; Nathan Smallwood, a cook; and the elderly William Florville and Moses McDaniel. At the rink, William Herndon addressed the crowd with "an appropriate and interesting speech," but the bulk of the speaking was done by local black leaders. The Reverend George Brent of the Zion Baptist Church, who had been born a slave in Kentucky, asked that his fellow black Springfielders remember that the Republican Party was the party of Lincoln and emancipation and that the Democratic Party was the party of slavery and treason. All black citizens should teach their children this truth, said Brent, "in case they should ever be permitted to cast a vote." Spencer Donnegan and Landon Coleman followed Brent with speeches of "considerable length," which were frequently interrupted with applause and cheers.[51]

Similar celebrations occurred throughout the 1870s, when a Fifteenth Amendment celebration was added to black Springfield's social calendar. In 1870, anticipating the announcement of President Grant's ratification message to Congress, "quite a number of the colored population" of Springfield assembled at one o'clock in the morning to await the news. When it was received, there followed a two-hour impromptu celebration in the small hours of the morning, featuring the firing of cannon, singing, "and other demonstrations of delight." The Rogers Cornet Band serenaded the offices of the *Illinois State Journal* at two o'clock—for which the editors later offered their somewhat dubious thanks—and by three o'clock, all was quiet once again.[52] Less than a week later, on the eve of the first local election in which black men were able to vote, a "large and enthusiastic meeting" was held in the African Baptist Church. Again, local black leaders, including the barber Henry Bailey and the shoemaker Cyrus Donnegan, as well as sympathetic white friends such as William Herndon, took the pulpit to inspire the black voters of the city, and probably also to give them practical information about how, when, and where to vote.[53]

Two weeks later, after the elections were over, Springfield's blacks held a more formal celebration for the ratification of the Fifteenth Amendment, including another parade that visited Lincoln's house and ended in a large rally. Many of the most active participants and organizers of these events were not wealthy or well known; both community elites and ordinary residents worked together. At the 1870 celebration, a local porter named Elias Rollins was the parade's chief marshal, assisted by the drayman William Head and the laborers John Clark, Isaac Parks, and Lewis Williams. The meeting at the rink was presided over by Landon Coleman, a shoemaker, along with James Johnson, a laborer; Nathan Smallwood; Charles Parker, a laborer; and Moses McDaniel.[54] The procession was again headed by the Rogers Cornet Band, by now a staple of such celebrations, "which favored the public with some excellent music." Behind the band marched standard-bearers with signs that read: "Peace on earth and good will to men"; "The Lord said: I have seen the affliction of my people who are in Egypt"; "The ratification of the Fifteenth Amendment is good news of great joy to the down-trodden"; "Our Watch-word is Liberty"; and "God speed the rights of every man." Next came a wagon bearing young black girls dressed all in white, each bearing the name of a state of the union. At the center of the wagon, on an elevated platform, stood "a tall negress, as the Goddess of Liberty." The liberty wagon with its bevy of young girls representing states was widely used in black celebrations across the country as a symbol of patriotism and a statement of belonging. Including such symbols in their parades allowed newly enfranchised blacks to lay equal claim to the principles they represented and the right to deploy them. After the wagon came a brass cannon and squad of black gunners, a troop of horsemen, and finally a group of carriages.[55] A similar procession was held the following year, drawing visitors from Decatur, Jacksonville, and other nearby towns, and was judged "unusually strong in numbers" by the local press. The Rogers Band again led the procession, and the costumes from the previous year were reused for the Goddess of Liberty and the states of the union. There was also a large national flag and a portrait of Abraham Lincoln, along with banners "inscribed with appropriate mottos." The local black lodge of Masons and a contingent from the Young Men's Aid Society completed the procession, along with a large number of black citizens on foot, on horseback, and in carriages.[56]

When the 1871 parade disbanded to hear speeches, Governor Palmer gave an address similar to the one he had given in 1869, but he made a special point of addressing the black audience now "as fellow-citizens." Palmer urged Springfield's blacks to make a stronger assertion of their rights, including their right to send their children to any of the city's public schools. Palmer was followed by Landon Coleman, who had been elected to chair the rally. Coleman's speech demonstrated a more complex understanding of the practical problems blacks still faced. Like the governor, Coleman urged the desegregation of the city's public schools, but expressed doubts that Democrats-turned-Republicans, like Palmer, would truly act in the best interests of black citizens. Coleman highlighted the problems black Springfielders still faced in the exercise of the rights they had gained. Coleman was followed on the stand by a white speaker who praised black Springfielders for their "advancement in intelligence and morals" and urged them to obtain real estate in order to make material progress. As the Democratic *Register* noted in its report of the celebration, the "enthusiasm of the audience was visibly dampened" at the conclusion of the speeches. Even celebratory rallies meant to highlight recent advances inevitably called attention to problems that remained unsolved. Black Springfielders likely came away from the event not simply with "dampened" enthusiasm, but with the realistic understanding that progress on paper did not always translate into practice.[57]

National and statewide conventions of black citizens helped black Springfielders place the challenges they faced in their community within a broader spectrum of black experience in the state and the nation. During the war, the national black convention movement became imbued with a new sense of urgency and significance that drew Illinois blacks more actively into the work. In 1864, J. Houston of Springfield was selected as the Illinois representative to the national convention in Syracuse, New York, where he heard Frederick Douglass declare that "freedom, progress, elevation, and perfect enfranchisement, of the entire colored people of the United States" were the most notable goals of the convention movement. The necessity of national and state organization was clear, said Douglass, because of the "state of feeling in the country toward the colored man."[58] Houston returned to Springfield with this message, which would hardly have surprised most black Springfielders. Although much positive work was being done—or promised, at least—by the federal government, black communities and activists across the nation must be the agents of their own advancement and must not rely only on whites for assistance, since much racial prejudice remained.

Community activists such as Landon Coleman, Hezekiah Hicklin, and George Brent, encouraged by the successes and motivated by the failures of the Reconstruction amendments and civil rights legislation, also attended statewide conventions on behalf of Springfield's black community. The messages they delivered continued to combine enthusiasm and optimism tempered by harsh experience and the reality of ongoing discrimination. In 1866, Hicklin and Brent attended the Illinois State Convention of Colored Men at Galesburg, returning with the convention's message that all black citizens must work for "equal rights for colored men, both at the *ballot-box* and in courts of justice." They also returned with a renewed commitment to "utterly remove those prejudices against us as a people," those less tangible and pernicious racial prejudices, "which still obtain in the minds of so many—prejudices which are the effect of slavery." When they spoke to black Springfielders of what had transpired at the convention—most likely before the congregations at the Colored Baptist and Colored Methodist churches—Hicklin and Brent also emphasized the common theme of equal access to education, an antebellum cause that remained unresolved. They communicated the convention's indignant protest: "We are *disfranchised* in the State of our residence, without the commission of any crime by ourselves, as a reason for our disfranchisement. . . . The colored citizens of this great State, that prides itself on its 'system of free schools,' must, under the present partial and unjust enactment, submit to see their children driven from the well organized and ably conducted schools in the districts where they reside, for no other delinquency than the crime of being created with a darker skin than their neighbors." In words that Hicklin and Brent very likely repeated verbatim, and with equal emphasis, to their white friends in Springfield: "To

God, the universal governor, and to you, we commit it, and ask you to decree by your suffrages, *Equality of rights for all loyal men in America, before the bar of American law!*"[59]

Other local, state, and national conventions followed in the 1870s, and Springfield representatives took part. In 1873, Mark Williams, a hotel waiter, and B. F. Rogers, a barber, were appointed as local delegates to the National Convention of Colored Persons in Washington, DC, called to urge greater enforcement of the Fourteenth Amendment. They were joined by representatives of other black communities around the state, including prominent anti–Black Laws activist John Jones of Chicago.[60] Together, they "articulated more developed and cohesive demands for rights" and "helped shape the legal concept of citizenship that emerged during Reconstruction."[61] When they returned to Springfield, like Hezekiah Hicklin and George Brent before them, Williams and Rogers would have brought new ideas and a greater sense of unity and purpose to others in the community working for local rights.

Political rallies, celebrations, and conventions combined optimism and enthusiasm with serious discussion about black citizenship, and provided a link between black Springfielders and other communities throughout the state and the nation, but there were also more immediate ways for black Springfielders to assert their place within the community. Participation in civic organizations was an important way for black Springfielders to involve themselves in the associational life of the community and to refute Democratic claims that blacks were fundamentally unfit for citizenship. In addition to black lodges of the Masons, Odd Fellows, and Knights Templar, there were other smaller fraternal orders, a baseball team, a brass band, and at least two militia companies. These organizations served dual roles as community-building institutions and as ambassadors to the skeptical white population, who found that blacks not only participated in, but also excelled at the same institutions that had long been staples of the white community. Even the Democratic *Register* acknowledged in 1870 that "Springfield now has the champion nigger base ball club of the United States."[62]

Black militia companies were particularly significant among the new organizations. The postbellum rage for volunteer militia companies harkened back to the independent militia clubs of the antebellum decade, but with the significant difference that many working-class veterans now joined the volunteer companies. Although still retaining their social aspects, local postbellum militias served both as colorful parade participants and as a nascent National Guard. Participation in black militia companies demonstrated engagement in local organizations that were centrally concerned with maintaining community standards. They were significantly different from the political clubs of uniformed black Republicans that Democrats perceived as a threat during elections. The *Register* described the latter as little better than organized political mobs, which seized control of the polling places and stormed the streets on Election Day benders (see chapter 4). The organized black political companies often participated in "dramas of intimidation" on Election Day as statements of their legitimate right to access the polls, but frequently ended up providing fodder for whites' fears and suspicions about disorderly black voters and irresponsible citizens.[63] The more formal militia companies in Springfield, in contrast, were expressly intended to uphold community norms. Although they rarely acted in a truly military capacity, local militias were a source of civic pride, traveling often to parades and exhibitions around the state in much the way sports teams would later in the century.[64]

In August 1871, Chicago's Hannibal Zouaves performed drills and maneuvers in Springfield as part of the annual Emancipation Day celebration, which even the Democratic *Register* described as "very creditable." Cyrus Donnegan was apparently inspired by their performance and decided to form his own local zouave company, which he called the Springfield Zouave Guards.[65] A second company was formed shortly by Nelson Bacon, a local laborer, which he called the Capital City Guards.[66] Neither Donnegan nor Bacon included any reference to race or color in the names of their companies, a practice that had predominated during the Civil War, when titles like "Native," "African," or "Colored" clearly marked segregated units. Excluding such labels from their organizations, Donnegan and Bacon asserted that their companies were intended to exist on equal terms with the city's white militia companies, not as second-tier auxiliaries.

The city press was less inclined to ignore the racial composition of the new local militias, but was generally supportive and even effusive in its praise for their aptitude, precision, and appearance. In September, the *Register* reported that "there are two colored militia companies organized in this city" and in October that the "new colored military company under command of Capt. Cyrus Donnegan" received arms from the state arsenal and, together with two white militia companies, departed for fire-ravaged Chicago to act as guards against the "cut-throats and villains who are pilfering its people."[67] Functioning as agents of law and order, and as adjuncts of the state government, the members of the black militia company were firmly on the side of established traditions of civic responsibility.

The next spring, for a Fifteenth Amendment celebration in Jacksonville, Donnegan's company performed a less martial, but no less significant role as community ambassadors when they made their first public appearance outside of Springfield as a crack drill squad. Springfield's *Illinois State Journal* reported that the "Springfield colored Zouave Company . . . in their showy and beautiful uniforms," accompanied by Roger's Cornet Band, "marched through the streets, made a splendid appearance and won the admiration of all by their soldier like appearance and strict attention to orders."[68] In 1874, at the dedication of the monument and tomb to Abraham Lincoln in Springfield's Oak Ridge Cemetery, the Springfield Zouaves were judged of sufficient quality to march in the procession's First Division, along with the Rogers Band, in the company of distinguished white militia companies.[69] Their presence in the parade demonstrated to a national audience that black citizens were willing and able to engage in the public pageantry of patriotism and nationalism. For the members of the company and their supporters from Springfield, such approbation signaled their successful participation in an acceptable and sanctioned patriotic display.

―

At the same time that Southern blacks began to arrive in Springfield in greater numbers, a monumental shift in public policy had occurred so that they could no longer be prosecuted simply for entering the state. Removing the ban on immigration facilitated the integration of the public schools, the growth of black businesses, and the granting of suffrage. Rather than tighten its laws and enhance its enforcement to keep out the expected flood of Southern blacks, as many Democrats advocated in 1862, Illinois removed its legal barriers and seemingly welcomed blacks into the state. Nearly three-quarters of the Illinois-born black children in Springfield in 1880 had been born into a nation without slavery and raised in a state without fear of persecution under the Black Laws. As the historian Jack Blocker has observed, "Although white racism lingered in both midwestern law and custom during the late nineteenth century, the legal and institutional changes that had occurred as a result of the Civil War gave grounds for hope that racist structures and practices could be further eroded in the years to come."[70] There were many black families in Springfield during the late 1860s, 1870s, and 1880s who fervently harbored this hope, and community activists who actively nurtured it. Every black child in school, every professional or skilled craftsman, every fraternal order, every parade, every election seemed to bring local blacks that much closer to the hope of greater equity, if not full equality.

Despite the significant gains and the substantial growth of black communities, blackness as a marker of difference remained a convenient source of whites' fear and suspicion. As Andrew Cayton and Peter Onuf have observed, "What made racial exclusion particularly galling was the degree to which the relatively small black communities in the nineteenth-century Midwest adopted middle-class values."[71] Although blacks participated in the civil and political affairs of the community in ways they assumed would demonstrate their ability and right to be community stakeholders, their efforts continued to meet with persistent race prejudice. Black Springfield by 1880 reflected the uneven success of the struggle against race prejudice: blacks attended public schools, but in small numbers; they worked in a greater range of occupations, but unskilled laborers still dominated; many owned property and participated in civic clubs and organizations, but segregated neighborhoods were already emerging. If greater opportunities were available to some of Springfield's blacks by 1880, it was only after more than a decade of struggle to define and assert their rights.

The nature of black citizenship underwent a fundamental transformation at the same time as the demography of black Springfield changed in the postemancipation period. Both of these were reflected in the ways black Springfielders lived, worked, and socialized. They were also reflected in the actions of black criminals like Gus Reed, who, either out of necessity or out of protest, consistently found themselves at odds with the agents of law and order. Continuing discrimination may have led him to seek opportunities in Springfield's small but active underworld, where he was joined by both whites and blacks who had also found themselves pushed out of the channels of success and prosperity during the turbulent economic times of the 1870s. In black criminals, many white Springfielders discerned a unique threat, and what they judged to be the true nature of the black population. Although most black Springfielders were respectable and hard working, decades of race prejudice were not easily erased either by law or by the good conduct of most local blacks. In the years following emancipation, Springfield's Democrats mobilized this pervasive prejudice as they pushed back against the advance of black citizenship and suffrage.

FOUR

A White Man's Country

> Let Illinois still shine in the galaxy with the
> clear light of a democratic state—one whose
> legislation is by white men, for white men.
>
> —Illinois State Register,
> *April 3, 1864*

JUST FOUR months after the body of Abraham Lincoln arrived in Springfield to the mournful welcome of his friends and neighbors, Democrats gathered on the front steps of the courthouse to praise the limited reconstruction policies of the Andrew Johnson administration and to make their case for the continued rejection of black citizenship. John McClernand, a Union general and a local attorney, addressed the crowd with an inflammatory speech, asking: "Is the elective franchise to be elevated and purified by admitting to its exercise the black men of the south? Are they qualified to exercise it intelligently? Have they not been degraded by bondage through successive generations? Are they not grossly ignorant and superstitious? What do they know of the forms or agencies of government?" McClernand continued: "I would see [the negro] a free man, but I would not make him the political equal of the white man." McClernand believed that irreconcilable racial animosity "would eventuate in violence and renewed subjection" of blacks and that political equality "leads to social equality or the amalgamation of the races." He concluded definitively, "I am opposed to the political and social equalization of the black with the white race."[1]

Illinois had long been protected by the Black Laws as a state governed by and for white citizens, but now it faced significant questions about what black citizenship would mean for a white democracy. Illinois Democrats, like others around the country, worried about the consequences of a decisive Union victory and the martyring of a president who had made emancipation a primary wartime objective. Victory seemed to justify the sweeping expansion of federal authority that Democrats had resisted during the war; the ratification of the Thirteenth Amendment validated the abolitionist crusade against slavery; and the military service of blacks in the Union army led to arguments for black suffrage. Democrats feared that a strong federal government dominated by Republicans would force black citizenship on the states, allowing blacks access to public facilities, schools, courts, and the ballot.

The abolition of the Black Laws and the ratification of the Thirteenth Amendment convinced Democrats that the work of black exclusion was now in the hands of ordinary white Illinoisans. The 1864 *Nelson* decision had affirmed the right of the state to legislate on the issue of black exclusion, but although that decision became moot after 1865, the conviction that the state alone should determine its racial policies still brought Democratic voters to the polls. As historian Joel Silbey has observed of the Democratic Party in the Civil War era, the party's use of "emotive symbols and code words" forged "an intense community of like-minded individuals" that remained in lockstep with the familiar doctrines of the antebellum era.[2] Racism in particular remained effective in local politics because it tied problems at home to the national process of Reconstruction and the negotiation of black citizenship. White Americans encountered and either rejected or legitimized the new black citizen within their own communities, and local Democratic rhetoric relied on deep-seated traditions of racial exclusion to craft their response to the questions raised by emancipation.

As early as the 1870s, northern Democrats especially began to court black voters in order to increase their own electoral pool, and disenchanted black Republicans joined the Democratic Party of their own volition. Democrats gradually turned away from explicit race agitation in national politics, and the party realigned its relationship to blacks after the failed presidential election of 1868, which historian Lawrence Grossman has characterized as "a simple referendum on white supremacy." By the 1880s, the race issue no longer played a central role in mobilizing national electoral opinions and "no longer could one generalize about a man's stand on Negro rights simply by examining his party label."[3] But concerns about increasing black migration and the attendant social problems were still frequently articulated in Democratic discourse. Racial antipathies and explicit race agitation influenced local politics, and a stubborn Democratic tendency to express white supremacy continued to motivate constituents in places like Springfield even as the national party walked a more centrist line.[4] Far from reluctant to voice their critiques of emancipation, or shortsighted in their political goals, Democrats retained race rhetoric even as they abandoned black citizenship as a political issue during the late 1870s and 1880s. Members of both parties continued to imbibe and confirm ideas about race difference through minstrel shows and other popular forms of racial entertainment, and stereotypes and assumptions about blacks fostered by political rhetoric continued to shape views on race well into the early twentieth century. Racism and white supremacy may have been uncoupled from partisan politics, but they were consistently mobilized for political purposes because they proved so popular, resonant, and relevant to many white citizens.[5]

Although the national and state Democratic organizations suffered during the war, the local organizations that sponsored the smaller party newspapers continued to shape political life in counties and towns throughout Illinois. These smaller branches and party organs remained vital because they spoke primarily to local concerns.[6] In Robert McClaughry's Hancock County, the *Carthage Republican* consistently tied local problems and concerns to critiques of emancipation and black suffrage. In October 1863, James M. Davidson, a printer and former editor of Lewiston's Democratic newspaper took over editorship of the *Republican* from McClaughry and Griffith. Davidson had developed a reputation as "an uncompromising democrat," and the *Republican*'s editorial tone changed dramatically once Davidson took control, becoming more critical of the Lincoln administration, the conduct of the war, and the Emancipation Proclamation.[7] One of Davidson's friends described him approvingly as "thoroughly anti-war" and believed that he was firmly devoted to "the great work of Democracy and white liberty."[8] But Davidson's editorial stance alienated the soldiers in the field. Samuel Gordon wrote home to his wife from the field: "I have not seen but one paper since I left Memphis and that is the *Carthage Republican*. I got awful mad before I got through reading it." Gordon opined that the editor should come down to the front lines and "he would be taught better doctrine than he publishes."[9]

Experience at the front changed many Democrats into more moderate partisans who were temporarily willing to place other concerns ahead of fears about emancipation and black rights. This seems to have been especially true for Robert McClaughry. When he rode in Abraham Lincoln's funeral procession to Oak Ridge Cemetery in May 1865, he was struck most by the "pathetic sight" and "intense grief manifested by the colored people, thousands of whom had journeyed for days in order to be in Springfield."[10] A year earlier,

McClaughry made his first foray into politics when he entered the race for clerk of Hancock County on the Union Party ticket. The stakes of the election were not particularly high, but county-level politics were as contentious as ever. Davidson attacked McClaughry in the columns of the *Republican* as a party traitor and an advocate of emancipation and black equality. A vote for Robert McClaughry, wrote Davidson, was a vote for abolition, and "a vote for the abolition ticket is a vote for the negro." Davidson scoured the files of the *Republican* for editorials from McClaughry's tenure as editor, finding plenty of criticism of the Lincoln administration, Republicans, abolitionists, and the war. Davidson explained: "It shows that before the present administration invested that gentleman with his shoulder straps and his stipend . . . he was as much opposed to Old Abe and the abolitionists as any 'copperhead.'" It was now up to the voters, said Davidson, "whether the Major's abolition friends will deem his recent conversion to their faith of sufficient genuineness to justify their supporting him for the office of circuit clerk."[11]

McClaughry's Democratic rival defeated him by more than three hundred votes in 1864, but McClaughry ran again for the same office one year later as a full-fledged Republican. With the war over, the Thirteenth Amendment all but ratified, and the Black Laws repealed, the campaign against McClaughry focused on his position on emancipation and black citizenship. The election in Hancock County embodied the political confusion of postbellum Illinois writ small, and many believed the future of their county, state, and nation lay at least symbolically in the balance. The *Republican* told its readers: "Our state [is] becoming Africanized to an unendurable extent. . . . Anybody not hell bent on nigger equality [is convinced] that to repeal the black laws would ruin the state. But, the repeal was passed; republicans did it; the black swarm is upon us; let republicans have all the glory!" Robert McClaughry, claimed the *Republican,* was now an advocate for black suffrage and equality. "Will he deny it?" asked an anonymous "Returned Soldier" in a letter to the editor.[12]

In the weeks between the *Republican*'s confrontational query and McClaughry's answer, the 118th Illinois Regiment, including what was left of McClaughry's old Company B, returned home to western Illinois. Although the ladies of Carthage had prepared a grand breakfast for the discharged troops, the veterans—most of whom lived in the surrounding countryside—departed the depot directly for their homes. One soldier reportedly even jumped from the train a mile outside of town and ran across the fields to get home sooner. Other veterans of the regiment came home in a much different fashion—the body of Private Thomas Mix arrived in Carthage with the train full of discharged soldiers. The *Republican* reported that the funeral service "dwelt feelingly upon the virtues and sacrifices of the brave deceased in behalf of his country's cause" and "inspired every beholder with feelings and memories they will never forget. Peace to the ashes of the brave dead, and blessings on the living heroes who thus honored them!"[13] The returning men deserved a world of peace and prosperity, and they deserved above all to be counted again as private citizens, rather than private soldiers. Their war was over, their sacrifices made, and now they returned to the state they had fought so hard to protect. Was it fair to these self-sacrificing citizens to allow the state to become overrun with freed slaves, who would compete with white veterans for jobs, whose children would crowd white children out of the schools, and who would undoubtedly soon make claims on suffrage, property, and other hallmarks of citizenship? Was there any loyal white citizen who would assert the equality of blacks before the law and constitution? These were the questions Davidson posed to McClaughry, and which went unanswered as the men of the 118th Illinois arrived home and laid to rest one of their comrades. For many, it must have seemed as if Major McClaughry's response and the pending election would provide a definitive answer to the question of just what the sacrifices of the war would finally mean.

On October 26, Robert McClaughry responded to the letter of "A Returned Soldier" in the columns of the *Republican*, making clear that "I am not in favor of extending the elective franchise to negroes in the state of Illinois." But he then ventured into controversial territory: "In denying them the right of suffrage I do not deny that it is our duty to protect them in their freedom, to instruct, educate and elevate the race; nor do I seek to disguise my belief that the negro soldier who has given his blood in the hot battle for the defense of a government under which he has always been oppressed, will rank immeasurably higher in the judgment of impartial history than the highest of the pampered and petted traitors who sought its ruin."[14] As he might have expected, McClaughry's response did not satisfy "A Returned Soldier," whose reply appeared on the same page. In a four-point denunciation, the anonymous writer maintained, "The question of negro suffrage *is* an issue" and not only in the state of Illinois, and he went on to criticize McClaughry for muddling the issue with "electioneering twaddle about negro soldiers."[15] One week later, in the last issue of the *Republican* before the November 7 election, "A Returned Soldier" revealed himself as John W. Burnett, formerly of the 3rd Iowa Volunteer Cavalry, and he wrote another long and caustic letter focusing on McClaughry's federal commission, his "Copperhead" editorials from the early days of the war, his recent reply on the subject of black suffrage, and his somewhat tame war record as reasons why "no returned soldier or consistent citizen ought to vote for you."[16]

But this time McClaughry won his race with thirteen of twenty-five voting precincts, including the town of Carthage, his home township of Fountain Green, and the city of Warsaw. The *Republican* was stunned by the Democratic failure, and uncharacteristically blamed Democratic voters rather than a Republican plot.[17] In 1865, Republicans were the party of the victorious Union, and Democrats were the party of treason and disloyalty. Returned soldiers such as Sidney Little, William Rand, and George Safford likely followed Robert McClaughry into the Republican Party, not because they supported rights or suffrage for blacks, but because they rejected the antiwar stance of the Democratic Party. Their military service had forged a tie to the Union that transcended old party affiliations and even racial prejudices. This was enough, at least in 1865, to overcome their strong antiblack feelings—which in many cases had also been strengthened by military service—and enable such men to vote Republican.

Local political reconfigurations in 1864 and 1865 seemed to indicate a growing, if somewhat grudging, consensus in support of emancipation, as well as future measures that would begin to integrate former slaves and other blacks into the body politic. But there were still many devoted Democrats who burrowed deeper into their partisanship and the principles of white supremacy that had long formed a basis for party identity. In Springfield, Elliott Herndon was among these Democratic faithful, working to mobilize white voters in defense of Illinois's remaining racial restrictions.

Springfield's economy underwent a transformation during and after the Civil War as the development of manufacturing and extractive industries tied central Illinois ever more closely to an industrializing regional and national economy. Farming was joined by coal mining, steel rolling, and manufacturing as major industries. Although hard times struck in the 1870s, the period between 1865 and 1880 on the whole was one of growth for Springfield and Sangamon County. The combination of tenuous prosperity and rapid growth produced tensions and troubles that had once seemed confined to larger cities. Crime in particular appeared to be on the rise and was often associated with the larger population of rootless transients who now filled the city. Especially unsettling to many white citizens was the influx of Southern blacks, portrayed in the Democratic press as dishonest, lazy, ignorant, and fundamentally dangerous to the institutions of law and order that had been established by and for white citizens.

As in Hancock County, many Democratic voters in Springfield turned to the Union Party in 1864 or to the Republicans a year later to show support for the military and the Union. Sangamon County as a whole remained

Democratic in 1864, but went for the Union/Republican Party across the board in local elections in 1865. After the war, Democrats quickly regrouped around resistance to federal authority and the threat of black equality. Republicans, they warned, would try to insert black suffrage and other measures into the Illinois constitution, and would dismantle the state and local laws that still prevented blacks from voting and sending their children to integrated public schools. In the local elections of 1867, Democrats won a few offices, and only one Republican won in the county elections of 1868. In 1870 it was a clean sweep for Democrats, and Republican candidates rarely won the county for the rest of the decade.[18]

In 1865, Elliott Herndon chaired a committee to draft the Sangamon County Democratic Convention's campaign resolutions, and produced a clear statement of postbellum Democratic priorities. Sangamon Democrats pledged their thanks to the military for their "heroic and self-sacrificing conduct in upholding, through every peril, the flag of their country" but expressed their approval for President Johnson's lenient reconstruction policy, affirming that "the civil should replace military authority, military trials be abolished, and the *habeas corpus* restored." The committee declared the "imposition by federal power of negro government" to be "subversive to the purity and dignity of free people" and asserted that *"we are now, as ever, opposed to negro suffrage and opposed to the political or social equality of the negro race"* (emphasis added).[19] The convention unanimously adopted the resolutions, and Elliott Herndon was elected to a post on the county party's central committee. He was selected as a delegate to the state Democratic convention a year later, and in 1868 he served as a member of the state convention's executive committee. He played a key role during the Democratic resurgence over the next decade, serving in various administrative positions in the city and county Democratic Party. He chaired the city party's convention in 1871 and was a delegate to the local "Liberal" fusion party in 1873. He also served as supervisor for the city's conservative Second Ward, home to a Democratic militia association called the "White Boys in Blue," which drilled, marched, and demonstrated at rallies and events, and occasionally tussled with the Republican-affiliated "Loyal Boys in Blue," who held their own similar events. Other all-white organizations came and went with the ebb and flow of the election cycles, most of them affiliated in some way with the Second Ward. During a torchlight procession through the city in August 1868, the Second Ward delegation, the largest in the parade, marched under a banner emblazoned with the words "Second Ward White Men." The Democratic *Register* described the ward approvingly in 1870 as "the white man's ward."[20]

The white supremacist principles voiced by Elliott Herndon and his fellow Democrats made clear that black citizenship and suffrage were manifestations of the erosion of white control over structures of political and social authority. They used the same language with which they had condemned the wartime expansion of federal authority to allege that the rights of free white citizens across the nation would be subordinated to "negro government" in the process of Reconstruction. Democrats knew that the ratification of the Thirteenth Amendment and the repeal of the Black Laws left open the question of black citizenship in Illinois. The removal of legal restrictions was not accompanied by any guarantee or definition of what rights black residents now possessed, and the Thirteenth Amendment said nothing about what rights and duties came with freedom from slavery. In the legislative void, Democrats argued that black citizenship was profoundly dangerous to the basic structures of law and order, citing fundamental racial qualities that prohibited blacks from the full exercise of citizenship duties. Even if blacks could be taught to mimic the values of whites, they would not fully understand the significance of and responsibilities inherent in citizenship, representative government, and free society. Democratic arguments appealed to a strain of antebellum racial conservatism throughout the Midwest that remained strong after the war. Historian George Fredrickson observed that "Northerners approached Reconstruction with their basic racial prejudices largely intact," and these were increasingly deployed for Democrats' electoral purposes. Even as Democrats suffered politically from a wartime and postbellum backlash against perceptions of disloyalty and Copperheadism, the white supremacist intellectual tradition from which they drew many of their ideals continued to flourish.[21]

For most Democrats, and indeed for many Republicans, white supremacy was less a cohesive ideology and more like a series of observations derived from both natural history and demonstrable fact. Senate candidate Abraham Lincoln voiced the opinion of many Illinoisans in 1858 when he said, "There is a physical difference between the white and black races which I believe will forever forbid the two races living together on terms of social and political equality.... I as much as any other man am in favor of having the superior position assigned to the white race."[22] The generally accepted racial hierarchy, sketched simply by Sidney George Fisher in *The Laws of Race as Connected with Slavery* (1860), was: "The white is the highest in the scale, the black the lowest." Fisher's statement that "the white race must of necessity, by reason of its superiority, govern the negro" resolved the question of slavery for many, since "the difference and natural inequality of the two races, white and black, therefore govern what is called the slavery question.... The negro is the inferior,—born for subordination and servitude, which has been his lot in all ages, when brought within the sphere of the white race."[23] Democrats cared little whether emancipation had been a wartime expedient or the culmination of an abolitionist agenda; the result was the same: the natural order of white supremacy had been ruptured, a race of barbarians had been loosed upon the body politic, and Republicans seemed determined to protect and guide them as they sought its ruin.

In 1863, Reverend J. M. Sturtevant, president of the Illinois College at Jacksonville, published his thoughts on "The Destiny of the African Race in the United States" in the *Continental Monthly*. Although ostensibly reflecting on the future of blacks in the postemancipation United States, Sturtevant was most insightful about the state of antiblack prejudice at the moment of emancipation. The "deeply seated aversion to the recognition of the equality of the white man and the black man is a potent force, which has been incessantly active in all our history," observed Sturtevant, and was the chief source of the national agitation over slavery. Sturtevant believed that popular aversion to emancipation was due to the fact that "to many it seems perfectly clear that the universal emancipation of the negro carries with it by inevitable necessity his admission to the full enjoyment of all equality, political and social, and his becoming homogenous with the mass of the American people." As Sturtevant argued, this was unacceptable to most Americans, himself included, for "the negro is, to a large extent, a barbarian in the midst of civilization." Sturtevant praised "prejudice against color" as "one of the most remarkable and one of the most respectable features of the English colonies wherever found." In contrast to the French, Spanish, and Portuguese colonies, which had "amalgamated freely with their savage neighbors," the English social, political, and biological heritage, to which nineteenth-century Americans were heir, had remained unsullied by racial mixing. This, argued Sturtevant, and the entirely reasonable prejudice it bred were the remedies to the current crisis. Dismissing concerns about a postemancipation black population explosion, economic competition with whites, and social or political equality, Sturtevant presented a complex argument for the inferiority of the African race and their speedy extinction. Blacks had always been excluded, both by popular prejudice and by their inferior nature, from the free democratic institutions of the nation, and they would continue to be until they simply faded away.[24]

Although Sturtevant theorized that racial inferiority and extinction obviated hysterical Democratic concerns about black rule and the pollution of white-only institutions, others were fearful that fanatical Republicans would nevertheless foist black equality upon the nation. In places like Springfield, where Democrats witnessed the daily growth of the black population, and the apparent validation of their wartime fears, the party newspapers advanced a racial view that encouraged their subscribers not only to reject black citizenship in general but also to fear and despise local black residents. Although the *Illinois State Register* agreed with Sturtevant that "it is almost certain that a single generation will witness the decadence and final extinction of the black race in the United States," it foretold that the inevitable functioning of "God's great laws of race" would necessarily involve white communities, which "*must perforce assist in [the negro's] extinction*" (emphasis added).[25]

As the black population of Springfield grew, Democrats warned of an increase in crime, job competition with returning white soldiers, and the potential horrors of black suffrage. In the election of 1865, with white soldiers returning from the front and mingling with the new larger population of blacks in the city, the *Register* seized on the ironies of emancipation, pointing out that blacks were now taking jobs left by the same white soldiers who had fought to free them from slavery. The week before the election, the *Register* described the choice facing local voters: "Whether we shall elect men to office who love the negro more than the soldier, or men who would keep the darkey in his place."[26] The *Register* asked its soldier readers: "You who have been fighting the battles of your country. . . . You can see what abolitionists have done by inviting negroes to immigrate to Illinois. . . . Will you vote for these men who have thus acted while you were in the field . . . or will you cast your ballots for those who opposed the repeal of our state laws, which prevented negroes from coming to Springfield?"[27]

When President Johnson vetoed congressional Republicans' Civil Rights Bill in 1866, the *Register* called on its readers to support the president by voting Democratic. The bill was the first congressional effort to define what sort of freedom the Thirteenth Amendment had created, designating all persons born in the United States (excluding Indians) as citizens of the nation without regard to color, and conferring on them the right to make contracts, bring lawsuits, and enjoy "full and equal benefit of all laws and proceedings for the security of person and property." These, declared Republican Illinois senator Lyman Trumbull, were "fundamental rights belonging to every man as a free man."[28] In the days between Johnson's veto and the Congressional override, the *Register* printed a front-page denunciation of the bill, asking Springfielders to consider the impact on their own community if it should pass. Democrats alleged that "the so-called civil rights bill, if it should become a law, will abolish all discriminations in local, municipal or state laws between negroes and white people. Make the application to our city, and what do you see?":

Our city council has provided for separate schools for colored and white children. The "civil rights bill" abolishes all such discrimination.... Negro children would at once enter all our city schools, and any attempt by teachers, or the city council, to keep them out, would subject them to a fine of $1,000 and imprisonment in the county jail for one year.... Apply the bill to the churches: By its provisions, negroes may occupy front seats in any church in the city.... Apply it to places of amusement: When Randolph's new hall is completed, negroes will take up the front seats and the private boxes.... Apply the bill to all the walks of life, and the same startling results are exhibited. Every legislature that ever met in Illinois, and every city council that ever convened in Springfield, have passed acts or ordinances which, if enforced, would subject all concerned in the enforcement to a fine of $1,000, and imprisonment for one year!... People of Springfield! do you want such a bill to become law? No, never![29]

Shortly after the congressional override of Johnson's civil rights veto, in July 1866, the *Register* complained about the "intermixture of black and white passengers, full blooded Africans sitting next to delicate ladies," on the cars of the city railway, where blacks seemed to feel "on full terms of equality with anybody." This was the result of the civil rights legislation, claimed the *Register*, but "we submit that no railroad company has a right deliberately and forcibly to offend the prejudices of any large portion of our citizens." The *Register* offered two solutions to the problem. First, given the hot weather and the close proximity that streetcars forced upon the passengers, "it would be more acceptable to the general wishes of the community if colored people were excluded." Failing that, however, "let a car be provided for them.... Do not force upon those of us who have the misfortune to be white, this dilemma, either to walk or having a substantial negro seated on each side of us."[30]

Congress responded to such discrimination with another Civil Rights Act in 1870, known as the first Enforcement Act. Although primarily targeting the states of the former Confederacy, less than one year after its passage a case under the law came before the federal district court in Springfield. Cyrus Donnegan, a long-time black resident of the city, bought two tickets to the Springfield Opera House to see the visiting magic show of Professor J. M. Macallister, "the Great Wizard of the World." Macallister's show would have been one of the few traveling performances to visit the city that Donnegan and other black residents could enjoy, since many of the shows that came through Springfield's theaters in the late 1860s and 1870s were blackface minstrel shows in which whites mimicked and mocked the speech, songs, and culture of blacks—likely not the kind of fare that Donnegan, a successful black businessman and community activist, would have found amusing.[31] In contrast, attending Macallister's "wonderful eastern delusions" with the promise that "100 elegant and costly presents all purchased of the leading merchants of this city, will be given away every evening" would have given Donnegan an opportunity to demonstrate his good standing and reputation in the community.[32] Donnegan purchased two tickets from the box office for the "parquette" section, the best section at the front of the house, on Wednesday of Macallister's weeklong run. When Donnegan presented his tickets at the door, however, he was turned away by the doorkeeper, who suggested that he return to the box office and get tickets for the gallery and have the difference in price refunded. Donnegan refused and returned with the captain of the night police in an attempt to gain entrance to the section for which he had purchased tickets. He was turned way again, and the offer of seats in a different section was repeated. Donnegan claimed that Macallister himself had been at the door to refuse him the second time.

Donnegan went to the federal court and claimed that his right to enforce contracts under the Civil Rights Act had been infringed. The complaint named Macallister as the one who had refused him entry. When Macallister was arrested, the magician immediately filed for a writ of habeas corpus. For witnesses, he produced the ticket seller and the doorkeeper, the former to claim that he had never sold the tickets to Donnegan in the first place ("he never sold tickets for that part of the house to colored people"), and the latter to claim that Macallister had not been present at the door when Donnegan was turned away the second time.[33] The court, presided over by Judge Samuel Treat, a prominent local Democrat, decided that there was not enough evidence to hold Macallister, and the magician was discharged. The case amounted to Donnegan's word against Macallister's, and even with the Civil Rights Act in place, there was little chance that a Democratic judge would take Donnegan's accusation seriously. The next morning, Donnegan filed two suits against Macallister in the Sangamon County circuit court, but when a deputy tried to locate the magician to arrest him again, he had appropriately vanished. In their final remarks on the case, the *Register* was satisfied to see Macallister escape the machinations of the "vexatious" civil rights legislation Donnegan had tried to utilize. For the time being, the ability to refuse equal service to blacks continued unabated, regardless of federal legislation.[34]

A more significant fight over access to public facilities came in the Springfield school desegregation controversy of 1873. The issue gained national attention in the 1870s as larger and more politically active black populations began to push local school boards to admit black students. In Illinois, the question of desegregation forced individual school districts to confront the extent of local race prejudice, and maintaining segregation became a rallying point for Democrats. As portals to public life and incubators of civic responsibility, schools were particularly vulnerable to what Democrats described as the insidious contagion of black participation. Before 1874, the Illinois public school system allowed individual districts to decide for themselves whether to admit black students to their public schools. In the face of federal civil rights legislation, it was one area of public life that Democrats could still protect with the weight of local opinion, and because school boards and superintendents were responsible to elected city councils, the will of the people frequently determined the issue.[35]

In his biennial report of 1865–66, Newton Bateman, state superintendent of public instruction, estimated that there were as many as six thousand black children in Illinois and lamented that the retention of the word "white" in the state school laws prevented many of them from receiving public education. Bateman did not mince words when he alleged that "it is plainly the intention to exclude them from a joint participation in the benefits of the free school system." Only in places with large black populations could sufficient tax funds be allocated for the construction of separate schools, and most of Illinois's blacks were too geographically dispersed to form their own schools. Bateman estimated that fully half of the state's black children were thus being prevented from attending school, and since "the law does not contemplate their co-attendance with white children . . . they are without recourse of any kind."[36] In his next report in 1868, Bateman called on the legislature to strike the word "white" from the school laws, urging them to "expunge this last remaining remnant of the unchristian 'black laws' of Illinois, and proclaim in the name of God, and the Declaration of Independence, that *all* the school-going children of the State, without distinction, shall be equally entitled to share in the rich provisions of the free school system." Bateman anticipated the objections likely to be raised by Democrats and others who feared the classroom mingling of the races: "Nor need any one be scared by the phantom of blended colors in the same school-room. The question of co-attendance, or of separate schools, is an entirely separate and distinct one, and may safely be left to be determined by the respective districts and communities, to suit themselves."[37] But any small district that could not afford to construct a separate colored school was unlikely to welcome black students into a one-room schoolhouse with white children, regardless of how the state's school laws were worded.

With the new state constitution of 1870 opening public education to all children in the state regardless of color, and with the ratification of the Fifteenth Amendment, which allowed black citizens to participate in electing school board members and superintendents, Bateman hoped that the question of school segregation would finally be settled. The question of separate versus integrated schoolhouses, claimed Bateman, was "one of very secondary importance, and should never be permitted to disturb the peace and harmony of any school district or community." According to Bateman: "What our colored citizens need, what they and their friends have been struggling for, is the means of educating their children . . . not the paltry privilege (if it be such), the empty name, of sitting in the same seats, or in the same house, with white children." Still, Bateman acknowledged, "In all places where the old prejudices exist, it would be better, in all respects, for their children to attend separate schools." Bateman believed, "When the continued indulgence of a mere prejudice is found to be expensive, it is not probable that it will be very long persisted in." Once white citizens determined that maintaining separate schools was too expensive, they would simply integrate black children into white schools. After all, reasoned Bateman, the state constitution stated that black children "*must be provided for,*" and no school district would fail to comply, for "the net value of the caste-feeling that lies at the bottom of it all, will be apt to be very thoroughly reviewed, and most likely given up."[38]

Four years later, Bateman was less inclined to believe that race prejudice could be so easily given up. He interpreted the Fourteenth Amendment to guarantee that "the two races shall be provided with *equal* public school advantages. This . . . is the only essential point—the only thing worth contending for. The schools provided for colored children must not be *in any respect inferior* to those provided for others." For Bateman, and for most other Illinoisans in the early 1870s, separate but equal became not only an acceptable standard, but the ideal outcome for all of Illinois's schools. In 1874, Bateman surveyed all of the county school superintendents to determine whether the black children in their counties attended separate or integrated schools. Forty-one counties reported that their schools were integrated; ten counties reported exclusively separate schools; and sixteen reported a mixture of the two systems. Thirty counties reported that there was no objection to school integration, with several "unimportant exceptions," and twenty-seven reported "trouble, of a more or less serious nature." Some superintendents reported only positive results from mixed attendance, while others, "including some from counties where co-attendance is the rule, express the opposite opinion in strong terms." In his concluding remarks on the issue, Bateman judged that "comparatively few cases of willful injustice and wrong to colored children . . . have been reported to this office during the past year," but acknowledged that "some very deplorable instances of that kind have, however, occurred." Bateman also revised his assessment of the durability of "mere prejudice" and acknowledged that "the extirpation of inherited, deeply seated and long cherished opinions and tastes in relation to social questions and customs, cannot be accomplished by legislation, but only by reflection and time, if at all."[39] School laws in 1873 and 1874 had reinforced the constitution of 1870 in providing that the public schools be opened to all children regardless of race, but the transition had not been as smooth as Bateman's reports indicated. Desegregation was undermined by pervasive patterns of prejudice that resisted the mingling of races in all public institutions, especially schools, where the plastic minds of children might be molded into unacceptable contours of racial equality.

Springfield's small public Colored School had served the community since 1858, but by the early 1870s, it was unable to accommodate the growing black population. Its four grades provided no opportunity for students to advance beyond a primary education. White students in the ward schools could apply to the city's high school if they wanted secondary education, where they received more rigorous instruction and preparation for either higher education or the professional fields. Black students were not explicitly prohibited from attending the high school, but none had ever applied until a student named Gertrude Wright in 1873. The school board was forced to decide whether to admit Wright, thereby setting a precedent for the desegregation of all of the city's schools. Wright's application was received at the school board's October 7 meeting. The members present included John Rosette, who had helped William Herndon represent the fugitive slave Frederick Clements in 1857, and former governor John Palmer, who was in the midst of a final campaign to strike the word "white" from the state's school laws. One of the board members moved that Wright's application be referred to a special committee. Rosette, Palmer, and two other board members voted against the special committee and suggested that the entire board undertake the question immediately. The motion to admit Wright to the high school passed on a vote of four to three—the same four who had voted against referring the application to a special committee voted in favor of accepting her into the high school. What happened next appears so abruptly in the board's minutes that it might easily be overlooked: "Resolved. That section two (2) of chapter seven (7) of the rules and regulations of this Board be amended by expurging therefrom the word 'white' and repealing the Provision in said section. Unanimously adopted."[40] Although the resolution must have come from either Rosette or

Palmer, there is no indication in the existing minutes who actually proposed it or why it was unanimously adopted; the typically meticulous minutes leave a notable gap at this crucial juncture. The resolution by itself was not especially radical since the school board had long since nullified its own racial exclusion by creating the Colored School. However, by repealing the provision at the same time as they admitted Gertrude Wright to the high school, the school board effectively desegregated Springfield's entire public education system.

The school board's action was the culmination of a fight that had been several years in the making. In 1870, the *Register* had resisted Palmer's school desegregation efforts on the basis that many people already found the current public school system flawed and warned that allowing black children into the public schools would "excite so much opposition as to destroy, not only their pet measure, but the school system itself."[41] Later that year, the *Register* reported that a meeting of black citizens had resolved to send their children only to the ward schools, rather than the Colored School. In this, the *Register* was sure that it smelled the meddling of "radicals" who were only using unwitting blacks as a means of "working out their schemes of insult to white children, degradation of white teachers and outrage upon white parents." The *Register* discerned a looming Republican presence that threatened "the subversion of every institution which is dear to the American people. Already the political rights of the states are abridged, and those of the white race degraded by the admission of the negro to a share therein. The free school system is now attacked; the other pillars of our government as well as of civilization, are already in the hands of the Sampson whose locks of strength can only be shorn by the united action of all the white citizens of the nation." The *Register* claimed that Republican politicians had little to lose by integrating the schools, and thus forcing them to close, since, "their ill-gotten wealth enables them to send little Coupon or little Grabbie to some select school or college. . . . We speak . . . to the people; to the farmers, mechanics and laborers, in order to urge them to the defense of the educational system. . . . If this opportunity is neglected all is lost in the sea of radicalism, negro equality and miscegenation."[42] Democrats positioned themselves as the guardians of yeoman values against a corrupt federal machine, and placed the responsibility for maintaining the old racial order squarely on the shoulders of the people and their prejudices. In this, the *Register* was sure that Democrats everywhere were "ready to stand by their rights, and to defend our institutions from the contamination of negro equality."[43]

The question of desegregation was raised again in 1872, when black Republicans in the First Ward discussed nominating one of their own for a position on the city council, or failing that, petitioning the city council for a position on the school board. Although blacks failed to gain a nomination, the election was a Republican success, owing in part to promises that a Republican city council would appoint a sympathetic school board that would strike the word "white" from the local school laws. The *Register* called the election "a more important event than has yet transpired in the history of Springfield" and tried to mobilize the Democratic constituency with warnings that "the republican leaders in the city have already made some pledges that the colored children shall be . . . admitted."[44] An anonymous letter from "First Ward" printed in the *Register* protested "the prostitution of our school to the negroes" and admonished Democratic voters to "*do what you can to save us from being driven from this last little piece of territory which the white people yet hold distinct from the negro race*" (emphasis added).[45] But Republicans prevailed, and the school board gained several new members who were sympathetic to school desegregation, including John Rosette and John Palmer.

In the fall of 1873, when Gertrude Wright applied for admission to the high school, Rosette and Palmer helped accomplish what Democrats had feared. The Republican *Illinois State Journal* explained that the board had little choice but to strike the word "white" from the city's school regulations because of changes to the Illinois school law, which specified that racial distinctions were now prohibited. As the *Journal* explained: "The Board has not abolished the [colored] school. . . . That will still be continued, not as a *distinct* colored school, but in order to accommodate such of our colored citizens as may prefer to send their children there. We have been told that the great majority of them would probably rather do this, even while possessing equal privileges in the ward schools." The *Journal* was confident that the citizens of Springfield would see that the school board was only complying with state and federal law, and it was sure that "its action will be duly appreciated and quietly acquiesced in by all our citizens."[46]

As the *Journal* might have suspected, however, its Democratic counterpart did not simply acquiesce to what they viewed as an usurpation of local authority likely to increase racial animosity. "There is no use denying that a prejudice does exist between the whites and blacks," said the *Register*, and "the introduction of colored children will give full vent, on all occasions, to this prejudice."[47] The *Register* seized upon a letter sent to them by James Jenkins, "a sensible colored man," who argued against desegregation on the grounds that "the unenviable position of being where they [the black students] are not wanted, will more than counterbalance the benefits they will derive from convenience of position or better teachings. . . . Would it not be better to be colored children in their own schools, than to be 'niggers' among white children." The *Register* took Jenkins's letter as an indication that not all blacks had been duped by "their pretended white friends," the Republicans.[48] The next day, in an extensive front-page review of the "law of the case," the *Register* contended: "We have no prejudice against the colored people. We oppose the admission of colored children to our public schools as much on their own account as otherwise. It will subject them to taunts and insults and continued annoyance." But the *Register* could not sustain its benevolence much further:

> If the negro race were the equal or even the superior of the white race, we should still be opposed to the mixing of white and black children in our public schools for the reason that such intermixing of children tends to establish social intimacies, which will result in intermarriage and amalgamation. Let the two races be kept as separate as possible, but give each all the privileges and immunities of the other. This ought to be acceptable to the negroes. At all events, the white population will insist upon it.[49]

After the board adopted the resolution to strike the word "white" from the school regulations on October 7, black children began to attend the public schools in their own wards for the first time, although some apparently still continued to attend the Colored School. In the Third Ward, seven white children withdrew from a single classroom when black students arrived, and the *Register* reported that when the school in the Fourth Ward was forced to admit eighteen black students, a number of white students walked out.[50] On November 1, Dr. Benjamin Griffith, one of the school board members who had opposed desegregation from the start, presented the board with a proposal to ease the difficulties of integration. Griffith noted: "The admission of the colored children to the Ward Schools of the City has created much dissatisfaction among the pupils and the parents of the pupils of the Ward Schools, caused the withdrawal of many children from these schools, produced an unsettled and unhappy feeling among many of those remaining." He proposed as a solution renting a separate room in each of the wards for the instruction of black students, essentially creating new segregated schools in each ward. Griffith's proposal attempted to solve the problem of access that many black residents had complained about without forcing black children into classrooms with white students, but also went one step further by suggesting that the board rescind its resolution allowing blacks to attend the ward schools without discrimination. The board split four to four on the proposal and the resolution was lost.[51]

Three days later, when the board convened again, it considered the issue of what to do with the existing Colored School and the teachers employed there. As the *Register* noted, since so many children from the Colored School now attended the ward schools, "attendance there has been greatly lessened, so much so that the school would have been abolished and the teachers discharged some days ago, but for the fact that some of the colored people, seeing the trouble likely to arise from sending their children to the ward schools, continue to send them to the separate school." At the same time, the *Register* claimed that more white children had withdrawn from the ward schools than the number of black children that entered them. As a result, not only were the two teachers at the Colored School virtually idle, two teachers in the ward schools also had no students to teach. As the *Register* noted: "It seems that the taxpayers of the city are paying dearly for the privilege of having their children educated with the blacks."[52] What finally became of the former Colored School is unknown, since it disappears entirely from the school board's minutes after 1873. If Springfield was like other cities around the state in the late nineteenth century, it maintained some semblance of segregation within its school system, with black students likely attending separate classes or otherwise unofficially segregated schoolhouses. The fact that the 1880 census listed a number of black children "at school" indicates that there were opportunities for black students, but they were likely severely circumscribed by continuing prejudice and segregation.

At the heart of the school fight in 1873 were issues raised by the Fourteenth and Fifteenth Amendments, which Democrats claimed took rights away from whites by nullifying state and local laws that preserved racial distinctions. The *Register* claimed in February 1870 that the Fifteenth Amendment was "no less than a complete revolution of the government of our fathers," and threatened "to take from the people of the states their control of the right of suffrage; *to reconstruct the northern and loyal states;* to convert a white man's government into a mongrel, piebald oligarchy" (emphasis added).[53] With ratification imminent, the *Register* commented gloomily: "Long ago [we] insisted that these things would come to pass. We said civil, political and social equality tread quickly upon the heels of each other. . . . We denounced the pretended necessity to yield our birth-right to an inferior race."[54] Before 1870, Illinois's constitution restricted suffrage to only white male residents, precisely the kind of discrimination the Fifteenth Amendment sought to end. Democrats attacked the suggestion that a federal constitutional amendment or other provision could force black suffrage on the states. When the new state constitution of 1870 removed the word "white" in keeping with the state's ratification of the

Fifteenth Amendment, the *Register* opined that it was "an admission that an inferior and barbarous race were needed to assist white men in conducting the affairs of Illinois" and pledged resistance, asserting that "this is still a white man's government."[55] Even after it reckoned the amendment unlikely to be repealed, the *Register* continued to oppose the removal of racial distinctions from the state constitution. "Let them vote," the paper said of blacks, "but do not consent to expunge from [the state constitution] the word that marks the distinction between the superior and inferior races."[56]

If the legal mechanisms Democrats had long relied on to maintain white rights were to be undermined by federal authority, the people would need to take up the work of excluding and stigmatizing blacks that had once been the purview of the Black Laws. The *Register* articulated this duty as early as 1865, when it reported on the "disgraceful row" that had occurred on a train from Chicago to Springfield when "a lot of discharged negro soldiers" attempted to sit in the ladies' car. If the police would not stop such conduct, "*The people ought to take the matter into their own hands,* and teach these 'cullod gemmen' that they are not entitled to any more privileges than white people" (emphasis added).[57] The press, said the *Register,* had a duty to warn the people of "their great peril," while to the courts, "devolves the power of stemming this black flood and shameful injustice."[58] With this mandate before the people, the *Register* and other Democratic newspapers devoted themselves to illustrating the consequences of black suffrage and the ruin that was sure to follow.

When Springfield's black citizens had their first opportunity to vote in the local elections of April 1870, the *Register* described the "disgusting spectacle" of blacks taking "possession of the polls and for hours preventing old citizens, gray haired veterans, men who have periled life in defense of their country, from exercising the right which it was supposed originally belonged to the white men." For Democrats it was "humiliating to the last degree to be compelled to stand back while these new fledged patriots, these colored gentry, this 'black vomit,' was poured into the ballot box." Although it was only a township election, the *Register* reported the next day: "The first fruits of the new dispensation were presented to the people yesterday, in such a manner as will not be speedily forgotten."[59]

Mocking a popular phrase from the war, "the colored troops fought nobly!" the *Register* portrayed black voters as a rogue army of toughs, pushing "old citizens, white men" away from the polls. The *Register* reported that blacks gathered early on Election Day before the polls opened and kicked down the door, and "took possession of the hall . . . elected one of their own kidney, Geo. R. Weber, moderator, and then held the polls for two hours or more."

Before the polls were due to close that evening, "The black allies of the radicals gathered their forces, and marching on the polls, ordered the voting to cease, while some hundred or more white men stood waiting for an opportunity to vote."[60]

Despite this outrage, Democrats elected many of their candidates, which the *Register* claimed was due to "a triumph of principle rather than of party, for a number of good citizens who had hitherto voted the [R]epublican ticket, refused longer to support the party which seeks to ride into power by negro votes." Whether this was true or not, the *Register* warned, "The negroes, under the direction of their radical fuglemen and file closers, inaugurated a system of fraudulent voting such as excels anything of which we have ever heard." Black voters from around the county supposedly came to vote illegally in the Springfield township election, and every black voter who cast a ballot "did so in pursuance of a fraud, concocted by the governor and secretary of state of Illinois." This was because the governor had issued a proclamation on April 4 that the Fifteenth Amendment had been ratified, when the official notice was not received by the governor's office until April 5. Although there was nothing they could do about it after the election, Democrats rallied their supporters against the "frauds and violence practiced by the negroes and their abettors at the polls" by warning that "such conduct will not be tolerated without trouble." Again using the language of conflict, the *Register* added: "The descendents of the men who wrested this land from British rule, and of the men who delivered it from the possession of American savages, will not tamely surrender their franchises to Africans."[61]

When the city elections were held a week later, the *Register* again used military terminology: "Despite the array of black men armed with a new weapon, of whose just use they were ignorant, the [D]emocratic [P]arty . . . beat back the enemy and elected the entire city ticket." The newspaper claimed that black voters were "mere tools . . . in the hands of designing plunderers, demagogues and office seekers" and characterized the entire local Republican Party as "a black mongrel faction, expiring like the stinking wick of a tallow candle, sputtering into stench and darkness." The *Register* claimed that future electoral success against the "negro cloud" would ensure that "the fifteenth amendment proves abortive. . . . This is still a white man's country."[62] The *Register* urged moderate and conservative Republicans to bolt the party and "unite with those who have faith in the doctrine that as yet white men are competent to care for the interests of this country and preserve it for their white descendents forever." Together, whites would reject party divisions in favor of racial ones and seek retribution for the breach in their last bastion of privilege. The *Register* warned that "Our colored 'brudder' must be taught that we have not yet consented to yield the administration of affairs entirely into their hands," and added chillingly, "This lesson . . . will be more impressively taught on the next occasion in which their scurvy leaders prompt them to similar outrages."[63]

The political realignment of 1872 did not distract Democrats in Springfield from utilizing race in local elections. The *Register* became a "Liberal" paper, joining a coalition of Democrats and Republicans in support of Horace Greeley for president over the reelection of Ulysses Grant. The newspaper intensified the language of anticorruption that Democrats across the country wielded against the Grant administration, portraying Grant's supporters as criminals and hoodlums interested only in looting the public and exploiting working whites. In the spring city elections, the *Register* alleged that over one hundred black votes were placed in Springfield's Third Ward, a portion of the city that the newspaper claimed had only thirty-five legal black voters. The problem was that "political bummers and dead beats hanging around the polls" had sworn in the illegal voters in hopes of gaining city patronage positions. The *Register* urged the mayor to "kick these vagabonds out . . . these leeches on the public treasury."[64] The problems of political patronage and corruption were tied explicitly with the problem of black suffrage. By alleging that much black voting was illegal because of the frauds committed by patronage seekers, the *Register* helped its white readers imagine that all black votes were potentially suspect and that blacks' political strings were pulled by corrupt Republicans.

Not only were their votes potentially illegal, black voters themselves frequently behaved in unlawful ways. During the same city election, the *Register* alleged that black citizens again closed the polls early in the First Ward, and that in the Second Ward, "A mob of negroes, armed with razors, bludgeons and brickbats," marched on the Second Ward polls "with loud shouts, and rushed up to the polling place, demanding, as near as was understood, that the polls be closed." Again, the *Register* used martial language to describe the confrontation:

> [The negroes] were met by a few of the policemen and a number of citizens, who acted with the utmost firmness and not less prudence. Without any offensive movement, the police and citizens forced the mob back, and the negroes retreated until they reached the middle of the block on Jefferson, between Third and Fourth streets. Here they made a stand, and here the police charged in, and one or two arrests was made. An attempt to rescue the prisoners was

threatened, but was not made in such force as to oblige the police to use their pistols."

Looking ahead to the November elections, the *Register* warned, "These facts . . . will not fail to have their effect on the public mind in the not distant future."[65]

As the election year proceeded, the *Register* continued to portray Grant's black supporters as unruly, disruptive, and criminal. When Greeley's nomination for president on the Liberal ticket was announced in July, his Springfield supporters held a massive rally at which "a few young negroes disturbed the audience and annoyed the speakers by profane and indecent exclamations and insulting remarks." Although most of the blacks in the audience "showed by their conduct that they appreciated the responsibility of voters," the *Register* noted that the disturbance "would certainly not be permitted by white men, and if indulged in again will be punished by broken heads if nothing else."[66] The same month, two local black men were scheduled to debate the question, "Will the interests of the colored people be subserved by the election of Horace Greeley?" Arguing in favor of Greeley, the *Register* championed Cyrus Donnegan, the same man who had been denied admission to Macallister's magic show the year before. Arguing against Greeley was Thomas Killion, a local barber, whom the *Register* had described in April as "a likely negro" and the "leader of the Africans," who had allegedly forced the polls to close early in the First Ward.[67] The debate was supposed to occur on August 1 as part of the Emancipation Day festivities, but Killion apparently did not show. Donnegan instead addressed the gathered crowd and "made a strong speech in favor of Greeley, and urged all colored men to support him," although the *Register* again noticed that there were some "colored men who endeavored to interrupt the speaker with profane and indecent insults." Their support of Donnegan as a black advocate for Greeley notwithstanding, the *Register* asserted, "It is such conduct as this which leads honest and unprejudiced men to seriously doubt the propriety of the measures which have given colored men the right to vote." If blacks could not participate with civility in the electoral process and instead would "insult and defame those who discuss publicly the questions in which all the voters of the country are alike interested, those doubts will be confirmed."[68]

Over the following weeks, further breaches of campaign etiquette provided more reasons to doubt the wisdom of allowing black votes, and the *Register* continued to cast black citizens as dangerous and destabilizing elements within the body politic. During a Greeley meeting one August evening, "There arose from a crowd of negroes in the street, a chorus of profane and indecent exclamations, with execrations on Greeley and cheers for Grant." The disruptive blacks had just come from a Grant rally, and as they passed the Greeley meeting, "took the opportunity to show their qualifications for the ballot by interrupting a meeting of gentlemen and ladies." Combining a sort of sympathy with their usual contempt, the *Register* (supposedly quoting John Palmer, who joined the Liberals) noted that the blacks "seem to have caught the inspiration of their master, Grant, and are performing his work, for which they are the proper instruments." To the relief of the civilized "gentlemen and ladies" at the Greeley meeting, "the negroes passed on up the street to their dens, and quiet was soon restored."[69] In response, the pro-Grant *Journal* claimed that the blacks had done nothing more than what a squad of white Democrats had done the week before by interrupting a Republican meeting with cheers for Greeley. The *Register* rebutted that blacks interrupting a white meeting was something altogether different from the political pranks whites played on one another during elections, and was appalled at the *Journal*'s attempt to "assure the negroes that they did nothing wrong in attempting to interrupt a meeting of white people." Even if it were true that white Democrats had barged into a Republican meeting, the *Register* claimed that it was "no excuse for the conduct of the negroes, whose language was such as would disgrace the lowest slums of the city."[70] In another article, the *Register* described the "demoniac yells of the negroes" and the fact that only Palmer's intervention prevented the audience from making a violent effort to repulse the "brutal intruders." Again, the *Register* hinted at a looming battle, for if black voters did not cease their violations of proper campaign etiquette, "there can be but one result . . . and this result will be such as all good citizens must deprecate." The allusion was to nothing short of a race war on the streets of Springfield, for if the "right of people everywhere to meet and peaceably discuss political questions . . . is invaded in Springfield, then Springfield is the very place to settle the question."[71]

As the election drew nearer, skirmishes between black "Tanners" (so-called after Grant's nickname, "The Galena Tanner") and respectable white citizens continually surfaced in the columns of the *Register*. In August, a "serious riot" broke out in nearby Clinton when a group of pro-Grant blacks insulted a white woman and attacked her male defender with razors. When the police intervened, the "gang" fought back, and when one of them was arrested, the rest broke into the jail and freed him. According to the *Register*, "Such are the fruits of emancipation and the works of republicanism."[72] In October, with less than one month before the election, such skirmishes seemed to intensify, and the *Register* published an excerpt from the *Cincinnati Enquirer* as a warning to Springfielders:

We do not desire any war or antagonism of races, and it is on that account that we desire to speak plainly in regard to the conduct of the negroes in our city [Cincinnati] during the present political campaign. . . . Whenever they have turned out blood has always been the result—not their blood, but the blood of innocent bystanders and unobtrusive whites. Riots and rapine have marked the course of their processions. . . . Strong as may be the prejudices of nationality or religion, they are nothing really compared to those of race and color, whenever the latter are allowed to break forth. Although the negro has a ballot, he is not the less an object of dislike than he was before. . . . If he goes around like a roaring lion, seeking whom he may devour—if his impulse is to slay or kill all whom his passions or caprice may suggest, we shall soon have dreadful scenes enacted in our midst.[73]

The political uprising of blacks was portrayed as frighteningly similar to the imagined slave rebellions antebellum Southerners had once dreaded. With bands of savages loosed on the streets—worse, on the ballot box—the inevitable result would be a race war such as the nation had never seen. The *Register* cautioned its readers in Springfield to "let the warning work" and be prepared to meet the threat.[74] The same issue of the *Register* also made use of less threatening allusions to antebellum stereotypes by describing the "plantation breakdown" dancing performed at a pro-Grant rally by "two negro women, dressed out in a ludicrous imitation of the prevailing fashions." Around the scene of the dancing were gathered "a crowd admirably adapted to suit those who wish to study low life," including a group of black thieves debating how to divide the spoils of a chicken coop robbery, a "burly colored man giving a grotesque imitation of Gen. Logan's last speech," and a "big black unreconstructed plantation darkey."[75] The images the *Register* presented to its readers might have come from any caricature of antebellum plantation life and were meant to confirm the impression that black voters remained mired in the ignorance of their recent past, unable to take seriously the momentous questions they were asked to decide.

The plantation "darkey" might well have repulsed white readers and confirmed their prejudices that blacks were unfit for the privilege of suffrage, but it was the savage side of the stereotype that the *Register* mobilized most often. In late October, the warning issued earlier in the month seemed to become reality when black Grantites stormed through the city "on the rampage." Disappointed that a promised free train ride to Decatur to attend a Grant rally had been canceled, the blacks "raised a frightful yell of rage" and dispersed in small "squads" across the city, still wearing the quasi-military costumes they had donned for the trip. The black Republicans, claimed the *Register*, "swore that they would not be cheated out of the glorious spree which the Grantites had promised them," and by midafternoon "the streets were full of drunken negroes, reeling from side to side, fighting, quarreling, and exhibiting all the characteristics of barbarians, heightened by drunkenness, and these made the air ring with their savage yells."

While this saturnalia was carried on in the center of town, the rest of the city fell into the "practical possession" of the blacks. In the First Ward, "they paraded up and down nearly all day, shouting and yelling." As dusk fell in the Second Ward—the "white man's ward" where Elliott Herndon lived—a black crowd marched along Jefferson Street until it encountered "a number of white men who did not seem disposed to submit to any insolence" and dispersed. The Third Ward was the scene of a "battle royal" when one of the crowd stood up to declare that he had been duped by the Republicans for the last time and would not vote for Grant. He was shouted down by the rowdy crowd and, when he attempted to flee, was chased, beaten, and stripped. By nightfall, the crowd had gathered in the "low grog shops," where "many disturbances occurred." A police officer was badly wounded by "a razor in the hands of a negro," and the *Register* noted that "almost all the Tanners are habitually armed with razors, and . . . most of them displayed the gleaming blades at all times." The *Register* believed that "no such display of drunkenness, disorder and bestiality has ever been so publicly made in this city. . . . For some hours the city was practically controlled by these negro ruffians." The Tanner riot was "upon a different footing from any cases of ordinary import" because it was "enacted by a body of negroes organized for political purposes, and wearing the uniform of their club."

The *Register* blamed Mayor John Smith for failing to put down the riot because the black Tanners were of his own party and warned the people of Springfield that "they must protect themselves and their property from the barbarisms of the negroes enlisted for Smith, Grant, Cullom and Hay."[76] The next day, the *Register* called Mayor Smith's city government complicit in the "high carnival" that had held the city hostage. Smith's government, charged the *Register*, "encourages instead of represses vice, crime and disorder, and the negroes . . . are organized in his political interest."[77] A few days later, another pro-Grant rally resulted in the arrest of "drunken and disorderly negroes," who attacked a police officer with razors, clubs, and "a loaded whip."[78] The next week, the *Register* reported a similar scene from Chicago, where pro-Grant blacks "attacked a street car full of passengers, beat the driver with torches, drove off the passengers, and when the police tried to suppress the riot, they turned on the officers and hacked them with razors."[79]

Voting day itself proceeded more calmly, with none of the poll-storming of 1870. The only incident was in the First Ward, where "a crowd of negroes" attacked a black voter who they believed intended to vote for Greeley and drove him away from the polls.[80] At a postelection parade to celebrate Grant's reelection, the worst the *Register* could muster was to point out that the "companies of white men . . . made a very good appearance," while the "the negro companies" in the victory procession "wore all sorts of uniforms, and expressed their feelings in various barbaric yells and whoops."[81] Although there were no other "riots" of the kind that took place in 1872, the decade following ratification of the Fifteenth Amendment saw the continuation of the *Register*'s race agitation and continued allusions to the civic incapacity of black voters.[82]

In 1870, the *Register* spoke only in a rhetorical sense when it condemned "the leading radicals, who hope by the aid of the negro to rob the people," but as the economic troubles of that decade wore on, the actual criminal activities of local blacks increasingly filled the newspaper's pages and were often reported with partisan overtones.[83] Allusions to black criminality were central to Democratic critiques of Republican politics. Reporting on a minor case involving the theft of a harness in 1874, the *Register* referred to the black defendants and other convicted thieves as "republican politician[s]." Just before the election of 1876, the *Register* reported that George Johnson, a "colored republican" was found guilty of horse stealing in the circuit court. A few days later, James Hunter, a "young colored man and sound republican," was convicted of robbing a grocery store and sentenced to one year in the state penitentiary. Hunter's "chief concern" according to the *Register,* "was his unavoidable absence from the [Republican] wigwam meeting last night."[84] That same month, an officer attempted to arrest Isaac Parks, a "burly negro," for disorderly conduct. The *Register* joked that "we knew Isaac was a sound republican, of course, but we did not know until this morning that he was high up in the counsels of the party. It seems, however, that he is 'captain' of the Capital [Rutherford] Hayes and Wheeler club, and as such is entitled to the sympathy and support of his party in his hour of trial." Not to worry, said the *Register,* "this won't affect him seriously . . . as the republicans have a liberal campaign fund on which to draw."[85] When an unidentified "colored republican" stole some cash from another black man, the *Register* ended its brief note on the crime sarcastically, "'Rah for Hayes."[86] Pairing criminality with Republican partisanship was clearly a political tactic, but it was impactful because perceptions of black criminality resonated well beyond political rhetoric. Crime seemed to be on the rise, and Democrats pointed to the growing black population as a likely source of the problem. With decades of judicial precedent and discriminatory legislation now dismantled by Republicans, Democrats' dire predictions about emancipation and black citizenship seemed to be coming true.

FIVE

The Underworld

> Behold the crime-stained blackness of the negro.
>
> —*Hinton Rowan Helper, 1868*

IN OCTOBER 1874, while Gus Reed awaited sentencing in the Sangamon County jail for "various robbing exploits" carried out that spring and summer, he would undoubtedly have overheard the festivities that accompanied the dedication of Abraham Lincoln's memorial tomb at Oak Ridge Cemetery.[1] The crowds in the city that week were almost as large as they had been when Lincoln's body first arrived home in May 1865. Then, emancipation had loomed large over the proceedings—as Philemon Stout complained, the funeral orations had been "ultra abolition"—but in 1874 the speeches focused almost exclusively on recalling the sacrifices of the war, the preservation the Union, and the continuing need to reconcile the still-divided nation, with scarcely a mention of emancipation, black citizenship, or civil rights.[2] The failures of emancipation and reconstruction were more acute in 1874 than they had been in 1865, and many would have considered Gus Reed, sitting in his dingy cell in the county jail, to be one of them. During the twelve years between his first arrest in Springfield and his death at Joliet, he spent more than seven and half years in local jails and the state penitentiary. His Springfield was quite different from the one respectable citizens wished to create and promote. Whereas black militias, fraternal orders, and community activists strove to participate

97

as equals in the maintenance of the city's respectability and prosperity, criminals such as Gus Reed raised concerns about correlations between the new larger population of black migrants and the postbellum increase in crime. He belonged to a growing criminal population in Springfield during the late 1860s and 1870s, and although he may not have been aware of it, his actions were taken by many as evidence of inherent black criminality and as justification for rejecting black citizenship. Although Gus Reed and other black criminals represented only a tiny part of Springfield's black population, many whites saw in black criminals all they had feared in the antebellum era. As they sought to reestablish or maintain racial boundaries in certain areas of civic life—education, the courts, electoral politics, and public facilities—white residents who resisted the inclusion of blacks in the body politic increasingly portrayed their city's black residents as "likely transgressors of what whites regarded as community mores."[3] The first black convict from Sangamon County was sent to the state penitentiary in 1863, the year of the Emancipation Proclamation, and black criminals seemed thereafter to constantly appear in the local newspapers as perpetrators of crime.[4] As all sorts of crimes seemed to increase throughout the city, Springfielders blamed a growing "class of vermin" that plagued the city.[5] For whites worried about both the race problem and the crime problem, blackness was a convenient and significant indicator of potential criminality.

Gus Reed probably began to commit crimes shortly after he arrived in Springfield. We do not know what led him to those activities, but the fact that he so frequently returned to thieving suggests that his were not only crimes of necessity. The types and quantities of goods he stole also indicate that he was doing more than supplying his own needs. He found an economic niche in Springfield, albeit an illegal one. If he did not have some compelling reason to return time and again to Springfield and the surrounding towns, a man who had already come from as far away as Georgia would probably have been willing to move on again. It may have been family that kept him coming back, but it may also have been that Gus Reed was more successful at thieving than his arrest record indicates. We know that he ranged over central Illinois, from Jacksonville in Morgan County in the west to Taylorville in Christian County in the east, with Springfield as a home base. In all three places, he would have found protection within networks of fellow thieves and others whose activities put them on the wrong side of the law. In Springfield, he would have gone to Greasy Row, where some of the barrooms and brothels readily—and others reluctantly—admitted black patrons. There he would have gathered with other thieves, burglars, pickpockets, confidence men, and fencers of stolen goods. He would have associated with both black and white working men, prostitutes, and drifters, seeking sociability in lower-class, mixed-race establishments, described by one of the *Register*'s concerned readers as "hot holes of hell."[6] In these places he would have arranged with underground dealers to buy and resell the commodities he stole, and he would have kept an ear out for news and gossip. If he had just completed a heist, he would want to know whether the police were looking for him and who would buy his loot; if he was planning a new job, he would want to know about recent shipments, piles of unattended merchandise, and the condition of the locks on certain doors and windows. He would likely have maintained connections with draymen, porters, janitors, and others who had reason to be aware of the flow of goods in and around the warehouses and shops of Springfield's grocers, merchants, meatpackers, and shippers.

Shortly after he first arrived in Springfield, Gus Reed stole four dollars' worth of flour—probably a barrel—from a local mill. This was not a particularly serious crime, and it may have been among his first forays into thievery in his new home. His accomplices were two other black men named Beverly Jackson and William Nelson. We do not know whether they had a chance to profit from their crime, since all three were quickly arrested. Gus Reed initially pleaded not guilty, but a jury convicted him and sentenced him to one year in the penitentiary.[7] Likely due to the harshness of the sentence, his court-appointed attorney motioned for a new trial, but the second jury could not agree on a verdict and was discharged. On a separate larceny indictment, he pleaded guilty and received just one month in the county jail. The short sentence could have been due to his youth—he was just twenty at the time— or the judge might have considered his time served, since he had already spent seven months in the county jail.[8] When he was released, he managed to keep himself out of trouble for only a few months. In late April 1867 he was fined three dollars in the police court for fighting with Isaac Kelsey, a thirty-five-year-old black laborer from Missouri. Less than a month later, Gus was involved in another fray with three other men, "indulging in a great amount of obscenity, profanity, and abuse, winding up with a free fight." This time he was charged with using "language calculated to provoke a breach of the peace" and again fined three dollars.[9]

Gus Reed worked with at least six other black thieves at different times between 1866 and 1878: Beverly Jackson, William Nelson, John Fisher, Scott Burton, James Burns, and Perry Braxton. For most of these men, thieving was not their sole occupation. Gus Reed was listed as both a laborer and a farmer on penitentiary documents; Scott Burton worked as a gardener in 1870 after he was released from Joliet, and later became a barber; John Fisher claimed he was a barber, but he does not appear in the census or city directories; William Nelson was a servant; and James Burns and Perry Braxton were both laborers. Braxton had a wife and two young children, and the other men may also have had families.[10] Gus Reed and Scott Burton were both from Georgia; Fisher and Nelson were from Kentucky; and Braxton was from Virginia. Did these men bring the complex moral economy of a slave society with them to Illinois? Did their actions as black thieves imply the same ambiguous morality as slave theft? The historian Roger Lane has observed of black criminals in Philadelphia in the late nineteenth century: "To steal successfully from whites or to sell illicit goods and services in the wider market was potentially to add to the slender resources available to the city's Afro-Americans . . . and, from a purely economic point of view, to compensate them for their exclusion from more legitimate activity."[11] But was this the same moral economy at work in resisting slavery?

Like the path he may have taken from Georgia to Illinois, the line between Gus Reed's experiences with slave theft and his postbellum larceny is not a straight one, but both clearly operated outside the legal marketplace. Although most local black citizens worked within the mainstream economy in Springfield, their roles were often circumscribed by popular prejudice. Even as discriminatory laws were removed, social and cultural barriers remained to limit their opportunities. Not all disillusioned black residents turned to crime to combat their marginalization, nor was it only blacks that worked in low-paying jobs and could not afford to participate as fully as their more affluent neighbors in the mainstream economy. Poor whites were also left out, especially during the postbellum population boom and the national financial troubles that followed in the 1870s. Local newspapers commented frequently on the great numbers of idle young men and women, black and white, who congregated on street corners and in taverns, brothels, alleys, and abandoned residences in Springfield. They were part of a growing, migratory army of the unemployed, many of them with criminal histories from similar shiftless stints in other midwestern cities. They faced exclusion, for one reason or another, from the legitimate commerce that drove the capricious prosperity of the postbellum decade. As unemployment soared, warehouses, storerooms, freight depots, and even private homes seemed ripe targets for those who crafted their own economic morality with pilfered goods and illicit commerce. Although Gus Reed and his associates may have viewed their activities more as appropriation and redistribution than as outright stealing, the mainstream economy, and the legal structures that kept it functioning, regarded them as dangerous to both the market and the public safety of the community.

In April 1869, Gus Reed and three accomplices stole about three hundred pounds of bacon, the single largest theft he is known to have committed. Gus was arrested the next morning, and apparently gave up his three accomplices in the hope of receiving a lighter sentence. John Fisher, Scott Burton, and Eliza Lewis were all arrested within days. The *Illinois State Journal* ran a brief story on the crime titled "A 'Dark' Transaction"—a pun that emphasized both the race of the criminals and the illegal nature of their activities.[12] Despite Gus Reed's willingness to reveal his accomplices, he received five years of hard time in the penitentiary, but was released on May 12, 1873, one year early for earning "good time."[13] He returned to the Springfield underworld, and extended his reach into the surrounding communities.

In early 1874, Gus Reed was arrested with Perry Braxton and James Burns and charged with larceny. The *Register* described the three as part of "a gang of plundering negroes," who had "about a wagon load of plunder that they had secreted at a house in the eastern part of the city." Gus Reed was identified as "the probable leader of the gang, who is said to be one of the most desperate characters in the country." Braxton and Burns pleaded guilty and were sentenced to one year in the penitentiary, but Reed apparently escaped from jail in the week after his March 6 indictment. When his codefendant James Burns pleaded guilty on March 13, Gus Reed was already gone. He eluded officers for three months, perhaps hiding in Jacksonville, and, according to the *Register,* "declared that he would never be captured alive."[14] In July, he was captured alive, but only after he "nearly 'chawed off' one of the fingers of the Jacksonville officer who made the arrest." This was apparently not the first time he had tussled with officers, and the *Register* reported that he had once escaped capture in Christian County by "'carving with a razor' his would-be captor," an attack so severe that the Chicago *Inter-Ocean* claimed he had "nearly killed" the arresting officer. The *Illinois State Journal* labeled him a "notorious negro thief and desperado" and described his crimes as "various robbing exploits and other crimes committed here and elsewhere."[15]

Gus Reed spent the rest of the summer and much of the fall of 1873 in the county jail awaiting trial. He pleaded guilty to larceny, and in October was sentenced to three years in the penitentiary, where he apparently behaved well enough to get a six-month reduction to his sentence. When he was released in June 1877, he once more returned to Springfield. Just nineteen days later, the *Inter-Ocean* reported the arrest of "Augustus Reed, a colored desperado, who three years ago cut with a razor and maimed for life Officer McCartney, of Tayorsville [*sic*], Christian County. Reed has several times escaped from the officers, and is regarded as a dangerous fellow." The *Register* reported that a deputy sheriff from Taylorville was on his way to Springfield to take the prisoner back to Christian County for trial, and offered a different version of the attack, reporting that he was to stand trial for "chopping an officer up with an ax to avoid arrest."[16] On June 27, Gus Reed was booked into the Taylorville jail for a charge of "assault with intent to kill." On September 5, he was found not guilty by a jury and released. It probably took him less than twenty-four hours to arrive back home in Springfield.[17]

After his return from Taylorville, Gus Reed rekindled his acquaintance with John Fisher, who continued to have his own troubles with the law. Although he had stayed out of the penitentiary, Fisher had been a regular fixture in the local police courts. In May 1877, and again in September, he and his wife, Emma, were in the police courts with Abram and Eliza James, with whom they seem to have had an ongoing feud. In the fall, both John and Emma were brought before the police courts for separate assault incidents, and in January of 1878, a notice appeared in the *Register:* "John Fisher, who is notorious in police annals, was before Esquire Condell, yesterday, on a peace warrant, obtained by his neighbors, and in default of bonds of $100 to keep the peace for three months, was remanded to his old quarters in the jail." Such petty misdemeanors were hardly on the scale of burglary and larceny, so perhaps John Fisher had avoided committing any serious crimes while Gus Reed sat in the penitentiary, or perhaps he had just gotten better at avoiding capture.[18]

In the fall of 1877, Gus Reed returned to John Fisher's house on Ninth Street, and the two began again to circulate stolen goods. In the small hours of November 14, two night patrol officers spotted Reed, "who seemed very anxious to keep out of sight," two blocks from Fisher's house. The officers approached him and asked him his business. Reed replied that "he had been out to see his girl, and was on his way back to John Fisher's." The officers noticed that he "had on rubber shoes, and over them a pair of socks," to mask his footprints. The officers decided to arrest him "on general principles," but he escaped after a chase, earning a couple of parting pistol shots from one of the officers.[19] The police set up surveillance on Fisher's house, and after receiving information that several burglaries had been committed on Fifth Street that very night, they arrested John and Emma Fisher (the latter, noted the *Register* disparagingly, was "a white woman"). In the Fisher house, the police found a large quantity of stolen goods tied to several recent burglaries, including wine, tobacco, and clothing. A later report linked much of this stolen merchandise to robberies committed by Gus Reed.[20]

On November 22, a brief item in the *Register* indicated that the police were still searching for Reed, and speculated that he was himself "hunting" the officer who shot at him on the night of the raid at Fisher's house. In early December, three men came upon Gus Reed holed up in a horse stall at the county fairgrounds, surrounded by plunder. He fled on foot, leading his pursuers on a chase that lasted several hours through the city and into the countryside northeast of town. When he was finally captured, a railroad handcar had to be sent out from the city to bring him back. In his hideout at the fairgrounds, officers found stolen clothing, several dressed chickens, and a whole cooked turkey. At a nearby home, officers found more stolen clothing, and suggested that the "premises of a number of negroes" near the fairgrounds were other likely hiding places for plunder. In celebrating the bust, the *Register* noted that "Reed is a hard one, and but a few months since was released from the penitentiary, where he was sentenced for robbery."[21]

Newspaper reports at the time of his arrest made no mention of a robbery at Elliott Herndon's home, but a later piece indicated that Gus Reed and John Fisher had included Herndon's house in their thieving that fall, stealing an unspecified quantity of meat. Indeed, it was this particular crime with which they were finally charged.[22] Having lived in Springfield for at least a decade, both Gus Reed and John Fisher were probably aware that Elliott Herndon was a staunch Democrat and no friend of the city's black citizens. Was Herndon's house simply one among many the pair robbed that fall, or did they target him specifically? In any case, Gus Reed was indicted on two counts of burglary and larceny on February 25, while Fisher was indicted only for burglary. Reed pleaded guilty on March 21, while Fisher pleaded not guilty and was subsequently convicted by a jury and sentenced to one year in Joliet. Reed's sentence was pronounced two days later, and notwithstanding his guilty plea, he received one year for each of the two indictments against him. On March 26, Sheriff Temple Elliott escorted four prisoners—Gus Reed, John Fisher, George Fox, and Christopher Carroll, all convicted of burglary or larceny—to the penitentiary at Joliet. Springfield was finally free of Gus Reed, the "notorious negro thief and desperado."[23]

The Civil War and its aftermath brought many newcomers like Gus Reed and John Fisher to the city, and not all of them achieved—or sought—the kind of success that marked them as valuable members of the community. When their sort encountered the justice system of Springfield and Sangamon County, their first contact was often with police officers and magistrates. The city's police force had been created in 1854, and by the 1870s employed only a dozen officers, on whose shoulders it fell to regulate criminal behavior, as well as ordinance violations, domestic disputes, and other citizen complaints. Despite complaints about the small size of the force and allegations of bribe taking, Springfield's officers were active on the streets of the city. From late April through August 1871, the police made 310 arrests, including 75 drunk and disorderly arrests, 81 prostitution arrests, 28 disturbing the peace arrests, and an array of others ranging from fast driving to "mayhem" and domestic violence.[24]

When the police conducted raids on criminal hideouts, tippling houses, and brothels, those arrested ended up in either the city or county jails. The city jail was reserved for the lowest class of petty lawbreakers, gamblers, prostitutes, drunks, and vagabonds who had no place else to sleep, whereas the county jail housed those convicted of minor offenses in the circuit court, as well as those awaiting trial in the county, circuit, and federal courts. In March 1874, the *Register* described the scene in the county jail as "the criminal crop" was mustered before being sent on to the penitentiary at Joliet: "The convicted criminals were brought out into the halls to be chained together preparatory to being forwarded to Joliet. . . . The rattle of the long chain to which they were to be secured, and that of the handcuffs which were to clasp their wrists, was heard on the floor. . . . It was a motley crowd, comprising men of various ages, classes and conditions. . . . Some of the men were bright, intelligent fellows, and with proper training in their youth might have graced society. Others were lacking in intelligence, stolid and beetle-browed, with countenances repulsive in the extreme." Among the offenders in this criminal parade was Ike Williams, "that rollicking son of Ham," who faced three years for larceny, along with Gus Reed's accomplices James Burns and Perry Braxton, both of whom also faced sentences for larceny.[25]

Once they had been lodged in either the city or county jails, the accused would appear before the police courts, the county court, or the circuit court, depending on the seriousness of the offense. The police courts—also known as the justice of the peace courts, or simply justice courts—handled ordinance violations and nonfelony crimes like disorderly conduct, fighting, public drunkenness, gambling, and minor prostitution charges. The justices were authorized to impose fines on those found guilty and to imprison them in the county jail, usually for relatively short periods. The county court typically handled only legal and chancery cases, but after 1872 also began to handle some minor criminal cases, including liquor and gambling charges, in order to relieve the overtaxed police and circuit courts. More serious justice was meted out at the circuit court, which handled most of the criminal cases in the county. The court was primarily responsible for committing local convicts to the state penitentiary at Joliet but also sentenced convicts on lesser charges to the county jail. The circuit court convened regularly and frequently throughout the 1860s and 1870s, a typical year consisting of winter, spring or summer, and autumn terms, with breaks of a few weeks between each. Between 60 and 140 cases were heard each term, about half of these being continued from previous terms.[26]

Of the three courts, ordinary Springfielders were probably most familiar with the police courts. In 1865, the *Register* painted a lively picture of their daily business:

> The little room in which the daily tribunal is held . . . is filled or partially filled. . . . Upon one side . . . is a group of men and boys leaning over a railing which divides them from the other portion of the room. These are spectators, those who may have come in through simple curiosity, or perhaps the friends of a party who is to be tried. . . . Upon a pine bench which has been nicked and carved by many an idle jack-knife, and which faces the judge's desk, are seated perhaps three or four, or it may be a dozen miserable creatures, their eyes sunken or blood shot, their faces unwashed, their hair uncombed, their general aspect, in fact, indicating, we might say speaking, "a night in the calaboose." These are the prisoners—the victims before the altar of justice, the prey of the police, the bread and butter of the magistrates and petty attorneys. The grist to be ground in the judicial machine. Near them . . . there are perhaps a couple of watchmen, a lawyer who wants a client . . . it may be a witness also, and this is the audience and the actors in the little drama which is daily represented here.[27]

Among the most common cases before the justices of the peace were the ubiquitous drunk and disorderly, breach of the peace, assault, gambling, and prostitution charges. There were also minor infractions like "driving a horse at an immoderate speed" and "repairing a wooden building in fire limits." If found guilty of these minor violations, the accused was ordered to pay the costs of the case and a small fine that typically did not exceed ten dollars.[28] In other cases, especially misdemeanor criminal cases, the verdict was more creative, as in the case of Edward Wilson and Annie Smith, who were found together inside one of Springfield's many active brothels. The two might have tried to reason their way out of the charges by claiming to be lovers, so the justice called their bluff and agreed to dismiss the charges if they would be married. The two acquiesced, and the justice married them on the spot. Other prostitutes and their clients were not so lucky. While many prostitutes escaped the justice's court with a small fine, brothel keepers were often sent on to the circuit court on the more serious charge of "keeping a house of ill fame."[29] Aside from prostitution, by far the most common complaints brought before the justices of the peace involved private conflicts that spilled over into public spaces: loud noises at late hours, unruly dogs, real or imagined insults, and unpaid debts. One day in the spring of 1878, Lucy Dunham reached the end of her rope and charged her husband with "being in a beastly state of intoxication." The justice ruled that "being a man with a family and sick wife [he] is dismissed with a reprimand." Like many of the contesting parties that entered the police courts, Lucy Dunham very likely left unsatisfied.[30]

Black Springfielders had the same opportunities as whites to experience partial and unsatisfactory justice in the police courts. John and Emma Fisher appeared frequently as complainants or defendants against Abram and Eliza James. The two couples sometimes fought with words, sometimes with fists, but seem to have always been at odds. On September 9, both Abram and Eliza were arrested and charged with "assaulting and striking" John Fisher and with "using language and conduct calculated to provoke a breach of the peace." The next day, Fisher was charged with exactly the same against Abram James. Their cases were almost always dismissed; only occasionally did one party or the other have to pay a small fine or face short-term confinement in the city jail. John and Emma Fisher also sometimes appeared on the complaints of others for disorderly conduct. Otherwise respectable black residents also came before the city courts to answer charges made by their white neighbors. William and Clarinda Head (he a drayman, she a housewife) were relatively prosperous by the standards of Springfield's black community, with an estate valued at $2,000 in 1870, and at least one young daughter. In 1878, they were brought before a magistrate on the charge of "rending premises for houses of ill fame." The charge could not be sustained, however, and the case was dismissed.[31]

It was all too common for cases in the police courts to be dismissed for one reason or another: witnesses failed to show; complainants dropped charges; evidence was lacking; or the accusations were spurious to begin with. Between May 1877 and May 1878, a total of 851 cases were brought before the several justices of the peace, ranging from 106 cases during the month of July (including 8 arrests for disorderly conduct and fighting on the Fourth of July) to just 8 arrests for the entire month of February. Between 18 and 88 percent of the cases were dismissed each month. Overall, 26 percent of that year's cases were dismissed entirely, and many more ended in a simple payment of fines or an order to leave town. The worst punishments a justice of the peace could threaten in most cases were confinement to the city jail—which was never large enough to handle all the petty lawbreakers in Springfield—or an order to leave the city, which if complied with at all, was quickly remedied by retracing one's steps. When George Fox was found in Kate Flanagan's brothel on December 10, 1877, he was given thirty minutes to leave town forever. Twelve days later, he was back in court on the same charge.[32] The police courts often amounted to little more than a source of income for the city and a nuisance for its citizens. Month after month, the justices saw the same sorry parade of prostitutes, gamblers, saloon keepers, loiterers, and drunks march in and out of their shabby courtroom. Many defendants probably walked from the court to the saloon or brothel, only to be dragged back again by the night police within a few hours. As the *Register* editorialized in 1865: "The police court is the most imperfect piece of judicial machinery. . . . Wanting all the dignity of whatever moves moderately, it goes quickly, and frequently quite confusedly."[33]

Although all of the local courts could be frustrating, their central role in the maintenance of law and order was never seriously questioned. The repeal of the Black Laws in 1865 meant that blacks could now potentially serve as jurors and witnesses against whites, a prospect that threatened to undermine both the racial and the legal order. There had been no separate courts for blacks in Illinois during the antebellum era, which meant that many aspects of the justice system before 1865 were inaccessible to them. White critics of desegregation feared that standards of truth, equity, and justice—concepts they did not believe blacks understood—would be compromised if blacks were allowed to participate in the justice system. When the Black Laws were repealed, the *Register* noted with alarm, "The field is open to Sambo, and we may expect his *debut* at any day."[34]

In November 1865, a discharged white soldier named Charles Buckley was sentenced to one year in the state penitentiary for stealing five dollars from a black man. Buckley was convicted on the testimony of his victim, apparently the first time a black witness was allowed to testify in the Sangamon County circuit court. The Democratic *Register* ran the story under the headline, "The Beginning of Negro Equality—A Negro Sends a Discharged Soldier to the Penitentiary." The editors noted, "We were struck with the appearance . . . for the first time in our life, of a nigger, as black as ebony, as a state's witness in a pending criminal case." If that was not enough to turn the world on its head, the *Register* explained that the prosecuting attorney for the state on behalf of the black victim was a Democrat, Cincinnatus Morrison (who had been named along with Elliott Herndon in 1864 as a member of the Order of American Knights), and that the attorney for the white soldier was a Republican. The defense claimed that the black man "as a witness . . . was not yet one year old" and that "the accused had fought four years to secure to the nigger the privilege of sending [the soldier] to the penitentiary," while the Democratic prosecutor "told the jury that the nigger proved himself truthful by his consistent testimony." The *Register* summed up the reversal of the typical partisan positions sarcastically: "What a beautiful commentary all this is upon the course things are taking, in consequence of our recent great and glorious war!"[35]

Despite their worries, the progress of "Negro equality" in the judicial system did not proceed as quickly as the *Register* feared. In 1866, a local attorney tried to convince a justice of the peace to impanel a black jury in the case of two black men and one white man charged with fighting, but the justice "couldn't see it, and a white jury was selected." When the first jury could not agree, a second all-white jury was impaneled and all three defendants were found guilty and fined twenty-five dollars each.[36] It was another four years before a black juror would have the opportunity to sit in Springfield, but with no greater success. In another justice court case in 1870, "the first colored juror was summoned in Springfield," but when the man took his chair, the white jurors refused to serve, and "the officer appalled at the result of his operation told the darkey to go likewise, and again set himself at work to get a jury."[37] In 1873, a local barber named Thomas Flynn was apparently the first black juror to successfully sit on a circuit court jury, a situation the *Register* called a "novel spectacle," commenting that, "such sights are common enough in some sections of our country, but are rarely witnessed in our midst."[38] Progress in the local courts was thus uneven; blacks could and did give testimony against whites, but persistent race prejudice often kept them from full and equal participation in all aspects of the judicial system.

In the commission of and conviction for criminal behavior, Springfield's black residents seemed to find the greatest opportunity for equality with their white neighbors. Both the police courts and the circuit court saw alleged black offenders routinely dismissed, convicted, sentenced, fined, and jailed without apparent discrimination. The crimes that most often brought both blacks and whites in Springfield and greater Sangamon County into the courts in the 1870s were property crimes: arson, burglary, forgery, larceny, robbery, receiving stolen goods, confidence games, embezzlement, and other crimes involving physical property or money. Of nearly 1,600 criminal cases in the circuit court between 1870 and 1880, more than 800, or 52 percent, were charges of property crimes. Ranging from 16 cases in 1872 to 167 in 1877, property crimes kept law enforcement busier than any other offense.[39]

These crimes were regularly documented in the crime columns of the local newspapers. Even if they were not violent, property crimes made their own lasting scars on the community's sense of safety. Young Anna Ridgely confessed to her diary: "Our home was entered on Wednesday. . . . It was very alarming and I have been afraid ever since. They unlocked the door with a jimmy and walked right in. It is the first time our house was ever entered and we are very much frightened."[40] The frequency of burglary and larceny ensured that they were a primary concern of the courts. During a crime wave in August 1873, the *Register* lamented that it was "almost every day now . . . called upon to chronicle the entrance or attempted entrance by burglars of the residences of some one or more of our citizens."[41] The municipal police were engaged in "a relentless warfare against the horde of vagabonds that infest the city," who the *Register* blamed for "the almost nightly depredations of burglars."[42]

Just one month before Gus Reed and his gang of bacon thieves were apprehended in 1869, the *Journal* reported, "There is evidently an organized gang of petty thieves in the city. The smoke house of a well-known citizen of the First Ward was robbed night before last. The scoundrels took away several hundred pounds of hams, shoulders and sides of bacon." The crimes are so similar that perhaps the *Journal's* prediction that "the police are on the track, and, perhaps, will catch some of the gang" may have come true with the capture of Gus Reed and his accomplices.[43] There were dozens of others waiting to take their place, however, and frequent charges of receiving stolen goods attest to the ubiquity of an underground market in stolen commodities.

The property crime required to support this market was such a problem in Springfield that even petty thieves received sentences that seemed out of proportion to the seriousness of their offenses. Thefts on a smaller scale were punished just as severely as large-scale heists, and sentences for property crime often exceeded those for violent crimes. In 1873, William Weiss and Patrick Carroll lured a man into the suburbs, far from the gas-lit streets of downtown, and robbed him of the cash and property on his person. For this seemingly mundane crime each man received three years in the state penitentiary.[44] During the same term of court, Moses Williams, whom the *Register* described as "a somewhat notorious character in this city," received no less than six years and ten months in the state penitentiary for robbing a crippled pensioner of forty-eight dollars he had just collected from the pension office.[45] Such crimes were perceived as especially threatening because "larceny tended to be committed by the poor against the politically and judicially influential propertied classes."[46] The kind of people who stole were the kind of people respectable Springfielders wanted off their streets for as long as possible.

Although property crime was the first choice for most criminals, Springfielders worried almost as much about vice crimes, and often linked the two by referring to brothels and unlicensed drinking establishments as the dens and hideouts of thieves. Over the course of the 1870s, more than three hundred vice charges, almost 20 percent of the criminal caseload, were brought before the circuit court, most of them involving illegal liquor sales, gambling, and prostitution. There were occasional cases of adultery, fornication, incest, and bastardy, but these were relatively rare.[47] More commonly, the courts were full of cases resulting from regular raids on Springfield's many "tippling houses" and "houses of ill fame." The brothels and barrooms of Greasy Row were particularly attractive destinations for both whites and blacks who enjoyed getting drunk and causing trouble. Springfield's brothels were no secret in the community, but there was a special stigma attached to those that housed prostitutes of different races. During a series of vice raids in October 1874, the *Register* commented on a particularly "motley crowd" of "black and white prostitutes, the former males and the latter females," who were arraigned for "herding together in a house on Reynolds Street, presided over by a young woman of white skin." To say nothing of the violated gender norms embodied by this arrangement, the apparent confirmation of black criminality and immorality, combined with fears of racial fraternization and miscegenation, led the *Register* to label the affair "a disgusting exhibition."[48]

The dives along Greasy Row combined alcohol and sex, two potent incendiaries for violent crimes like murder and rape, but such crimes were not often reported. Violent crimes represented the fewest charges before the circuit court, only about two hundred between 1870 and 1880, about 15 percent of the total criminal charges. The majority of these were varieties of assault: with intent to kill, injure, rape, or rob. Threats are also included in this category, since many of them involved threats against life, and these were the second most common.[49] Actual murder, rape, and manslaughter were the rarest crimes in Sangamon County but were the most sensational and best remembered. Homicides typically occurred as the result of drunken quarrels or as revenge for perceived wrongs; most were unpremeditated and usually accidental. When barkeeper Fritz Triever bludgeoned a knife-wielding patron several times over the head in 1867, he likely had no intention of killing the man, but the unfortunate victim died the next day. In another instance, a drunken customer got into a dispute with a local merchant and killed him by striking him with a wagon spoke, the nearest weapon at hand, and not the best choice for cold-blooded murder. Premeditated murder was so rare as to arouse considerable excitement when it did occur. The most sensational murder of the period was the killing of Sharon Tyndale, a former Illinois secretary of state, in the spring of 1871. Tyndale was assaulted as he left his house to catch an early-morning train, bludgeoned and shot in an apparent robbery attempt.[50] The story received extensive coverage in the local newspapers, but the killers were never apprehended. The attention given to such cases indicates that they were the exceptions that proved the rule.

Because violent crime was so rare, and because threats and assaults rarely translated into full-blown cases of rape or murder, juries may have been more likely to forgive these infractions, or to punish them less severely than property crimes. When James Gilmore, a black thief and troublemaker like Gus Reed, assaulted a black woman with a corn knife in 1873, he was charged with "assault with intent to kill," but when found guilty by a jury, was sentenced to only ten days in the county jail. At the same term of court, Gilmore was also tried on the charge of stealing an ox from a white farmer, for which he received three years and four months of hard time in the state penitentiary.[51] Although it is possible that Gilmore might have received a lengthier sentence had he assaulted a white woman, his treatment did not deviate from either the overall patterns of crime in the community or sentencing in the courts.[52]

When it came to the courtroom exercise of justice, whether in the police courts or in the circuit court, it seems that blacks in Springfield experienced a relatively impartial justice system. But the docket books provide an incomplete picture of how Springfielders perceived the relationship between race and criminality, for although the courts seemed color-blind, most Springfielders were not. James Gilmore's case, like dozens of others involving black defendants, also received coverage in the city's newspapers, which played a central role in shaping public perceptions of the crime problem. The editors cited Gilmore, and the specter of the black criminal, as a chief example of the crime problem in the city and county. Like Gus Reed, Gilmore was portrayed as a marauding "colored desperado" and a "desperate character," and when he was sentenced to Joliet for stealing the ox, the *Register* characterized him as "one of the roughs—white and black—which has long invested the city, and the fact that he has gone where all ruffians ought to go is a fact which will please all good citizens."[53]

As the crime rate rose during the 1870s the local press constantly lamented the need to chronicle the "nightly depredations of burglars."[54] Although black criminals represented a minority of those convicted for all types of crime, newspapers frequently emphasized the threat posed by black criminals. Through stereotypes of black degeneracy and criminality, white Springfielders tried to maintain the line they had long drawn between honest white citizens and dangerous black interlopers. Illinois's laws had once made it easy to tacitly assume that all blacks were potentially guilty of something, whether it was violation of the Black Laws or more heinous crimes, but as black residents gained some state and federal protections through the civil rights acts and legitimacy as citizens through the Fourteenth and Fifteenth Amendments, the old line between white and black no longer seemed to clearly separate the typically law-abiding from the potentially criminal. Springfielders sought new ways to describe the biracial criminal element that harbored in their city, but all too often, blackness remained a convenient marker of possible criminality.

The newspapers were the surest way for most Springfielders to learn of criminal and judicial activities in the city and county. They carried detailed information on the justice courts, police matters, county and circuit courts, and the federal courts. The names of grand jurors and sitting circuit judges were printed at the beginning of each term of the circuit court, as were the anticipated dockets of the several courts. Each day, the doings of the courts were briefly reported (usually the defendant's name and charge were listed), and some of the more sensational or noteworthy cases received detailed coverage. The crimes themselves, both successful and unsuccessful, were reported as well. Occasional rashes of robberies and housebreakings received extensive coverage and were often accompanied by editorials decrying the inefficacy of the police to prevent crime. In general, the Democratic *Register*'s crime reporting was more comprehensive and consistent than that of the Republican *Journal*, but both featured stories about crimes or courts on their local news pages every day. Both also called regularly for reforms to the justice system in order to suppress Springfield's active criminal element. Criminals of all races were referred to as a "class of vermin" that plagued peace-loving citizens, but crime reporting could also be an exciting section of the local news page.[55] In the fall of 1873, the *Register* lamented, "We are just now experiencing one of the dullest seasons we have ever passed through," noting that "money is so scarce that people can't get drunk, and as a consequence there are no murders; no 'cutting and slashing,' not even an ordinary street brawl." While the situation was "discouraging in the extreme to the collator of local news," most citizens probably did not mind such dull periods.[56] More typically, the city columns were peppered with sensational and frightening reports from the courts and streets of Springfield.

Black criminals, in particular, appeared in the Democratic *Register* with alarming frequency. Editorials, headlines, and derogatory wordplay drew on antebellum stereotypes of thieving slaves and duplicitous "darkeys" to implicate Springfield's black citizens as likely perpetrators of local crimes. In December 1872, the *Register* reported that "a Springfield darkey, who was arrested with a chicken in his sack, declared, 'De man dat put 'em dar was no fren of mine.'" The piece was intended as humor, but in order to resonate as such, relied on the assumption that the "Springfield darkey" was, in fact, a thief.[57] A similar story in the winter of 1872 noted that "a colored girl, whose name would do the public no good," had recently tried to rob a local shoe store. The girl made it outside before the clerk caught her, where she reasoned by way of explanation for her crime that "a body can't go ba'foot this cold weather." The "kind hearted" clerk took the shoes back and sent the would-be thief on her way, "rejoicing at her fortunate escape from arrest, but sorrowing over the loss of the coveted foot gear."[58] The same combination of inherent criminality and humorous ignorance was manifest in a vignette published in the *Register* in 1863, when Democratic outrage over the Emancipation Proclamation was at its peak. The *Register* described a fictitious, but apparently instructive, situation at the state penitentiary: "'Let me out ob heah!' said an old darkey confined in the penitentiary at Joliet, after old Abe's manifesto was published in the west—'I wants to go out!' 'Want to go out; what do you mean?' 'I want to go home. Massa Linkum set all the darkeys free—me and all de balance.' The poor darkey thought the proclamation made a free man of him. So it did, just as much as any body else."[59] This ironic vignette was meant to deride the Emancipation Proclamation and the motives of its supporters, but it also suggested that in a postemancipation world, prison and the de facto slavery implied by incarceration, may well be the best and most likely place for the new black citizen.

Even as Springfielders may have chuckled at the image of the "old darkey" clamoring to be released from the penitentiary, underlying apprehensions gave this humor a bitter flavor. As William Van Deburg has observed of nineteenth-century stereotypes of black villainy, "Attempts to comfort the public with less troubling visions [of blacks] were deceptive and dangerous. In the end, it was the brute black—more precisely, the brutishness and villainy of blacks—that would have to be faced."[60] Although the *Register* used imputations of black criminality explicitly as a political tactic, the specter of the black criminal was more than just a means of mobilizing white voters against black suffrage and civil rights. For those who already harbored suspicions about black citizens' civic fitness, black criminality was a threat not only at the polls on Election Day, but throughout the city and throughout the year. In the aftermath of emancipation and the repeal of the Black Laws, black crime seemed an even greater threat. When Gus Reed was arrested in March 1866 for stealing flour, the *Register*'s headline announced "Another Descent of the Freedmen" and added his crime to another recent robbery by "a posse of negroes" as evidence that "freedmen" were wasting little time subjecting

Springfield to their malicious intent. Playing on the title of the Bureau of Refugees, Freedmen, and Abandoned Lands, the *Register* commented, "What a pity it is that there cannot be a special tribunal established here for the trial of 'freedmen and refugees.'"[61] An 1868 editorial titled "Respect for the Rights of Negroes" rebutted an accusation by the Republican *Journal* that the *Register* was opposed to granting rights to blacks. "Not exactly that," claimed the editor, "but the *Register* begs leave to differ with the *Journal* when it insists that robbing, plundering and murdering are rights of the negro which the white man is 'bound to respect.' . . . The *Register* is opposed to all this, and would put it in the power of the whites to protect themselves against negro violence and outrage." Republicans, claimed the *Register*, wanted to "protect the negroes in their right to rob, and plunder, and murder" by "keeping up a large standing army, whose duty it shall be to compel white people to respect these negro rights." In the end, the *Register* objected, "We should be compelled to excuse ourselves on the ground of prejudice against crime, more than our prejudice against niggers," but the rest of the editorial left little doubt that crime and "niggers" were meant to be tightly joined in the imaginations of the *Register*'s readers.[62]

The editors of the *Register* and other Democratic newspapers nationwide relied on several stylistic elements to effectively communicate the degeneracy or criminality of blacks. In addition to sarcastic quips and degrading jokes, editors deployed intentionally provocative wordplay, carefully positioned and worded their headlines, and casually conflated actual instances of black crime with unsubstantiated stories, jokes, and anecdotes. Most commonly, when an alleged criminal was black, the *Register* gave the race of the criminal in parentheses after his or her name, a distinction not granted to white offenders. Simply identifying "negro," "colored," "black," "nigger," or "darkey" offenders exaggerated the frequency of black crime and emphasized the threat posed by black criminals.[63] Playing on the word "dark" also suggested evil or threatening activities performed by black criminals. When George Cook stole a "baby wagon," his activities were jokingly described as "*dark* doings," and when Morrison Wilson "being possessed by more evil spirits than those with whom he quenched his thirst" stole forty-three dollars from a fellow saloon patron, the *Register* described the robbery as "A Dark Deed, Indeed." Even the Republican *Journal* could not resist labeling Gus Reed's bacon theft in 1869 "A 'Dark' Transaction." Beyond mere editorial wordplay, the connection between blackness and moral darkness or criminality would not have been lost on readers.[64]

Notorious repeat offenders were also often portrayed as criminal caricatures in the columns of the *Register*. A particular favorite was Isaac "Ike" Williams, who was described as "that rollicking son of Ham" and "that irrepressible darkey." Williams seemed always to be involved in some crime, fight, or disturbance, and in its reporting, the *Register* crafted a real-life caricature of the black criminal, apparently unable to control his criminal propensities. "Ike is not to blame for being a negro," the *Register* joked, "for he cannot change his skin any more than can the leopard its spots."[65] Ike Williams and other black criminals seemed to steal or fight as part of their nature, including "The Duke," who liked to start fights, and "Black Martha," "a fat, greasy wench," who became a kind of corrupted Mammy figure in the pages of the *Register*.[66]

The stereotypical black criminal established by the *Register* exhibited a set of common characteristics that were alternately humorous and threatening. Black thieves had a tendency to run "like a quarter horse" when they were discovered, a feat that continually confounded the police.[67] Black criminals were also supposed to prefer razors and knives to more sophisticated weaponry, indicating a particular kind of brutality. Reporting on a fight between two white men in which one drew a razor, the *Register* joked: "The right to use which we supposed belonged exclusively to negroes."[68] Black criminals were also known to prey on each other, another point of some humor for the *Register*. When "a semi-intoxicated negro" attacked a black woman and then fled, the *Register* reported that "the woman was not much hurt, and it is believed that if left alone she would have got the better of the brute, as she was just in the act of going for him with a 'little hatchet.'"[69]

Blacks appeared to lack common levels of restraint and intelligence, and this made them as much a point of humor as a danger to the community. A story headed "Fugitive African" from April 1871 spoofed the abolitionists of the 1850s while showing the negative results of their benevolence, noting sarcastically that "'a man and a brother' who sighed for freedom" was recently seen being pursued through the First Ward by a police officer, or as the *Register* joked, "by 'the hell hounds of the law' as Wendell Phillips used to say in the fugitive slave law days." The fugitive, said the *Register*, was named Johnson, "a nigger who has caused more trouble and committed more crimes than anybody in this neighborhood."[70] Exhibiting the special propensity for great speed that the *Register* assigned to all black criminals, Johnson eluded his pursuer. The message of the article, which most readers would have understood, was that far from being the innocent objects of misguided benevolence, blacks were a suspect population now set loose from the necessary restrictions of slavery and prejudicial laws.

Whether or not Springfield's black criminals actually imbibed a sense of moral economy akin to slave theft, the fact that so many of Springfield's black citizens in the 1870s had been born into slavery seemed—to many whites, at least—to suggest this population as a likely source for the recent rise in local burglaries. In April 1876, the *Register* ran a story that began: "Some people say a nigger won't steal, but there are those who doubt the truth of the proposition."[71] The *Register* implied not only that blacks *would* steal but that *every* black person was potentially prone to larceny. Considering the frequency with which black criminals seemed to appear in the columns of the *Register*, there would have been few readers who did not believe a "nigger" would steal. Indeed, many would have been convinced that most of their black neighbors could hardly keep themselves from it.

The image of the childlike black thief, who did not seem able to keep from stealing, had a counterpoint in the more threatening image of the bestial black assailant, violent and lustful. Although violent crimes represented the smallest category of black crime, they also had the most potential to crystallize public opinion. Of the fifty black criminals sentenced to Joliet between 1870 and 1880, only four were convicted of violent crimes: one for manslaughter, one for assault with intent to murder, and two for rape.[72] Because violent crime was so rare, the *Register* often resorted to alarmist headlines about anonymous black assailants, encouraging fearful white Springfielders to imagine skulking criminal blacks waiting in back alleys. In a column headed "Assaulted by a Negro," the *Register* began: "These times are fruitful of thieves," and after several pieces of general advice, it reported that a young white man had bravely fought back against an unknown black thief and driven him away "a few nights ago." Assembling the story from vague reports and warnings, and emphasizing the race of a single alleged criminal, the *Register* encouraged readers to suppose that black criminals were the main scourge of the city.[73]

Anonymous black criminals also preyed on anonymous white females in the columns of the *Register*, incidents that were usually reported without any evidence that such crimes were actually taking place. In the summer of 1873, the paper reported that "a poor Irish woman, who earns her bread by daily labor, was assaulted by a negro man, whose name we have forgotten, and subjected to a good deal of rough handling."[74] Supposedly forgetting the black assailant's name extrapolated a stereotypical black criminal roaming at large in the city; any black man encountered after dark might be this assailant. A similar story appeared in October 1873: "A respectable German servant girl was assaulted . . . by a stalwart negro, whose evident intention was the gratification of his beastly lusts." The girl's cries attracted the attention of a passerby, and "her brutal assailant" disappeared into the night. Again unnamed, and still at large, the black assailant became another feared black specter on Springfield's streets.[75]

In November 1876, the *Register* reported an "Attempt of a Negro to Ravish a White Woman," in which yet another servant girl was stopped on the street at night by a "a negro, who gave unmistakable evidence of an intent to violate her person." The girl succeeded in escaping "the beastly negro," and although she could not identify her alleged assailant by name, she was certain she would recognize him.[76] In another incident, a "negro wretch" attempting to satisfy his "beastly lusts" broke into a white resident's house and "approached his wife, evidently with the intention of committing an indecent assault upon her person." Neighbors scared the anonymous offender away, and the *Register* suggested that if the woman's husband were to find him before the police did, "It is more than likely that a coroner's jury will be called upon to determine upon the cause of his death."[77] In all of these cases, rape was the assumed intention of the black assailants. Reports of anonymous black criminals encouraged white readers to view all black citizens as potential threats. How could any white housewife or servant trust that the black porter who carried their bags or the black drayman who delivered their firewood by day was not the same brutal assailant who preyed on innocent women by night? The stereotypes the *Register* mobilized against blacks thus began to seem less like caricatures and more like real threats faced by ordinary citizens every day.

Black criminals were not the only lawbreakers, and criminals of every sort seemed to be flocking to the capital city in greater numbers than ever before. In 1873, the *Register* ventured to say, "There are not, in any city in the state of equal population with our own, as many disreputable characters, male and female, as there are in Springfield."[78] It was a remarkable and frightening change in less than a decade. Between 1860 and 1870, Springfield witnessed an 86 percent population growth, and between 1870 and 1880, another 13 percent.[79] Although most of the new arrivals, black and white, were respectable people, the population of vagrants, vagabonds, and career criminals also rose, and the *Register* led the charge against them. Politicians, military officials, and other dignitaries came to the city in droves during the war, but there were also unscrupulous patronage seekers, hawkers, confidence men, swindlers, pickpockets, housebreakers, drunkards, and other rowdies.

There had been some petty crime in the city in the 1850s, but before the war was over it seemed that crime had become an epidemic. In January 1864, a rash of burglaries led the *Register* to recommend "a good revolver, lodged in a proper place" as a cure for the "'take-things-that-don't-belong-to-you' disease" that seemed to be sweeping the city.[80] Later that month, the newspaper blamed a group of rogue soldiers for "a system of wholesale robbery" and even implicated a "spy" employed by the Republican mayor in the recent incidents of housebreakings and street robberies.[81] By the end of the war, the *Register* observed that "Springfield, at the present time, seems to be most unfortunately infested with thieves, desperados and outlaws of every description," and the houses of prostitution that flourished during the military presence in the city had become "an increasing evil."[82] In the Second Ward, Elliott and William Herndon united temporarily to drive out a brothel that stood directly adjacent to the ward's schoolhouse.[83] During the fall term of the circuit court, the *Register* reported over one hundred criminal cases on the docket, "which . . . gives evidence of an increase of crime and lawlessness in the community which is shocking to consider."[84]

The crime problem, and the obvious inability of the city police to deal with it, led to rumors in early 1866 that a citizens' "vigilance committee" was being formed "for the purpose of clearing our city of the murderers, thieves and pickpockets which infest it." The *Register* applauded the effort, observing that "the occasional arrest of an inoffensive drunkard or vagrant, does not satisfy a community that is overrun with vagabonds and criminals of the deepest dye."[85] The problem, implied the *Register,* was that the police focused on the crimes that were already committed instead of taking preemptive action against the "vagabonds and criminals" who committed them. The only way to drive out crime was to drive out criminals, and the only way to drive out criminals was to define and identify who exactly was a criminal, and what caused criminality. Fearful citizens shared with criminologists in the latter half of the nineteenth century a desire to discover and root out the fundamental causes of crime. If their language was less precise and their calls to action less nuanced, the crime columns of the newspapers provide a window into how ordinary people came to think about and define the new criminal class.

By the early 1870s, the *Register* had hit upon a solution that would provide the centerpiece of its anticrime reporting over the next decade: rid the city of "vagabonds" and other "unwholesome *debris*" that constituted a "class" from which criminals were produced. These included "bullies, strumpets, vagrants, and sneak thieves. It is from these classes of people that the full blown criminals who fill our jails and penitentiaries and finally ornament the gallows, originate. Left to themselves they disgust good citizens and finally become dangerous to life and property . . . we suggest in the interest of respectability, of peace and good order, that such an application be made of the vagrant laws and other wholesome ordinances of the city, that this class of people be driven from our midst."[86] The "low grog shops and brothels" were "hot beds of crime and disorder," and by breaking these up, the criminal element would find no place to harbor.[87] As historian Roger Lanes notes, the biracial composition of the taverns and brothels where the criminal classes gathered was particularly troublesome, for these "comprised the most racially integrated milieu in late nineteenth-century America, as gamblers and other criminals crossed the color line more easily than most."[88] In the dens of the criminal underworld, disreputable whites and blacks schemed, fought, and caroused together, and the line between the supposedly respectable white community and the potentially criminal or degenerate black community began to blur, threatening to destabilize a racial order already made precarious by emancipation.

When blacks and whites of the "criminal classes" gathered together, newspapers typically deemed the result a "motley" crowd. The term had made its appearance in the English language centuries earlier to describe a multicolored cloth, as in a jester's or fool's motley costume. By the late nineteenth century, the word had become slang for "mixed" or "varied," even "incongruous," especially with regard to race. As the *Register* used it, the term took on derisive and even sinister connotations, as it implied not only social race mixing, but potential miscegenation and biracial crime. From the "motley crowd at the negro quarters" that gathered to watch a "rollicking" performance by a "vagabond" entertainer, to the black and white prostitutes in a Reynolds Street brothel, the term always implied an improper degree of interracial fraternization among the city's lower sorts.[89] The presence of blacks in the "low grog shops and brothels" was evidence enough that blackness and criminality went hand in hand. Indeed, the fact that blacks were present in such places seemed to confirm not only their own immorality but also added evidence that such establishments were irredeemably debased. The implication for whites was that common association with blacks in such places led to vice and crime. When a young woman was brought before the police courts on vagrancy charges, the justice of the peace was about to dismiss the case due to the woman's youth until a witness testified to "seeing her frequently loitering in company with negroes of a very abandoned caste." With this new information, instead of dismissing the girl, the justice fined her ten dollars plus costs, a sum she was likely unable to pay, and confined her to the city jail.[90] In 1870, the *Register* reported under the headline "A Hard Lot" that a restaurant and bar on Greasy Row "has lately attracted much unfavorable attention. Every evening a large number of *men of all colors* have congregated in and around the establishment" (emphasis added). The only crime committed by the multiracial crowd was apparently prolonging their "noisy festivities" into the small hours of the morning, certainly not an uncommon activity. The solution of the city police was to arrest "a baker's dozen of darkies," who were taken to the police court and fined.[91]

In 1871 the *Register* described Greasy Row sarcastically as "one of the most delectable spots" in the city and, as evidence of its immoral nature, informed its readers that "it is the rendezvous of all the trifling, worthless vagabond negroes."[92] One night in March 1872, "a lot of drunken colored roughs" attempted to enter the Greasy Row brothel of a white woman named Sadie Bailey, "a very soiled dove," but were turned away, which led them to break into the house and assault one of the prostitutes. When the police arrived, three officers were slashed with razors when "the negroes made an attack in force upon the police." The next day, a citizen of the First Ward, where Greasy Row was located, wrote to the *Register* that the "cut-throat villainous ruffians of 'dark skin'" were just one problem in these "houses of infamous iniquity, *such like hot holes of hell*, where vice, prostitution, lawlessness and crime have been going on for some years." Vice attracted vice, the writer suggested, and thus attracted blacks, among other lower sorts. The *Register* urged "all good citizens" to "join together in such measures as will prevent the repetition of such an outrage" by "this part of our criminal population."[93]

Other stories of whites and blacks colluding in crime or vice required little or no editorial comment to send their message. In the fall of 1877, the *Register* described John Fisher as "a moke who is not unknown to the police" and his wife, Emma, simply as "a white woman."[94] When a black man named John Leonard was caught robbing a tailor's shop in 1870, the *Register* reported that "a white woman who had been living with Leonard as his wife" was also arrested on charges of assisting in the concealment of the stolen goods.[95] The association between blackness and criminality, and the consequences for white female virtue, would have been plain to readers. Similarly, in the case of "a negro named Clark [who] shot a white woman, who is married to another negro named Garrett," the *Register* left it to the readers to judge what sort of people would engage in such behavior and whether a bullet in the arm might not be the woman's rightful reward for keeping such company.[96] Whites who associated and schemed with black criminals were doubly guilty, not only of the crimes they committed, but also because of their association with blacks. By colluding with blacks, criminal or otherwise, unsavory whites demonstrated their membership in the criminal classes and were implicated in the characteristics of both racial and moral blackness. As the *Register* quipped when a white boy and a black boy got into a fight: "Hurrah for the bottom rail."[97]

When Gus Reed was captured in Jacksonville in the summer of 1874, the *Register* noted: "[He] is now snugly stowed away in the county jail, whence it is devoutly to be hoped he will never issue except to be taken to trial and then to the penitentiary." In summarizing his violent and larcenous deeds, the newspaper conjectured that "the prospect seems pretty good that he will be deprived for some time to come of that liberty which he will not enjoy except at the hazard of the public."[98] During the ten years between his arrival in Illinois and his capture in the summer of 1874, Gus Reed had become familiar with each level of the local justice system in Springfield, and through the crime reporting of the local newspapers, he had also become familiar to a reading public growing increasingly concerned about the epidemic of crime that seemed to be sweeping their community. As a criminal, Gus Reed embodied concerns about the civic unfitness of black migrants. Although thieves were only a tiny minority of the black population of the city, their actual crimes merged with racial tropes of black criminality and immorality that circulated within both popular culture and scientific discourse on race and crime. Like emancipated slaves, members of the criminal underclass were characterized as a population unequipped for participation in civil society and fundamentally unable to meet the demands of law-abiding citizenship. Narratives of racial incapacity and criminal degeneracy from the emerging fields of criminology and penology seemed to align with the fears of white Americans who had resisted black citizenship during and after the Civil War. As the problem of rising crime rates became more acute in the 1870s, renewed public attention was directed toward the institutions that were supposed to keep the public safe from "desperados" like Gus Reed. In Illinois, the state penitentiary at Joliet was the focal point for a new round of penological reform aimed at making the experience of incarceration better serve both the public and the criminal. When Gus Reed took his last train ride to Joliet in the spring of 1878, he was on his way to what was supposedly one of the most progressive penitentiaries in the nation.

SIX

The Penitentiary

> And the iron gates of Joliet
> Swung as the gray and silent trusties
> Carried me out in a coffin.
>
> —*Edgar Lee Masters,*
> Spoon River Anthology

ONE YEAR before Gus Reed was sentenced to the penitentiary for the third and final time, a Chicago real estate agent named Aaron Benedict Mead arrived at Joliet under very different circumstances. Mead toured the penitentiary with several relatives, one of them a deputy sheriff from Hartford County. Their law enforcement connections secured them a letter of introduction to Warden Robert McClaughry, which Mead described as "an extra good one" that provided them with a tour of the entire facility. Mead detailed his visit in a letter to his mother, beginning with the exterior of the prison, which he guessed looked like most others: "The high stone wall, too high to climb and sure death if one should by any chance reach the top and tumble off the other side, with armed sentinels pacing their beat on the top." Entering the prison proper, the heavy iron gate swung shut behind them, and Mead observed with a shudder that "only our dress distinguishes us from the 1,690 others who doubtless wait the opening of that gate for them with fierce impatience or staid endurance." Once inside, Mead reckoned correctly that the facility covered about sixteen acres of ground and was composed of two cellblocks, the hospital, and the workshops, all surrounded by high stone walls. Their first stop was one of the main cellblocks, which Mead described thus:

FIGURE 1. Hallway of solitary confinement cells, Illinois State Penitentiary at Joliet, ca. 1890. *Courtesy Chicago History Museum*

"Three tiers . . . one above the other, each cell about as large as a section in a sleeping car. The prison just now is quite crowded so that some of the cells are fixed for two persons. A long iron bar runs along the whole line of cells with a lever at the end by which the doors are all fastened or unfastened at once by the keeper throwing the lever back or forward, every thing was neat and tidy and I should judge the beds not uncomfortable though I can't speak from actual experience."

From there, Mead and his party visited the hospital and toured the cooper, harness, and shoe shops, brush factory, and the kitchen, all of which Mead summed up in this way: "A large number of striped men working silently so far as talking is concerned for that is not allowed. A superintendent who sits up on a little stand where he can keep his eye on all in the room and all with close cut heads and that horrid striped dress." In the kitchen, Mead observed that feeding nearly two thousand men "really seems at first like preparing to feed a lot of cattle." The group then toured solitary confinement, where unruly and troublesome convicts were locked away for infractions of prison discipline. Mead described the solitary in detail: "A double tier of cells on each side and the room lighted by a sky-light. . . . The cells . . . are twice as high as the ordinary cells and a little grated window near the top furnished light and air. It was elegantly furnished with a couple of large rings fastened into the wall and instead of a luxurious spring mattress, there was the soft side of the stone floor. . . . The rings in the wall are to fasten them to when they have been extra bad. I mean to behave myself when I am sent there and keep out of *that* dungeon." After they left the solitary and watched the prisoners marching to their midday meal, Warden McClaughry invited the party to his private rooms for lunch. Mead noted, "We had colored gentlemen in black and white stripes to wait on us and every thing passed off very satisfactorily." Although Mead obviously enjoyed his tour, he admitted: "I can see that a little change in circumstances would make a great change in the experience of my prison life and cause me to regard the whole thing, prison-officers and all with entirely different feelings from those I now entertain."[1]

The prison Aaron Mead and his relatives visited in the summer of 1877 was supposed to be a model of reform. In just three years, Robert McClaughry had transformed the penitentiary from corrupt, abusive, and costly to orderly, humane, and profitable. Convicts shuffled in lockstep through corridors that echoed only with the clang of cell doors and their own heavy footsteps as they made their way to the workshops, where they worked silently to mass produce articles the penitentiary's contractors would then sell for a profit. When prisoners misbehaved, they were sent to the solitary, where the "bull rings" Mead described, although still bolted to the wall, had been abandoned in favor of supposedly more humane punishments. Prisoners were no longer doused in cold water or left hanging from the rings as punishment, nor were they supposed to be whipped for infractions of discipline. These barbarous punishments had been replaced with a reduced diet, shackling to the cell door, and above all, the isolated silence of the solitary. Mead's visit fell during one of the brief periods in the 1870s when Gus Reed was not at the penitentiary, having been discharged from his second term just weeks earlier. Less than a year later, however, he was back in Joliet, passing through the iron gates, and into a solitary cell, where he died, gagged and chained to his cell door.

In most ways, Gus Reed's three incarcerations at Joliet between 1869 and 1878 were unremarkable. The labor regime at the Illinois State Penitentiary was like most others—disciplined labor in the prison's shops was intended not only to reform the minds of criminals but also to put their bodies to work for the benefit of contractors. As a prisoner, Gus Reed was subject to the only form of involuntary servitude still permitted by the Thirteenth Amendment. When he was received at the penitentiary for the first time in December 1869, he was put to work in the penitentiary's limestone quarry, where he dug, blasted, and hauled rock by the ton, day after day. It was the most physically demanding work he could have been assigned, but it was perhaps alleviated by the presence of his accomplices Scott Burton and John Fisher, who were also assigned to the quarry.[2] The work was difficult and dangerous, but the men were able to spend time outside the walls of the penitentiary, and they may have felt some small measure of freedom during their days in the pits. Gus Reed apparently performed this work obediently, and a notation beside his name in the penitentiary's register suggests that he may have earned "good time" during his first incarceration, qualifying him for early release.[3] He marched dutifully to and from his work and meals, kept his cell and striped uniform in good order, did not damage or lose his tools, obeyed orders, and most importantly, exceeded his production quotas. By all indications, Gus Reed was a model prisoner. The prison's officials may even have believed him reformed when they discharged him a year early in May 1873.

By the summer of 1874, however, newspapers described Gus Reed as a "desperate" criminal.[4] Instead of reforming or rehabilitating him, his time in the penitentiary may have only hardened his determination not to get caught. His escape from the Springfield city jail in the spring of 1874, his flight to nearby Jacksonville and Christian County, and his violent resistance to arrest were surely born of his desire to stay out of the penitentiary. We do not know whether he was again assigned to the quarry when he was incarcerated in 1874, but the fact that he was there in both 1869 and 1878 suggests that he also worked there during his second term. Although his criminal activities had become more extensive and aggressive, he was sentenced for only three years, and only served two and half of those. Despite his initial escape from the Springfield jail and his subsequent assault against the officers who arrested him, Gus Reed's second term at Joliet seems to have gone as smoothly as his first. He was discharged from the penitentiary early on June 7, 1877—although it would not be long before he was back again, this time to stay.[5]

When both Gus Reed and Aaron Mead entered the solitary confinement block at Joliet, they stepped across a motto painted in red letters on the floor: "NEVER TOO LATE TO MEND."[6] The hopeful message belied the punitive nature of the solitary: it was not a place to mend; it was a place for punishment. Each cell had two doors, one of iron bars, the other a thick wooden "blind door" behind which convicts were expected to sit in mute repentance. A card on the door of each cell identified the offender by his assigned number, described his punishment, and specified the number of days to be spent inside. On the evening of Sunday, May 5, 1878, Gus Reed was sent to the solitary for fighting with another inmate on his cellblock.[7] Because he could "read a little" by then, he may have been able to make out the message on the floor, but for him it was indeed too late. Two days later, he was dead in his cell, gagged, bound, and bruised from an illegal whipping. Gus Reed's treatment, his death, the subsequent investigation, and the public reaction to the controversy revealed a set of apparently contradictory impulses in late nineteenth-century attitudes about criminal justice. The brutal death of a prisoner in a public institution was widely condemned in the press, but so was the prisoner himself. As the expected role of penitentiaries increasingly became rehabilitation, rather than merely punishment, the bodies of criminals took on new significance. When Gus Reed entered the solitary, the latest criminological theories held that repeat offenders like him might, in fact, be physiologically incapable of mending their ways.

Gus Reed spent all of Monday, May 6, handcuffed to the iron door of his cell on the orders of Deputy Warden Benjamin Mayhew, the prison officer responsible for determining punishment. The position in which he was shackled required him to stand all day, his forearms before him at chest height. He was ordered to pass his hands through the vertical bars of the door, and his wrists were handcuffed above the horizontal crossbar, preventing him from sitting or lying down. He was unshackled Monday evening and permitted to spend the night on the bare stone floor of his cell, but after breakfast on Tuesday morning, he was again cuffed to the door. At eight o'clock, Adolph Heise, the prison physician, made his morning rounds, checked Gus Reed's pulse, asked him a few questions about his health, and judged him sound. Over the next two hours, however, something changed. At ten o'clock Gus Reed began shouting, which was strictly forbidden in the tense silence of the penitentiary. Warden Robert McClaughry later explained: "If noises were permitted in the solitary during the day time so that they could be heard by the gangs marching to and fro in the yard and by the prisoners [who] are continually about the yard . . . it would certainly tend to induce a revolt which would not only

FIGURE 2. A prisoner handcuffed to a cell door in solitary confinement, Illinois State Penitentiary at Joliet, ca. 1890. *Courtesy Chicago History Museum.*

imperil the lives of the keepers inside but actually destroy the discipline of the institution and render it impossible to manage." Though locked away where his echoing cries would be less troublesome, Gus Reed's repeated "halloring" was a direct threat to institutional order, and an indirect indictment of a penal system that claimed reform, yet seemed to produce only recalcitrance.[8]

Several weeks before Gus Reed arrived in the solitary, another insubordinate convict had raised the issue of malingering—pretending insanity—to get out of the solitary. Thomas Harris was a convict from Shelby County, where he had reportedly told the sheriff that "he could play insanity to perfection." Harris had been sent to the solitary because "he acted so foolishly, making all sorts of maneuvers and stating that he had once had an attack of insanity." In the solitary cell, Harris's behavior only worsened. Solitary keeper Stephen Reed (no relation to Gus Reed) later recalled that Harris "had dirtied his cell, had torn his bed-tick, and took a portion of the hay out of it and scattered it all over the floor, and he eased himself [defecated] on the blankets, and he had the cell in a terribly filthy condition." Dr. Heise reported more clinically: "He took his excrements and rubbed, and wiped them on the wall and he made a statement that the ventilator—that there was so much [air] coming through that he had taken his clothes and stuck them in there, so that when the air came in he should not take cold." What happened next was later a point of contention between Keeper Reed and Dr. Heise. The keeper claimed that the doctor ordered him to whip Harris to determine whether or not he was pretending. Dr. Heise claimed that he had given no such order and would never have ordered any punishment, since it was not part of his responsibility as a physician. Regardless of who ordered it, Keeper Reed constructed a leather whip with a wooden handle and used it several times to whip Harris into admitting that his insanity was a ruse.

Several weeks later, when Gus Reed began yelling, Keeper Reed initially gagged him, as was common when solitary prisoners became noisy. The gag, a straight wooden rod shoved between the convict's teeth and buckled around the back of the head with leather straps, had been on for only a few minutes when "he acted as though he was going to faint." Keeper Reed removed the gag and the prisoner was temporarily quiet. When Gus Reed began making noise again, Keeper Reed tried to apply the gag a second time, but as he later testified: "In gagging him he closed his mouth, and I had to force the gag into his mouth. I pulled down on his teeth to force it in. I put the gag in, and held the strap in my hand so it would not slip out—as the buckle had slipped from the strap." Keeper Reed's supervisor, Assistant Deputy Warden D. C. Sleeper, arrived a few moments later, and asked the prisoner if he would keep quiet and behave. Gus Reed nodded, and Keeper Reed released his hold of the gag strap. Not long after the second gagging, Gus Reed again began to shout. Rather than trying to fix the broken gag, Keeper Reed went to the closet where he kept his leather whip soaking in a bucket of water "to keep it pliable." With Gus Reed still chained to the door, Keeper Reed entered his cell with the sodden leather strap, pulled down the prisoner's trousers, and began to whip him, striking him across the buttocks three or four times. After this first whipping, Gus Reed fell silent. Later that afternoon, when fresh undershirts arrived from the prison laundry, Keeper Reed unshackled the convict and ordered him to put on a clean shirt. Gus Reed may have mistaken Keeper Reed's order to mean that he was going to be whipped again, and he refused to take off his shirt. It is not clear whether Keeper Reed entered the cell with the whip in hand, or if he then went to fetch it. In any case, with Gus Reed's shirt pulled up, Keeper Reed struck him again, three or four times with the whip across his bare back and shoulders. Still smarting from the blows of the soaked leather whip, Gus Reed was cuffed to the door for the rest of the afternoon. Whatever had motivated him to begin shouting that morning, whether it was resistance to a cruel penitentiary regime, or indeed some sort of psychological break, the painful whipping certainly did nothing to calm him.

When Park Leasure, the nighttime keeper of the solitary, reported for duty at six o'clock Tuesday evening, Keeper Reed took him aside, and over Gus Reed's continuing shouts, told Leasure that he would probably have trouble with the convict all night. Leasure went to the prisoner's cell and asked him if he would be quiet, but he only "continued halloring loudly." Leasure later went back and warned Gus Reed that if he continued yelling, he would be gagged. The third time he went to the cell, Leasure brought a makeshift gag he had fashioned out of a piece of broom handle and spare piece of leather. He put the gag on loosely so that Gus Reed could still make some noise and could articulate his name when asked. The prisoner continued making noise, and after ten minutes, Leasure tightened the gag. Reed immediately began to have difficulty breathing, and Leasure, although "under the impression he was doing it to deceive me," loosened the strap again. He tightened it later when Reed continued to make noise, with the same result. Leasure again loosened the gag and then left the solitary to fetch something from the washroom. Leasure also visited one of the other cell houses, where he spoke with the captain of the night watch. The two men could hear that Gus Reed had started shouting again, calling his own name over and over, perhaps mocking Leasure's request that he articulate his name to ensure that the gag was not too tight, or perhaps trying to assert some semblance of agency in his final conscious moments. When Leasure returned, the solitary had grown quiet, and Gus Reed was slumped down, hanging from his shackled wrists. Leasure sent for the night doctor, C. T. Dripps, and the two men lifted the unconscious prisoner to remove his handcuffs, then laid him out on the floor. Leasure recalled that "he made some noise although I could not distinguish anything he said." Dr. Dripps sent to the hospital for "restoratives," but he later testified that he believed Gus Reed was already as good as dead. The coroner's jury later determined that the cause of death was "pulmonary apoplexy," which a contemporary medical textbook described as "a haemorrhage which breaks up and infiltrates the lung . . . the blood will pour out of the mouth and nose, there will be gurgling in the fauces, frantic efforts at respiration, a deadly pallor will overspread the face, and, with a general convulsion in which the breathing ceases, all is over, but the heart will beat for a minute longer."[9] Dr. Dripps must have heard or felt those final futile heartbeats, and once they had ceased, declared the convict dead. Gus Reed's body was removed from the solitary and taken to the infirmary—imprisoned even in death, but quiet at last.

A coroner's jury convened at the penitentiary on May 9, and Gus Reed's body was moved to what the guards called the "school room" for an autopsy, presided over by the county coroner. Officials of the penitentiary, including Warden McClaughry and Dr. Heise, as well as the state's attorney and several other medical men, were witnesses. When the coroner's jury met to determine a cause of death, they discussed the results of the autopsy and examined witnesses, including Dr. Heise, Dr. Dripps, Warden McClaughry, the night watch captain, solitary keepers Stephen Reed and Park Leasure, and Deputy Warden Benjamin Mayhew. The jury determined that the cause of Gus Reed's death had been "pulmonary apoplexy caused by his persistent yelling with a gag in his mouth"; they noted that "neither the gag alone, nor the yelling alone, would have caused death." They also found that Keepers Reed and Leasure had both acted within the rules of the penitentiary, for "the gag is used for the purpose of preserving discipline and securing the safe keeping of the convicts." The jury thus laid the responsibility for Gus Reed's death at his own feet: "The unruly conduct and extreme obstinacies of said deceased" had necessitated the use of the gag. Gus Reed was an irredeemable, insubordinate, obstinate criminal, and although there was already debate within criminological circles about whether such men chose to be criminals, or if defective physiology dictated their deviance, the fault for his death was determined to be his alone.[10]

The conclusions of the coroner's jury did not close the matter. Because Gus Reed died within a state institution, the circumstances of his death quickly became known to the public. The *Joliet Republican* broke the story on Saturday, May 11, with coverage of the coroner's inquest. An article headed "The Fatal Gag" ended its account of Reed's death on the hopeful note that "the matter will be fully investigated and the bottom facts obtained."[11] The Chicago press was more sensational, with the *Daily News* proclaiming on May 17 that "a convict was done to death a few days since, in the Illinois Penitentiary, at Joliet, by one of Gov. Cullom's brutal minions," and the *Daily Tribune* headlines shouted: "TORTURE," "THE RACK," and "Deafness of the Officials to the Dismal Howls of the Tortured."[12] Papers as far away as Boston, New York City, and Washington, DC, picked up the story of Gus Reed's death. The Louisville *Courier-Journal* claimed that "the murder was committed under the direction of the prison doctors," and the *Washington Post* was even more sensational in claiming "the prison doctor and deputy warden did the killing."[13]

Under mounting public pressure, the penitentiary's commissioners convened a special hearing in which the prison's doctors, officers, and guards were again called to testify about Gus Reed's death and the general treatment of prisoners. Eighteen witnesses took the stand over two days, first among them Keeper Stephen Reed, who was questioned extensively regarding his use of the leather strap. The commissioners asked him about Thomas Harris, and Keeper Reed testified that, in his opinion, Harris truly was crazy, for when he was ordered to clean up the mess he had made, "he went at it in a kind of bungling way, and I strapped him."[14] Keeper Reed described the strap he made as "about two feet long, and about an inch wide, and it is fastened on to a soft wood handle . . . sixteen or seventeen inches long." He claimed that both Dr. Heise and Dr. Dripps knew about the strap and that Park Leasure, the nighttime keeper of the solitary, had seen it as well. Keeper Reed also said that he had taken it upon himself to use the same strap on Gus Reed when he began shouting, believing that his case was the same as that of Thomas Harris.

Stephen Reed also testified about the case of Michael Ryan, a convict he had gagged the previous November, and who had nearly died. Keeper Reed had left Ryan gagged and shackled to the door of his cell, and when he returned, the convict was slumped down, unconscious, with "blood and froth" at his mouth. Keeper Reed shouted to another convict who was cleaning the solitary who "blew his breath into Ryan's mouth" while the keeper ran to get the deputy warden. When they returned, Ryan was conscious again, although he required hospitalization. When Keeper Reed expressed his doubts about the use of the gag to Deputy Warden Mayhew, the latter had seemed indifferent. "I guess the Deputy has done probably all he can against me, and I may as well tell it now," said Keeper Reed, and continued: "When I spoke about Ryan, he said it didn't make much difference anyway; it would not make much difference whether he died or not, and I think he said—it was something to that effect. I cannot tell the exact words." The commissioners ignored Keeper Reed's accusation and continued their questions about Ryan and the use of the gag. They pressed him on minor points that he could not precisely remember, repeating their questions when they knew he could provide no further information, and apparently attempting to catch him in some inconsistency. By the end of the first day of questioning, it was obvious where the commissioners intended to place the blame for Gus Reed's death.

The next day, as they had done with Stephen Reed, the commissioners closely questioned Park Leasure, and he was forced to admit that he did not remember certain details of his conversations with Keeper Reed and that he had known about the strap but had not brought it to the attention of the prison's authorities. Keeper Reed, he testified, had told him that he considered the strap to be a safer method of discipline than the gag ever since Michael Ryan had nearly died. Leasure gave a thorough account of the night Gus Reed died, describing the convict's loud, unruly behavior and specifying for how long and how tightly he had fastened the gag. The commissioners indicated a gag lying on the table, and asked if it was the one used on Gus Reed that night. Leasure responded that it was not and that when Gus Reed lost consciousness, he had cut away the makeshift gag and tossed it into the baker's furnace. One of the commissioners asked Leasure why he had burned the gag, to which the keeper replied: "Well sir, it was to destroy it. . . . I didn't consider it worth while to repair that up again, and I destroyed it for that reason and no other." The commissioners were especially concerned with how long the gag had been in Gus Reed's mouth the night he died and how long Leasure had left him unattended, but Leasure stuck to his story, playing the obedient subordinate to the end.

After the two keepers had been subjected to the commissioners' scrutiny, the panel called on Dr. Heise. The doctor said that he had checked on Gus Reed the morning of May 7, as he did all prisoners in the solitary, and found him to be healthy. The next time he saw the convict was late that same evening, dead in his cell. According to his testimony, it was Heise who then set the investigation in motion, contacting the coroner and summoning the other penitentiary officials. Heise consistently testified that he had "no information at all" about Keeper Reed's strap until after Gus Reed's death. In the case of Thomas Harris, Heise thought that Deputy Warden Mayhew must have issued the order to whip the convict, since he was the officer responsible for determining punishment. Mayhew later claimed that he believed Dr. Heise had ordered the whipping as a medical treatment to cure the convict of his malingering. In hastening to clear themselves, and citing the errors of subordinates, Heise and Mayhew placed the blame for Gus Reed's death squarely on Stephen Reed and Park Leasure. Mayhew stated positively that "there never was a word named with regard to strapping, whipping, or punishment," and that he had never ordered the strapping of Harris or Reed.

Warden Robert McClaughry, who had been away from the penitentiary on business the night Gus Reed died, was the last to testify before the commissioners. McClaughry had occasionally interjected his own questions throughout the hearing and listened closely to the answers of his officers. McClaughry was now questioned on the policies and procedures of the penitentiary, especially the need to maintain absolute silence. McClaughry testified that without the threat of solitary and the use of the gag, "it would be absolutely impossible to maintain quiet in the prison. There are so many vicious men here who are only restrained by fear of punishment, that it would be impossible to restrain them if they didn't know that they would be punished for a violation of the rules." Warden McClaughry's responses closed the two days of testimony, and after some deliberation, the commissioners decided that there had been no official wrongdoing by the penitentiary administration, but recommended that Keepers Stephen Reed and Park Leasure be dismissed. The case was forwarded to the county prosecutor, who determined that there was no basis for charging the prison's ranking officials, and the investigation was officially closed.

The press was not so quick to consider the matter resolved. The *Joliet Republican* referred to the commissioners' investigation as "jug handle justice," and the *Illinois State Register* remarked: "It is strange that the death of a convict under such circumstances, taking place as it did on Tuesday night, was not reported until Friday evening. This may . . . be . . . a result of that policy of suppressing official facts, the disclosure of which, to use the slang of the officials, is 'incompatible with the public interest.'"[15] The *Joliet Republican* joined other newspapers in condemning the death and calling for a public investigation of the matter: "A prisoner has died under painful, not to say suspicious, circumstances. . . . The law consigns men to the Penitentiary as a punishment for their crimes, but it does not recognize the necessity of torturing them to death in order to maintain the discipline of the institution."[16] The *Chicago Tribune* labeled the commissioners' investigation "a star-chamber inquiry," criticizing the fact that "the Commissioners do not appear anxious to make the investigation a public and open one."¹⁷ The press assumed the role of watchdog on behalf of the public, who were taxed to support the penitentiary and thus had an inherent interest in its management. For almost the entire month of May 1878, the newspaper reading public around the nation knew something about the death of Gus Reed and the subsequent investigation. Moral and civic outrage combined in reaction to the corruption of the criminal justice system and its failure to perform the public service of rehabilitation. Extreme punishments that resulted in death were not only inhumane; they were ineffective. Gus Reed died during a transitional moment for the penitentiary system, for although stories about prisoner abuse had long aroused public anger, the stated goal of incarceration was now ostensibly shifting from punishment to rehabilitation.¹⁸

Penitentiaries were supposed to be places where the minds of criminals were reformed to meet the priorities of a disciplinary regime closely tied to industrial capitalism, but the body of the prisoner still remained of central concern. Because the punishment and rehabilitation of criminals was the responsibility of the state, presumably performed for the public good, the public took an interest in criminals both inside and outside of the penitentiary. As early as the 1830s, Alexis de Tocqueville and Gustave de Beaumont observed that the annual reports of state penitentiaries were widely published and thus "handed over to publicity and controversy. . . . There is not a citizen of the United States who does not know how the prisons of his country are governed, and who is not able to contribute to their improvement, either by his opinion or by his fortune."¹⁹ As state-administered institutions, the voting public assumed a right to know what happened behind the walls of the penitentiary, whether financial or disciplinary.

When a prisoner died at Joliet while undergoing another illegal punishment four years before Gus Reed's death, the *Register* opined: "It is the *right and duty of the legislature* to examine into all the affairs of the prison, financial as well as disciplinary, and this right should be speedily exercised, as well as this duty impartially performed" (emphasis added).²⁰ As the state assumed more direct responsibility for the bodies of its criminals, the more these bodies and the legal process through which they passed came under public scrutiny. Neither punishment nor rehabilitation had been removed from the body of the prisoner, or from the realm of public perception; both remained corporate and corporeal acts.

Physical punishments continued within the walls of nearly every institution, as guards and keepers found themselves outnumbered by criminals exhibiting dangerous or forbidden behavior. Punishments were used not only to maintain discipline and hierarchy within the prison, but also to "treat" offenders who seemed to need a shock to their bodies to force them to desist from their delinquent tendencies. When sensational exposés of prisoner abuse surfaced, as they did frequently, the reaction among the reformers and in the press was swift and unequivocal. The state did not have a right to treat men, even convicts, like brutes—or, more significantly, like slaves. The images of emancipated slaves with lacerated backs and evidence of malnourishment that had surfaced before and during the Civil War served as tangible reminders of the brutality of a system that exerted total control over the bodies of its subjects.[21] For antislavery activists and others sympathetic to this seemingly unique species of human suffering, these images signified a cruel system in which the lash, and its brutal agents, reigned supreme. The revelations in Gus Reed's case, as with other instances of prisoner abuse, brought this brutality into fresh focus, and located it not on the grounds of southern plantations, but within public institutions, where the rules of a well-ordered society should not only be followed, but exemplified and inculcated.

The national reading public had also been exposed to an even more emotionally charged discussion of prisoner abuse and mistreatment during and after the Civil War, as memoirs and exposés on the horrors of the wartime prison camps were published. One account of Union prisoners' experiences at Andersonville equated their treatment directly with the conditions of Southern slavery, asking, "Are not the cruelties and oppressions described in the following pages what we should legitimately expect from men who, all their lives, have used whip and thumb-screw, shot-gun and blood-hound, to keep human beings subservient to their will?"[22] The wartime prisons brought the capricious brutality of mass incarceration more widespread attention than it had had before the war. Stories of hanging by the thumbs, binding and gagging, starvation, physical abuse, and worse, focused public attention on the vulnerability of prisoners' bodies to corrupt penal regimes. Although the moral outrage fueled by such accounts drew on antebellum precedents, the scale and severity of the abuse of prisoners of war, together with the condemnation of similar treatment of slaves, contributed to the growth of a postbellum ethic that was less tolerant of abusive incarceration and more inclined to censure public institutions for excesses of punishment.[23]

In both the testimony before the penitentiary commissioners and in the press, the body of Gus Reed, as well as the circumstances of his death, received detailed attention. Graphic descriptions communicated the full extent of the outrage and gave the reading public an opportunity to demonstrate their own moral sensitivity. The physical condition of Gus Reed's body, before and after his death, received a great deal of attention. The coroner was bound by law to examine the body, and the involvement of so many medical men, both inside and outside of the penitentiary, produced details the newspapers used to enhance their calls for a thorough investigation of the case and censure of the prison authorities.[24] In one of the first stories to appear on the case, the *Chicago Daily Tribune* reported, "The whipping which the dead man received was administered on the naked body, the prisoner being partially divested of his pants and drawers and his shirt turned up over his head." In describing the use of the gag, the *Tribune* also gave a detailed explanation of the device's rough logic: "It was placed on their lips or teeth, the strap passed around to the back of their necks, buckled, and drawn up until they were forced to open their mouths and receive the instrument of torture.[25] The *Joliet Republican* gave an equally descriptive account of Gus Reed's final moments, "shackled like a wild beast to the iron bars of his dungeon door and unable to make his condition known as the murderous gag swiftly and surely accomplished its fearful work."[26] This potent prose of suffering, combined with a critique of the penitentiary as a publicly accountable state institution, expressed a powerful language of reform that went beyond merely indulging the morbid sensations of the reading public. The details of such a grisly death—even if largely conjecture—placed the guilty parties at the mercy of an outraged public, for as the *Chicago Tribune* noted, "The people prefer to form their own conclusions in so serious a matter as the killing of a convict by prison punishment."[27]

But the details of Gus Reed's death were only important to imagine or re-create because of how they reflected on the penitentiary and its officials, not because the prisoner himself was a subject of sympathy. As the investigation into his death progressed, the newspapers turned away from the convict's tortured last moments, and focused instead on the shameful conduct of the prison officials and the flawed ruling of the penitentiary commissioners. No matter how serious the case, or how grisly Gus Reed's death, he was a criminal who had damaged the social order materially by his crimes and, more fundamentally by his disregard for the law. When news of Gus Reed's death first broke in Springfield, the *Journal* was indignant that "a former citizen from Springfield" was subjected to "barborous [sic] and cruel" treatment, and even hinted at a racial motivation behind the torture by quipping sarcastically, "but then, 'it was only a nigger.'"[28] The next day, however, apparently after some further investigation, the *Journal* reported that Gus Reed had "the reputation at home of being a most violent, dangerous and lawless character, who, at the time of his death was serving out the third term for crimes of which he had been convicted in the Circuit Court of this county." The *Journal* even echoed the coroner's report by suggesting that "Reed's own violent resistance and perverse insubordination" had caused his death.[29] In just one day, Gus Reed went from a victimized black citizen to a "lawless character" who was responsible for his own demise.

Defining Gus Reed as a criminal—an especially bad and irredeemable one—made him the victim of both his irrational and erratic behavior and of a brutal prison system in need of reform. Gus Reed was guilty of his own irredeemable badness and powerless to resist his misbehavior, not to mention the lash of his cruel overseer. In either case, Gus Reed's life was so meager and so mean that he seemed to be able to exercise no practical control over it himself, and the events that led to his death had, to some extent, been preordained by forces that carried him inexorably to his fate. This view of the criminal aptly characterized a nation on the brink of a revolution in criminological and penological thought. While deep suspicions about abuses of institutional authority lingered from the antebellum period, Americans in the late 1870s were also increasingly concerned about rising crime rates and a growing transient underclass of potential criminals that threatened to undermine civil society and structures of authority and order. As they responded to Gus Reed's death and the subsequent investigation, newspapers generally expressed some form of outrage, but never questioned the fundamental legitimacy of the penal system that caused it. State-sanctioned torture was surely inhumane and unacceptable, but an unchecked criminal class posed a greater threat. Just as the criminal body in prison was a focal point for reformers and administrators, the criminal body at large became a point of concern for those alarmed at the rising crime rate. As criminologists turned to the study of the criminal classes, they focused their attention on the penitentiaries, where criminal bodies could be safely and conveniently studied and analyzed.

When he arrived in Joliet in August 1874, Robert McClaughry faced what the *Chicago Tribune* called "a grand muddle" at the penitentiary.[30] The governor, the board of commissioners, and the previous wardens had been at odds for years, and periodic scandals included prisoner deaths, allegations of corruption, political infighting, and ongoing financial problems. Until 1867, the state leased out the grounds, facilities, and even the prisoners themselves to a private contractor, who appointed wardens, guards, and other officials independent of state authority. The board of commissioners was supposed to oversee the operation for the state, but they lacked authority to make changes to the penitentiary administration. The contractor ran the shops and the quarry to turn a profit, but the arrangement cost the state money every year, while the contractor reaped the benefits of expanding facilities and a growing workforce. In 1867, reformers with the support of the governor argued that turning over convicts who had been tried and convicted under public laws to a private contractor was immoral and unjust. The penitentiary was brought under state control, and a new board of three commissioners was appointed to supervise the institution, assuming a more active role in administration.[31] The commissioners continued to argue with each other and the full financial burden of the institution fell to the state for the first time since the leasing-out system began in 1838. Between 1869 and 1873, the wardenship changed six times, frequently due to conflicts between the wardens and commissioners over the finances and discipline of the institution. In June 1869, political infighting on the board led commissioner Andrew Shuman to warn the governor: "It is impossible to keep such things from the convicts," but he noted that "discipline is maintained much better than could be reasonably expected under such circumstances."[32] In November 1869, forty guards went on strike against Warden George Perkins, whom they called "tyrannical," leaving only twenty-six guards to watch over more than one thousand convicts.[33]

As late as February 1874, Warden J. W. Wham sent a string of telegrams to Governor Beveridge warning him that "I cannot maintain the Discipline of this Prison under the present management you will have to come and settle matters or I will have to again demand an Investigation."[34] There were also scandals involving prisoner abuse, including a particularly infamous episode in December 1873, in which a convict died while undergoing a torturous cold-water bath supposedly intended as a medical treatment. In a case very much like Gus Reed's more than four years later, a coroner's jury decided that no official wrongdoing had been committed, and that the cold-water bath, prohibited by institutional rules, had resulted from a misunderstanding between the prison's physician and the guards. Democratic and Republican newspapers across the state united in decrying the coroner's verdict. The Democratic *Register* called the incident "the Joliet murder," and the Republican *Chicago Tribune* labeled the coroner's report "an absurd and disgraceful document."[35] In January 1874, a special committee conducted a general investigation, widely supposed to have been precipitated by the convict's untimely death. But, as the *Tribune* lamented, the resulting report "will impress most people as an ill-timed, if not unwarranted, mess of whitewash."[36] Political factors were clearly at work. Governor Beveridge was considering running for Senator John Logan's seat in 1877. Logan, who desired reelection and was friends with Wham, urged the warden to press for a further investigation, while the penitentiary commissioners, who were friends of Beveridge's, were happy to consider the case closed. Wham could be removed by either the governor or the commissioners if he pushed an investigation, and he was caught between his political friendship with Logan and a hostile board of commissioners until August 1874, when the board removed him and appointed Robert McClaughry, who was on good terms with both Beveridge and Logan.[37] As an outsider, McClaughry was a potential solution to the penitentiary's problems, and he had his war service, his friends in state government, and his business experience to recommend him. He was probably expected to do little in the way of disciplinary reform at the penitentiary, but McClaughry proved to be both a competent administrator and an innovative criminologist.

Robert McClaughry was among the last generation of professional criminologists to enter the field without formal training or practical experience. After his election to the Hancock County clerkship in 1865, McClaughry served in the post for four years, but he was defeated in 1869, due to a county-wide Democratic resurgence.[38] The temporary political reorientation of the postwar period had come to an end, at least in Hancock County. In the meantime, McClaughry entered the stone quarrying business, and provided rock for the new state house in Springfield, one of his largest contracts. By 1870, McClaughry was so invested in the business that he moved his family to Missouri, where he had purchased an interest in another quarry. But the business apparently took a physical toll on McClaughry, and after only two years in Missouri, he moved his family back to Illinois. In 1874, he began a run for Congress as a Republican, but called off his run when the penitentiary's board of commissioners selected him for the wardenship at Joliet.[39] The paper trail leading to his appointment is thin, but it seems likely that it had as much to do with politics as with McClaughry's quarrying experience. McClaughry's political friends included former Republican governors John Palmer and Richard Oglesby, both of whom he had served with in the war, as well as a host of friendly references. One of his former professors at Monmouth College assured Governor Beveridge that Robert McClaughry was "a Christian, a gentleman, and an able, discreet, executive officer. . . . He will study the task under his supervision with the care of a philosopher."[40]

Reforming the disciplinary system was a primary part of McClaughry's mission to improve the finances and productivity of the penitentiary. Discipline in the penitentiary came from the steady pace of labor, the expectation of quality work, and the demand for compliance—all of which were supposed to produce reformed citizens and tractable industrial workers. As the *Chicago Tribune* observed in 1875, if the goal of penitentiary confinement was

FIGURE 3. Robert W. McClaughry at the time of his appointment to warden of the Illinois State Penitentiary at Joliet, ca. 1874. *Courtesy Chicago History Museum.*

to "restrain criminals where they can be subjected to discipline . . . how can so favorable a result be brought about as by systematic labor?"[41] There was also a military aspect to the discipline imposed within the penitentiary; convicts were expected to march, turn out for inspections, and perform specific tasks within the shops, grounds, and cellblocks, all under the guidance of penitentiary officers. With Major McClaughry in command, the penitentiary ran as much like a military barracks as it did an industrial production facility. Shortly after McClaughry took charge, the commissioners of the penitentiary advertised for a new contractor to begin production at the penitentiary with convict labor. Their classified advertisement appeared in newspapers around the state, promising "the labor of from fifty to seventy-five convicts . . . sound and able-bodied, and adapted to most any or all kinds of labor," along with shop space and steam power. The advertisement assured bidders that "the discipline in the institution is excellent and will be maintained at its present standard."[42] Even the critical *Chicago Tribune* judged the Joliet penitentiary a "model prison" by the spring of 1875.[43] When a legislative subcommittee on the penitentiary reported financial inconsistencies and allegations of prisoner abuse, all of the allegations were of events that took place prior to McClaughry's appointment. The *Tribune* distinguished between "the old regime" and the present administration, lauding the penitentiary under McClaughry as "one of the model prisons of the country."[44] With McClaughry in charge, punishments had decreased by 40 percent, and discipline remained good. The most abusive punishments had been abolished, including the bull ring, the ice bath, and the practice of making convicts haul heavy bags of sand on their backs. Altogether, the *Tribune* found that "the plaudits of [Warden McClaughry's] management which have gone forth have been numerous, and in most cases well-deserved."[45]

This improvement in the discipline and efficacy of the penitentiary was timely, for by the time Robert McClaughry and his guards received Gus Reed into the penitentiary for the final time in March 1878, the problem of rising crime rates and, more significantly, concern about the sort of crimes being committed had become particularly acute. Before the Civil War, severe and chronic crime had been a problem primarily for larger cities like Chicago, and the crimes that did occur in smaller places could be frequently attributed to unruly passions, alcohol, or a small category of incorrigible troublemakers. By the 1870s, however, it seemed as though a vast crime wave was spreading across the country; financial troubles put many out of work and drove others to earn their living illicitly. As early as 1865, the Springfield's *Illinois State Register* chronicled a wide array of crimes that were becoming common:

"Robberies, larceny, knock-downs, murders and every species of outrage . . . houses entered, pockets picked in crowds, burglary and highway outrages"— all committed by an underclass of "pick-pockets, burglars, sneak-thieves and rascals of every sort."[46] Illegal grogshops and brothels attracted multiracial crowds of transient strangers who seemed unable or unwilling to conform to norms of law and order. As one reformer characterized such vagrants in the 1880s, they were "the chrysalis of every species of criminal. A wanderer without home ties, idle, and without apparent means of support, what but criminality is to be expected from such a person?"[47] Edward Morse, in an 1892 article in *Popular Science,* expressed the common view that "vagabonds, like criminals, spring largely from a degenerating stock. . . . The tramp horde is a nidus from which apparently a vast number of criminals spring."[48] Black migrants from the South were also characterized as an inherently rootless population, and thus a potentially criminal one, once they cast off the economic, legal, and social shackles that supposedly kept their criminality in check. With the addition of Southern blacks, unemployed white workers, paupers, and other vagabonds, many crime pundits and reformers argued that the criminal population itself was changing, and the justice system had to change with it in order to protect law-abiding citizens.[49]

Municipal police forces and state penitentiaries attracted renewed public interest after the Civil War, as cries for more efficient and professional law enforcement accompanied the alarm over crime and criminals.[50] The public called penitentiary administrators to task for punishments that seemed extreme, or even barbarous, but also criticized penitentiaries for failing to reform habitual or dangerous criminals. Gus Reed would not have been in Joliet for the third time in 1878 if the penitentiary had done its job when it first received him in 1869. Robert McClaughry was particularly sensitive to these calls for more effective incarceration. As warden at Joliet, he observed that "society has a deep interest in discharged prisoners, [and] it is equally interested in prisoners still in bonds. . . . [If the criminal] reenters the world hardened in heart and broken in spirit by the effect of years of prison discipline . . . it can hardly be expected that he will have strength to boldly face the distrust and doubt which will meet him on every side as he seeks for employment."[51] If criminals like Gus Reed returned unreformed and unrepentant to the streets, incarceration ultimately failed to protect the public from those who seemed intent on doing harm. In the penitentiary, the criminal body could be a victim, but loose in society it would certainly be a threat.

Much of the new penological and criminological work in the latter part of the nineteenth century was inspired by ideas introduced by Robert

McClaughry and carried out at the institution where Gus Reed died. Under McClaughry's wardenship, the penitentiary at Joliet became one of the first proving grounds for the new science of criminal anthropometry, a field that sought to identify known criminals by physical markers, anticipating the development of more rigorous scientific methods of criminal identification and marking a significant turning point in the modernization of the criminal justice system. McClaughry introduced the first English translation of the work of French criminologist Alphonse Bertillon in 1887. Bertillon's anthropometric identification system relied on a series of precise bodily measurements recorded on cards kept in vast reference catalogs. When an offender was arrested or incarcerated, a series of measurements were taken and cross-referenced with a massive index of cards shared between major metropolitan police departments and penitentiaries. In a nation of increasing mobility, rootless criminals could wander from city to city, changing names and superficial features like facial hair, but they could not change the length of their index fingers, the distance from elbow to wrist, or the shape of their ears. With these measurements, Bertillon specialists could recognize known criminals immediately, no matter what alias or disguise they used. Because of McClaughry's advocacy and endorsement the penitentiary at Joliet became the model Bertillon institution in the nation, and Chicago adopted Bertillon's system in its Bureau of Criminal Identification.[52]

Between 1891 and 1892, as the chief of Chicago's police, McClaughry employed the Bertillon system as a means of ridding the city of criminal types that would cause the most trouble during the World's Columbian Exposition. On a visit to Chicago a month before his official appointment, McClaughry praised the city's Bureau of Identification, saying that the Bertillon system had there achieved "a greater perfection than will probably be found elsewhere."[53] The Chicago bureau had photographs or descriptions of 3,000 known criminals, and access to more than 200,000 more descriptions from around the country. All of this was necessary, said McClaughry, for he anticipated "the greatest congregation of criminals that ever yet met in this country" to arrive in the city for the exposition.[54] A year before the dedication ceremonies, and almost two years before the fair opened to the public, McClaughry announced that he planned to accumulate the Bertillon records of every convict released from every penal institution in the nation between October 1891 and the beginning of the fair in order to be on the lookout for them in Chicago. McClaughry even suggested that Bertillon data be used to identify criminals arrested in the city before the fair, and hold them in jail until the fair was over, an incarceration without trial of more than two years.[55] Three months before the exposition opened to the public, McClaughry announced the debut of the "biggest rogues' gallery in the country" to detectives and police bureaus around the world. Both foreign and domestic criminals would be "confronted not only with detectives from their native cities but with their photographs and measurements showing the length of their index fingers and other portions of their bodies which it will be impossible to conceal." The functioning of the Bertillon system and the Chicago Bureau of Identification at the exposition would be the greatest test either had faced, and McClaughry envisioned that the city would become "the permanent headquarters for the United States for the identification of criminals."[56]

McClaughry's influence in Chicago helped establish the precepts of the Bertillon system as central to modern criminology and shaped the professional precedent for identifying, photographing, and fingerprinting criminals. It also highlighted the limitations of the system as a practical tool for fighting crime. As the problems of organizing and sharing Bertillon information for the purposes of convict identification became more evident, criminologists turned to anthropometric data to link physical characteristics with behavioral manifestations. In 1896, Dr. W. A. McCorn of the Illinois Eastern Hospital for the Insane used Bertillon data to determine and record what he believed were the physical manifestations of criminality. McCorn observed that the Bertillon system was not "merely for the purpose of identification" but also "aided in the collection of some valuable statistics as to the proportional size of the head of cephalic index of the delinquent class."[57] As more data was gathered, it would become easier to recognize and correct the physical traits of "congenital criminals." McCorn noted that criminologists and the scientific world had "come to recognize that the criminal, as a class, is a degenerate, and while his moral depravity, anti-social and perverse tendencies were apparent, the idea of ascertaining their true cause and proper remedy has been entirely overlooked until recently."[58] Institutions that recorded Bertillon measurements could provide vast pools of raw data through which criminologists, anthropologists, and anatomists could work to determine the marks that hereditary degeneracy left on the body. McCorn's proposed use of the Bertillon system created a class of degenerate criminals, which could then be further subdivided by type. These taxonomies of criminal characteristics would help penologists and psychologists reform individual criminals by more precisely identifying their particular hereditary defects, but it also created a vast suspect population on the basis of little more than superficial physical characteristics.[59]

Five years after McCorn's article, during the height of enthusiasm for criminal anthropology, Henry Boies, one of the field's most notable practitioners, claimed that Bertillon provided "*a largely sufficient substitute for judicial decision* by the identification of the 'Presumptive Criminal' before the crime" (emphasis added)." This class of criminals, said Boies, "is at large in society, the undetected, and those who are too young for conviction, but are the victims of a bad heredity or environment which will certainly in the process of time, if not corrected, develop into criminality."[60] This application of Bertillon's methods placed the system firmly within a broad set of theories and debates about heredity, environment, and criminality that had been circulating for decades, and which culminated with the late-nineteenth-century's professionalization of the social sciences. McCorn and Boies approached Bertillon data and criminal anthropology as the latest in criminological thinking, but race theorists had begun a conversation on the biological markers of degeneracy and criminality at least several decades earlier.[61]

In the 1850s and early 1860s, as the sectional conflict over the expansion of slavery grew more heated, two well-circulated treatises on race noted significant physiological differences when comparing blacks and whites. Josiah Nott and George Gliddon's *Types of Mankind; or, Ethnological Researches,* which first appeared in 1854, richly illustrated the physiological differences between the Caucasian, Mongol, and Negro races. The latter, claimed Nott and Gliddon, "possess about nine cubic inches less of brain than the Teuton."[62] In 1861, John H. Van Evrie in *Negroes and Negro "Slavery": The First an Inferior Race: The Latter Its Normal Condition* (reissued in 1868 as *White Supremacy and Negro Subordination*) asserted that blacks were the "lowest in the scale" of the several human races, as indicated by their physical characteristics. Although Van Evrie admitted that the cause of different pigmentation in the skin among the Caucasian, Mongol, and Negro races was "as absolutely hidden from us as the cause of their existence at all," he was confident that such physical differences marked substantial moral differences as well. "The capacities, the wants, the moral and intellectual nature of the negro, differ from our own to the precise extent that his physical nature or bodily structure differs from ours," argued Van Evrie, connecting the physical and the psychological. Any misguided attempt on the part of whites to force the Negro into white society "destroys the objects of its solicitude when it strives to give him the rights of the white man, or to force him to change his moral and intellectual nature into that of the white man."[63] This destruction and ultimate extinction affected not only the black race, for as their ultimately futile struggle to accommodate white social and moral norms went on, blacks became "vicious as well as idle and non-productive, and *every one of them a disturbing force—a dangerous element—which . . . are always liable to be made instruments of fearful mischief.* . . . [They exhibit] the same moral defects that [they do in their] physical nature . . . and though [their] subordinate nature renders [them] less likely to commit great crimes than the superior white man, the tendencies to petty immoralities are almost universal" (emphasis added).[64] What was worse, noted Van Evrie, "In the cities and larger towns, the vices and immoralities of the whites have an extended association with this free negro element," juxtaposing whites in their basest criminal state and free blacks in their natural state.[65] Such thinking was reflected in the Supreme Court's affirmation of the right of white Illinoisans to protect themselves against the immigration of free blacks or fugitive slaves; the court described them as "a population likely to become burdensome or injurious, either as paupers or criminals."[66] The court and many others likely agreed with the "negro specialist" Dr. Samuel Cartwright when he wrote in 1861 that "the negro must, from necessity, be the slave of man or the slave of Satan."[67]

When the work of European criminal anthropologists was introduced in the late 1870s and 1880s, most people in the United States were already familiar with the notion that criminality could be read on the body—blacks were widely acknowledged as a prime example of the linkage between primitive physiology and criminal tendencies. The work of the Italian Cesare Lombroso in particular meshed well with ideas about race difference. Lombroso's theories about born criminals gained widespread international attention beginning in the 1870s. Lombroso believed that criminals exhibited an "atavistic" or primitive nature, making them morphologically equivalent to lower or savage races. Although his work was not translated into English until the 1890s, the work of others in the Lombrosian school received wider circulation in the United States, and Lombroso's work was frequently summarized, quoted, and cited in American work.[68] When Dr. William Noyes of New York's Bloomingdale Asylum published an article on Lombroso's theory of the "criminal type" in 1888 in the *Journal of Social Science*, he remarked that US scientific criminology was still far behind the work of European scientists, and that the administration of penitentiaries, in particular, had focused primarily on convict labor and not on the actual reform of criminals. The result was a crisis in public safety, as convicts released from penitentiaries simply returned to the barrooms and brothels, where they resumed their criminal behavior. The new criminology, in contrast, "considers the criminal rather than the crime," an approach that came to characterize Progressive criminological reforms.[69]

The first concern in this new view of the criminal was to determine the causes of criminal behavior. In the work of Lombroso and other Europeans, US reformers found scientific evidence that criminality was a physiological disorder with physical manifestations. Lombroso's studies, according to Noyes, confirmed not only that the behavior of habitual criminals resembled that of primitive races, but that the marks of their inferiority could be read on the person. As the early phrenologists and race theorists had suggested, the brains and craniums of "lower" order humans—including criminals of all races—were of deficient size or shape, and criminal anthropologists found that other congenital physiological defects were manifested as well. In a study of seventy-nine criminal children under the age of twelve, Lombroso discovered that 69 percent exhibited "morbid heredity" or "physical anomalies," as compared with only 30 percent among "those who had no moral anomaly."[70] Given the proper training and education, Lombroso (via Noyes) argued, these children could be corrected, but if their moral and physical deficiencies were allowed to flourish in a criminal or immoral environment, they would become lifelong criminals. Noyes concluded his review of Lombroso's work and its applications for criminologists with "a pleasing solution of present evils" wherein sometime in the near future "the possession of certain *physical* anomalies will also be evidence that the person in whom they occur is an enemy of the race" and that "an individual such as those we have been studying, must give bonds, as it were, that the community shall suffer no harm from him."[71] This was eugenics in its earliest form, seeking to identify and isolate the biologically defective members of the population before they could pose a threat.

As sociologists and educators traveled to urban slums and tenements in search of the roots of poverty, crime, alcoholism, and violence, the environmental and social conditions that bred such problems did not escape their notice. Drawing on their own antebellum traditions, those who sought to reform society's ills by transforming the physical world in which they bred argued that criminality had less to do with heredity and more to do with social and physical conditions.[72] In 1890, Havelock Ellis's synthetic work *The Criminal* was published as part of Scribner's Sons' popular Contemporary Science series. Parting from the strictly biological school, Ellis asserted that "both biological and social aspects are fundamental in criminality, and they constitute the two essential data of criminal anthropology."[73] The notion of two possible roots of criminality guided US criminology as it developed during the 1890s and helped affirm an apparent link between race and crime.

In the early 1890s, criminal anthropologists in the United States began to publish their own studies of criminal behavior following the biological model of their European colleagues but striking a balance between biological and social or environmental explanations for crime. In 1890, Dr. Hamilton Wey of the New York State Reformatory, one of the leading figures in

US criminology, presented a paper on criminal anthropology at the annual congress of the National Prison Association that was sympathetic with Ellis's tendency to read social or environmental causes alongside biological markers of criminality. Wey spent a great deal of time describing the physical manifestations of crime, including cranial morphology in the tradition of Lombroso, but he was not convinced that physical markers indicated a predisposition to crime. For Wey, criminality was "bred in the bone and born in the flesh, and the etiology of crime to be looked for chiefly is heredity and environment, using the word environment in its most liberal sense, ante and post natal."[74] Wey compared criminality to insanity and inebriety—which he characterized as "manifestations of a defective organization"—hereditary tendencies contained within the defective individual from birth, waiting only for the environmental circumstances that would permit their expression. Wey concluded that early isolation and treatment of potential criminals while still in a "plastic age" was the only means for developing the "latent good" and neutralizing the "asserting bad" hereditary tendencies. The longer criminal propensities were allowed to flourish, the more degenerate the criminal brain would become over the life of the individual. Wey's conclusion that "all criminals are born, but predisposition does not exclude the influence of surroundings" guided most subsequent research for the next two decades.[75]

Progressive reformers embraced the ability of the individual to reform when guided by enlightened social policy, even if they bore the biological markers of degenerate criminality. Robert McClaughry admitted that "crime is hereditary . . . the disposition to steal, and even to commit crimes against person, is transmitted, like consumptive traits, from one generation to another," but he rejected the notion that "if we would eradicate or even minimize crime, we must separate the dangerous classes from the rest of mankind, and reduce their power of reproduction to its lowest term," as a course of action that would be "hardly practicable in this country."[76] To counter the idea that criminals were doomed from birth, prison reformers and criminologists, including McClaughry, turned to juvenile delinquents and to their environments.[77] The environmental school owed much to an Illinois reformer, Frederick Wines, who represented the state at the National Prison Association and served on the state's Board of Public Charities. Wines was the son of the prison reformer Enoch Wines, who worked with Robert McClaughry through the National Prison Association. The younger Wines joined Havelock Ellis in acknowledging a hereditary influence, but he emphasized the influence of environmental factors when it came to considering the possibility of reform. Wines's lengthy popular treatise *Punishment and Reformation*, published in 1895, gave equal weight to the biological and social explanations of crime. Wines observed, "Everything is, or may be, a cause of crime in those upon whom it reacts unfavorably," but likewise, a person with criminal propensities might never become a criminal unless confronted by the specific environmental factors that triggered his or her unique criminality.[78] For Wines, the key to preventing crime was for the state to intervene and train the potential criminal, while young, to resist his or her hereditary urges: "The first duty of the State is to the child," argued Wines; "Every child has a natural right to such education and training as will fit him for the discharge of the duties of citizenship."[79]

Similarly, in two studies of reformatory youth conducted in Massachusetts in 1896, George Dawson, a psychologist at Clark University, also accepted biological theories to an extent but believed the social causes of crime to be the most treatable. Like Wines, Dawson believed that "however bad the hereditary taint, there must be in every young child some saving elements which make an immoral course possible only after a certain hardening process."[80] The answer to juvenile criminality was to remove the children of alcoholics, criminals, and degenerates from their "evil habitat" and place them in reformatories and schools where the environment provided everything necessary for the virtue-starved portions of their brains to flourish, while working to repress the criminal instincts. Ultimately, Dawson concluded, the scientific determination of the causes of criminality would lead not only to the cure of existing delinquents but also to the prevention of future ones.

Eugene Talbot conducted studies similar to Dawson's on inmates at the Illinois State Reformatory at Pontiac and came to a similar conclusion about the relative influence of heredity and environment on criminal behavior. For Talbot, "although heredity plays a large role in the degeneracy of the individual, still environment in many cases exerts a greater influence in determining . . . the depth of degeneracy."[81] As criminals, paupers, and the insane succumbed to the vices of their naturally degraded environments, they gave rise to successive generations of morally and physically weakened children. These degenerate offspring traveled an opposite evolutionary course from the rest of humankind, descending into savagery over the generations. This left Talbot with the conclusion that "criminals form a variety of the human family quite distinct from law-abiding men."[82] Like Dawson, Talbot advocated carefully screening the children of such degenerates with both physical and psychological tests to determine their hereditary defects, then immersing them in specifically tailored reform programs to combat the degenerate tendencies. For Talbot and others who advocated a blending of biological and environmental factors, if the problem was found in the heredity of the criminal, the solution was found in the environment.

In 1901, the sociologist Frances Kellor of the University of Chicago effectively summed up the conclusions of two decades of criminological theory and practice with her comprehensive *Experimental Sociology*, which discussed anthropometry, criminal identification, and juvenile delinquents and directly addressed the question of race. Kellor downplayed the emphasis on physical characteristics obtained through anthropometry, noting that the use of this method had become prevalent only because anthropometry was already an accepted practice when criminologists began to investigate the causes of criminal behavior. As newer social science models from experimental psychology and sociology were developed, Kellor believed they would show that the conclusions of the biological school had been taken too far, and she noted that anthropometric identification systems like Bertillon's had never been intended to "prove any theory which has a strong hereditary or atavistic flavor."[83]

Pairing an acknowledgment of biological abnormality and its physical manifestations with an argument for environmental influences, theorists such as Wines, Dawson, Talbot, and Kellor suggested a potent solution for reformers. They also created a convenient model for racial theorists to argue for black degeneracy on both a biological basis and an environmental basis. The combination of biological and environmental theories condemned criminals for their degeneracy yet also placed the causes of it beyond their control. This merged unproblematically with theories that linked born criminals with primitive races, and it seemed to confirm the observations of racial theorists who argued for the inherent criminality and ultimate extinction of African Americans. In his chapter on race intermixture, Eugene Talbot noted that "whether the results of race intermixture prove degenerate or not *will turn largely on the environment*" (emphasis added) and observed that "the mulatto is certainly better adapted to the white environment than the pure negro, albeit less so than the white."[84] Talbot was convinced that, if left alone, blacks would be hereditarily unable to advance beyond their present and inferior racial characteristics, marking them as inherently degenerate without the hope of positive environmental influences, for blacks were "protected, by the very prejudices of race and caste, from any large intermixture with the white race."[85] Talbot's relative weighting of biological and environmental influences amounted to a determination that blacks, through a combination of each, were destined to be inherently degenerate and criminal.[86]

As the work of professional criminologists brought both environment and heredity to bear on the question of criminality, more accessible examinations of the crime problem exposed the concerned public to scientific data that also seemed to confirm linkages between race and crime. In his popular *Race Traits and Tendencies of the American Negro* (1896) the statistician Frederick Hoffman used both hereditary and environmental arguments to conclude that blacks were a doomed race. Hoffman cited the case of Chicago, where "the number of negro criminals is out of all proportion to the numerical importance of the race." Hoffman noted that blacks tended to congregate in the "worst sections of the city," but he claimed that "the conditions of life" did not constitute the only factor in producing criminal propensities among blacks. "The colored people are not alone in their tendency to congregate under conditions of vice and crime," claimed Hoffman, noting that Chicago's Italian population lived adjacent to "the negro colony" but contained a much lower proportion of criminals. Of all the races, claimed Hoffman (in a table conflating the constructs of nationality and race), "the colored race shows . . . the most decided tendency towards crime"; he concluded that "the criminality of the negro exceeds that of any other race. . . . Education has utterly failed to raise the negro to a higher level of citizenship, the first duty of which is to obey the laws and respect the lives and property of others."[87] The same year that Hoffman's work appeared, J. Sanderson Christison, a criminologist and psychologist, published a series of articles on "Jail Types" in the *Chicago Tribune,* which were subsequently reprinted in the volume *Crime and Criminals* (1897). Christison's work drew on data from criminal anthropologists that supported the assertion that certain types of people were more prone to negative influences in their environment, but that crime itself was not hereditary. The problem with blacks, claimed Christison, was not that they were naturally criminal per se but that they were "beings of rudimentary simplicity" and, when exposed to negative environmental factors, suffered from "an imposed degeneracy which lowers the brain tone and renders them subjective to fortuitous and unfortunate circumstances."[88]

Even sociologists who championed an environmental approach could not quite dismiss the suspicion that black criminality was more deeply seated than other types of criminality. Frances Kellor noted that blacks were prone to theft because "their beliefs regarding property and rights are erroneous."[89] Kellor claimed that blacks were equipped with a moral foundation that was distinct from that of whites, evoking Thomas Jefferson's observation that slaves' propensity to steal "must be ascribed to their situation."[90] As Kellor saw it, blacks had little understanding of crime and even failed to acknowledge that certain actions were criminal. They were thus simultaneously more prone to crime and too primitive to understand their actions as criminal. "Laws have been accepted by negroes from the whites," Kellor observed, "but it is *imitation* only." As a result, "[Negroes] are notorious and dangerous, but there is no criminal genius. . . . [They] are notorious thieves . . . but there are few bands or gangs." This lack of ability to organize and produce great criminal minds "shows that the race may be inferior."[91] Although Kellor laid much of the blame for black criminality on slavery and unreasonable postemancipation expectations, her suggestion of fundamental racial unfitness only confirmed race as a potential marker of inferiority.

Others working on race theories and the "negro problem" were more explicit in their conclusions. Between 1899 and 1908, Walter Willcox, a federal census statistician, published extensively on the US race problem, including an influential essay on "Negro Criminality" delivered at the American Social Science Association in 1899. Noting that black convicts represented a much larger proportion of the criminal population than whites, Willcox claimed that "these facts furnish some statistical basis and warrant for *the popular opinion, never seriously contested*, that under present conditions in this country a member of the African race, other things equal, is much more likely to fall into crime than a member of the white race" (emphasis added).[92] Willcox argued that the deficiencies of black family life and generations of slavery produced unstable and immoral environments for black children, and he concluded that "Negro criminals spring especially from the rising generation."[93] It was the same combination of environmental and biological determinism that other criminologists saw in juvenile delinquents: a hereditary predisposition to crime aggravated by negative environmental influences. George Winston, president of the North Carolina College of Agricultural and Mechanical Arts, made a similar observation in a talk before the American Academy of Political and Social Science in 1901, noting that "more horrible crimes have been committed by the generation of Negroes that have grown up in the South since slavery than by the six preceding generations in slavery."[94] As Winston saw it, black criminality flourished in a unique environmental milieu: unrestrained freedom from slavery. "The Negro is a child race," he argued, and "no legal enactment, no political agitation, no scheme of education can alter this fact."[95] Consequently, the descent into criminality proceeded much the way it would among any other degenerate or inferior population.

Charles McCord left less doubt about the causes and consequences of black crime and degeneracy in *The American Negro as a Dependent, Defective, and Delinquent* (1914). McCord, more than other students of black crime, fully integrated the hereditary and environmental approaches to criminality in his extensive study, seeking the root of black inferiority in both causes. McCord differentiated between four "classes" of blacks: the educated upper class, the ignorant but well-behaved middle class, "the great mass of ignorant . . . Negroes of unstable character," and "the lowest class, composed of vagrants and criminals and their associates of distinctively vagrant or criminal tendencies."⁹⁶ As Kellor, Willcox, and Winston had done before him, McCord emphasized that the white and black populations were diverging ever more in their social relations with one another. As blacks retreated to racial enclaves, eschewing the culture and refinement of whites, McCord observed a corresponding increase in degeneracy and crime. Surrounded only by their own kind, blacks had little choice but to yield to their defective heredity. For the truly degenerate among the black population, as among whites, McCord suggested the segregation of all defective individuals and "unsexing by surgery" so that they could not reproduce and further degenerate. As for the rest, McCord also believed that blacks represented a "child race," and his solution to their uplift was identical to the solutions for juvenile delinquency of the 1890s: "It is of supreme importance that [the] centers of feeling be properly appealed to—be trained properly to respond. For that means that right-thinking, right-doing, right standards, industry, and efficiency become habitual—become a part of the nervous system."⁹⁷ McCord drew upon a quarter-century of theory and practice in criminology and over a century of speculation on the nature of race difference. He determined that state-of-the-art social science methods and established criminological practices confirmed the racial theories advanced well before the Civil War; blacks belonged to an inferior, childlike race that was predisposed to vagrancy, criminality, and dependency, unless rescued and rehabilitated by benevolent whites.⁹⁸

As the biological and environmental schools of criminal behavior merged in the work of US criminologists, they remained grounded in the same basic theory of criminality, whether among whites or blacks: some were more prone to crime than others, and outward physical markers often indicated criminal propensities or susceptibilities. The concern about the race of the criminal and new theories about the criminal race complemented each other by allowing both everyday people and criminologists to assume that blacks, and the whites that associated with them, were likely to be criminals. The corpus of theories and popular knowledge of the biological causes of crime developed in concert with theories of and assumptions about race. Even as reforms to the system seemed to swing toward an ethos of individualized sentencing and punishment, the modern criminal justice system continued to turn on broad assumptions about race, crime, and criminals that amounted to little more than codified popular prejudice. Operating on the mandate created by increased public concern about the criminal in society, the professional criminologists of the Progressive Era installed the scientific state as the ultimate arbiter of justice, and the state itself thus became responsible for the perpetuation of that prejudice.

EPILOGUE

Springfield, 1908

> It is the presence of the negro among us that is responsible for lynch-law, and not the tastes of our people for such brutal horrors.
>
> —*R. W. Shufeldt,* The Negro; A Menace to American Civilization, *1907*

IN THE EARLY morning hours of Saturday, August 15, 1908, a crowd of white rioters appeared at the Springfield home of sixty-one-year-old barber Scott Burton, who stood at his front door armed with a shotgun. Thirty-nine years earlier, Burton had helped Gus Reed steal three hundred pounds of bacon, and spent a year in the penitentiary, but he had apparently put his criminal past behind him and had long since settled down to earn his living legally. It is unlikely that anyone in the white mob that night knew anything of the crime he had committed so long ago, but for the rioters, Burton's race alone identified him as a target. He had already watched his barbershop on Ninth Street burn to the ground and had sent his family out of the city for protection. As the rioters advanced, Burton fired two loads of buckshot and then ducked back into the house to make his escape through a side door. The mob reached him as he ran through his backyard and beat him senseless. He was still alive as they dragged his limp body through the streets until someone found a length of clothesline with which to hang him. Burton was strung up from a tree at the corner of Twelfth and Madison Streets, stripped, riddled with bullets, slashed with knives, and finally left hanging dead. The tree was gone by the next afternoon, carved to pieces by souvenir hunters.

The Springfield race riot of August 1908 began, as did many other such incidents, with accusations against alleged black criminals. In July, a drifter named Joe James was jailed for reportedly stabbing a white mining engineer. The case against James was circumstantial, but popular opinion convicted him quickly, and rumors of an imminent lynching circulated freely. Then, in mid-August, a black intruder allegedly assaulted Mrs. Mabel Hallam, the wife of a city streetcar driver, while she slept in her bed. Mrs. Hallam identified her assailant as George Richardson, part of a crew remodeling a house in the neighborhood. Although no other evidence was presented, Richardson was arrested and taken to the jail. The city, already on edge from the James case, simmered uneasily all day Friday, August 14, and by that evening, a crowd had gathered at the jail. Rumors began to fly that a white restaurant owner had helped Richardson escape. A mob attacked the restaurant, overwhelmed a small contingent of local militia sent to keep order, and began to roam through the city, burning black homes and businesses and attacking black citizens. In addition to Scott Burton, the mob also lynched William Donnegan, an elderly shoemaker who had lived in Springfield since at least 1845, and who was married to a white woman. Donnegan was pulled from his house and beaten senseless with bricks pried from his own front walk. His throat was cut and he was left hanging from a tree, barely alive. He was cut down and taken to a hospital, where he died the next day.[1]

The racial tensions of the 1860s and 1870s remained unsettled in Springfield in the latter decades of the nineteenth century. Although explicit race agitation had largely disappeared from Democratic campaign rhetoric, black criminals were still identified in the local newspapers, and sensational stories of racial violence and black crime still appeared regularly. Segregated ghettos on the west side of the city reflected a contraction of the opportunities for new migrants and established residents alike, and an area called the "Badlands" developed by the 1890s, a low-rent zone near the city center, where drinking, gambling, and prostitution reminiscent of the old Greasy Row seemed to attract black residents and business owners who had been priced out of other neighborhoods. This gave local whites reason to believe that blacks were bound—perhaps innately, some thought—to congregate in such places, a belief based on long experience and an understanding of race that was firmly grounded in the same suspicions that had driven antebellum Illinoisans to create and enforce the Black Laws. In August 1908, many of those same Illinoisans watched as the fruits of their long labors to delegitimize the black citizen were harvested.

In the aftermath of the Springfield riot, local newspapers decried the actions of "the element that created such infernal havoc . . . that undesirable class that did all the mischief," readily assigning criminality to those unlawful whites who were "no more representative of the real citizenry of Springfield than a rotten and foul smelling fruit is representative of true vegetation." Another newspaper claimed that the rioters were composed of "law violators, burglars, thieves, prostitutes, keepers of disreputable resorts, the riff raff, the scum of the community."[2] The parallels between these assessments and the observation of the criminologist Henry Boies in 1893 that criminals represented the "imperfect, knotty, knurly, worm-eaten, half-rotten fruit of the race" were hardly coincidental.[3]

By 1908, the "undesirable class" had been featured for several decades in the crime columns of Springfield's newspapers. Sometimes this ambiguous group included black criminals, sometimes it colluded with them, and sometimes it fought with them, but it always represented a threat to community law and order. The line between criminal blacks and lawful whites, a fiction from the Black Laws era, blurred in the latter decades of the century. The Springfield race riot of 1908 illustrated a key feature of the late-nineteenth-century reaction to race and criminality: even as evidence mounted that some whites seemed also to be naturally criminal, the long-standing assumption that blacks were especially predisposed to crime remained central to both popular and professional discourses. As social scientific and criminological thought seemed to confirm decades of race prejudice, places such as Springfield, Chicago, and East Saint Louis, all of which had seen increases in their black populations, erupted in violent race riots meant to purge them of their black populations. In East Saint Louis, after the first of a series of race riots in 1917, a local newspaper deflected responsibility from the white rioters by blaming "the large influx here of penal and shiftless negroes from the south" but noted that the "older, law-abiding and long resident" black population bore no responsibility. This was an argument informed by the social scientists' debates about environment and heredity. Overtly casting the problem as environmental by emphasizing the southern origins of the new population allowed the newspaper to claim that "the trouble is not really a race one," even as it characterized the new black migrants as inherently prone to criminality.[4]

The postbellum years also witnessed the continued growth of a popular culture that sanctioned and even openly endorsed white supremacy and racial violence. The cues that signaled black inferiority and criminality were ubiquitous: newspapers, stage shows, national magazines, and increasingly criminological, psychological, and medical theories all provided models for viewing blacks as inferior and as biologically degenerate. The epidemic of lynching and racial violence perpetrated by whites against blacks as a form of retributive extralegal justice grew out of a multivocal corroboration of black criminality. Race and crime were connected and reconnected to each other in different ways from the antebellum era through the turn of the century. Evidence came equally from the actions of actual criminals like Gus Reed and from Democrats' criticisms of emancipation. It came from the crime pages of the local newspapers, and from scientific, medical, and criminological journals. It came from penitentiary officials and police departments, from scholars and universities, and from well-respected popular magazines. All of these reinforced—and were reinforced by—popular depictions of blacks as childish, simplistic, and rudimentary, a lower order of human, and prone to base impulses. These depictions all drew from a deep well of continuing unease about the consequences of emancipation and the tentative advance of civil rights during Reconstruction.

In examining the nationwide epidemic of racial violence at the turn of the century, historians have emphasized specific factors that gave rise to collective racial antipathy: recent growth of local black populations, competition for scarce jobs, high-profile crimes, unfounded allegations, and other flashpoints.[5] The historian Jack Blocker has argued that the "unsettled nature" of race relations in the early twentieth century was actually symptomatic of a fundamental and convulsive refiguring of the national racial order. Blocker notes, "A society in which relationships of domination and subordination are well entrenched does not require spontaneous extralegal outbursts . . . to maintain the control of the dominant."[6] But if incidents of large-scale racial violence were precipitated by imminent threats to the racial order, the fears that drove angry white mobs to take extralegal measures against local black populations also had deeper roots. The racial violence of the 1890s through the 1920s was in part an outgrowth of more than a half-century of prejudices embedded within the popular culture of local communities, where concepts of race and citizenship were informed by experiences and challenges faced during the crises of the Civil War and Reconstruction.

Mob violence was a means by which local whites could wrest control of capital punishment and local justice from the courts and penitentiaries. As reformers sought to reduce the brutality and capriciousness of the criminal justice and penitentiary systems, there were others who came to believe that such systems had become anemic and ineffectual. Coupled with continuing unease about the inability to control the social and cultural consequences of emancipation, extralegal racial violence became a means of both enforcing the color line and the law. As Springfield's *Register* had advocated in 1865, "The people ought to take the matter into their own hands," when blacks transgressed against what whites deemed the best interests of the community.⁷ The postbellum period left Springfielders, Illinoisans, and all other Americans with choices to make about how to address the interwoven problems of race, crime, and racial violence. Many relied on stable and consistent tropes of black criminality and degeneracy that had emerged over the previous decades through legislation, judicial opinions, political rhetoric, and popular culture, and which were finally validated by social science. The new paradigms in sociology and criminology, in turn, reinforced theories of racial difference and granted implicit justification for lynching, race riots, and other forms of mob violence.

As Americans in the heartland and elsewhere confronted the epidemic of racial violence that spanned the turn of the twentieth century, historians such as William Archibald Dunning and his followers in the "Dunning School" of Reconstruction history reminded them that these struggles were firmly grounded in the Civil War era, and that even that self-sacrificing generation had its own significant doubts about the propriety of emancipation, black suffrage, and civil rights. For Dunning School historians, those doubts had been proven correct in subsequent decades, both by hard experience and now by modern scientific methods. James Ford Rhodes lamented in his 1906 *History of the United States from the Compromise of 1850 to the Final Restoration of Home Rule at the South in 1877* that the scientist and natural philosopher Louis Agassiz had warned during the Civil War about too quickly assimilating blacks into the body politic: "What the whole country has only learned through years of costly and bitter experience was known to this leader of scientific thought before we ventured on the policy of trying to make negroes intelligent by legislative acts."⁸ Rhodes believed that the heedless assimilation of former slaves into free society had induced convulsions that reverberated throughout society and throughout the decades. Whites had risen up in the face of federal policies that tried to secure black citizens an equal place in the nation, and were rising still as the century turned.

Gus Reed was dead thirty years before the Springfield race riot. His body, mangled from the autopsy, was buried in the Joliet penitentiary's cemetery beneath a rough pine board painted white and lettered in black, an inscription soon obliterated by the elements.⁹ In denying him the "good death" and idyllic final rest idealized by nineteenth-century Americans, the prison system confirmed that his had not been a good life. Gus Reed's story was a cautionary tale of criminality and irredeemable badness. Much of the latter part of his life was not even his—it belonged to the state, to the penitentiary, and ultimately to the hands of careless and brutal guards, who forced a gag between his teeth, chained and whipped him, and left him to scream himself to death.

Throughout his short life, he responded to the marginalization he faced with attempts to subvert the standards of law and order, and, in so doing, provoked both the criminal justice system and the ire of a white population unsettled by the postemancipation negotiation of black citizenship. In reporting on Gus Reed's life and death, newspapers drew on tropes of black criminality that were deeply engrained in Americans' assumptions about race. As a black criminal, Gus's activities—and indeed, his very existence—embodied two of the central concerns of the nineteenth century. Discourse on black crime took place within many contexts, including politics and popular culture, and emerged from worries about property and safety, as well as from concerns about black emancipation, citizenship, and civil rights. Identifying the black criminal and defining the nature of the criminal black were both fundamental to the foundation of the modern criminal justice system.

Gus Reed's life leads us to consider the nature and purpose of justice, not only as an admirable—if elusive—ambition of systems of law and order, but also as a sort of moral wellspring into which many seekers might dip many buckets. He was just one among many thousands of criminals, black and white, whose opportunistic notions of justice ran them afoul of the mainstream legal and economic cultures of the nation; he was not alone in stepping beyond the confines of the law to pursue an alternative morality. Gus Reed's crimes, the brutal whipping he endured, and the lynching of Scott Burton and William Donnegan were all illegal under the law, but they were each also responses of particular legal cultures to questions of justice, order, and morality. Each was uniquely oriented to the notion of justice and how to achieve it.[10]

For Gus Reed, who came of age in a legal culture that sanctioned the buying, selling, and stealing of human lives, the theft of commodities like meat and clothing represented both resistance and subsistence at the fringes of legal and economic cultures that overtly and implicitly excluded him. For the penitentiary keeper Stephen Reed, who illegally applied the lash to his prisoner's bare back, the failure of the convict under his charge to simply keep his mouth shut was a form of rebellion against institutional law and order, a threat to the orderliness demanded inside the penitentiary, and to the safety of the world outside. For the mob that stormed through Springfield in the summer of 1908, killing Scott Burton and William Donnegan was a kind of answer to a widespread consensus about black criminality. Making an example of two innocent black citizens demonstrated that the responsibility for black crime lay not just with the criminals and that the responsibility for justice lay not just with the institutions of law and order. All of these actions drew their power from the perception that they were illegal and yet in the minds of their perpetrators somehow also compatible with justice. They were moments of slippage between the letter of the law and the extralegal moralities of circumstance and popular consensus. The life and death of Gus Reed bring us into contact with a few such moments in which the disputed meanings of the long Reconstruction jostled for influence on the streets and in the courts of the nation's heartland.

APPENDIX A

Timeline of Known Dates in the Life of Augustus "Gus" Reed

1842/1846	Born in Georgia
1864	Arrived in Illinois
1866	**MARCH 4:** Arrested in Springfield for stealing flour with Beverly Jackson and William Nelson
	SEPTEMBER 2: Sentenced to one month in Sangamon County jail for stealing flour
1867	**APRIL 23:** Fined for fighting with Isaac Kelsey
	MAY 18: Fined for "language calculated to provoke breach of peace"
1869	**APRIL 22:** Theft of bacon with John Fisher, Scott Burton, and Eliza Lewis
	APRIL 23: Arrested for larceny
	MAY 7: Sentenced to Illinois State Penitentiary at Joliet, five years
	JUNE 7: Processed at Joliet penitentiary
	JUNE 1869–MAY 1873: Incarcerated at Joliet
1873	**MAY 12:** Released from Joliet one year early
1874	**MARCH 6:** Charged with larceny in Springfield along with James Burns and Perry Braxton

	March 13: Escaped from Sangamon County jail sometime between March 6 and March 13
	July 21: Arrested in Jacksonville
	October 21: Sentenced to Joliet for larceny for three years
	December 2: Processed at Joliet penitentiary
	Dec. 1874–June 1877: Incarcerated at Joliet
1877	**June 7:** Released from Joliet six months early
	June 26: Arrested in Springfield, extradited to Christian County
	June 27: Booked into Christian County jail for "assault with intent to kill"
	September 5: Found not guilty and released from Christian County jail
	November/December: Arrested in Springfield
1878	**March 24:** Sentenced to Joliet for larceny for two years
	March 26: Processed at Joliet penitentiary
	May 7: Died in solitary confinement at Joliet

APPENDIX B

Nativity of Springfield's Black Population, 1860, 1870, 1880

Place of birth Free states or territories (as of 1860)				Place of birth Slave states (as of 1860)			
	1860	1870	1880		1860	1870	1880
Connecticut	—	1	—	Alabama	4	30	15
Delaware	—	1	—	Arkansas	—	1	4
Illinois	**135**	**246**	**576**	Florida	—	—	2
Indiana	4	7	28	Georgia	1	10	14
Iowa	—	—	2	**Kentucky**	**35**	**128**	**109**
Michigan	—	1	—	Louisiana	2	12	6
Montana	—	—	1	Maryland	9	14	16
New Jersey	—	1	—	**Missouri**	**21**	**88**	**211**
New York	1	3	3	**Mississippi**	—	**43**	**41**
Ohio	3	3	11	North Carolina	9	9	18
Pennsylvania	3	2	2	South Carolina	—	16	8
Wisconsin	—	1	—	**Tennessee**	**10**	**52**	**41**
				Texas	—	—	2
				Virginia	**31**	**74**	**82**
				Washington, DC	2	4	7
Total	**146**	**266**	**623**	**Total**	**124**	**481**	**576**

Source: Manuscript Federal Census for Illinois

APPENDIX C

Sangamon County Convicts Sent to Illinois State Penitentiary by Year and Race, 1860–80

Year	Total	White	% White	Black	% Black
1860	12	12	100	0	0
1861	7	7	100	0	0
1862*	—	—	—	—	—
1863	13	12	92	1	8
1864	4	4	100	0	0
1865	16	14	88	2	12
1866	30	25	83	5	17
1867	12	10	83	2	17
1868	18	15	83	3	17
1869	34	28	82	6	18
1870	16	10	63	6	37
1871	11	9	82	2	18
1872	8	7	88	1	12
1873*	—	—	—	—	—
1874	27	22	81	5	19
1875	28	26	93	2	7
1876*	—	—	—	—	—
1877	45	38	84	7	16
1878	20	15	75	5	25
1879	25	21	84	4	16
1880	23	21	91	2	9
Total	349	296	85	53	15

*For 1862, 1873, 1876 microfilm copy of Joliet Penitentiary Register is illegible or incomplete.

Source: Illinois State Penitentiary at Joliet Register of Prisoners, Illinois State Archives

APPENDIX D

Criminal Cases in Sangamon County Circuit Court, 1870-80

Year	Property Crimes	Vice Crimes	Violent Crimes	Other	Total
1870	63	67	25	15	170
1871	59	23	25	45	152
1872	16	3	12	10	41
1873	39	14	14	17	84
1874	43	34	11	9	97
1875	120	60	22	31	233
1876	82	15	12	17	126
1877	167	24	27	17	235
1878	96	18	14	24	152
1879	88	30	15	29	162
1880	60	23	19	37	139
Total	833	311	196	251	1,591

Property Crimes: arson, burglary, forgery, receiving stolen goods, receiving goods under false pretenses
Vice Crimes: prostitution, selling liquor without a license, selling liquor on Sunday, public indecency, bastardy, adultery, fornication, gambling
Violent Crimes: rape, assault, manslaughter, murder, threats against life
Other: contempt of court, riot, mayhem, mischief, resisting a police officer, obstructing public road

Source: Sangamon County Circuit Court Criminal Docket, University of Illinois at Springfield, Illinois Regional Archives Depository

APPENDIX E

Disposition of Criminal Cases (Continuance and Appearance) in Sangamon County Circuit Court, 1870–80

(Includes appearances and continuances in which a verdict was rendered, plea made, or case was dismissed, stricken, bill ignored, indictment quashed, or nolle prosequi entered.)

Year	Plea of Guilty	Trial by Jury (plea of not guilty entered)		Dismissed, Stricken, Ignored, *Nolle*	Other*	Total
		FOUND GUILTY	FOUND NOT GUILTY			
1870	46	9	7	91	70	223
1871	33	3	2	62	45	145
1872	4	1	0	38	12	55
1873	20	5	4	31	30	90
1874	25	2	3	67	48	145
1875	54	7	2	100	64	227
1876	68	6	6	124	87	291
1877	60	24	9	134	57	284
1878	32	15	9	118	47	221
1879	59	13	5	62	32	171
1880	36	14	11	62	82	205
Total	437	99	58	889	574	2,057

*Cases for which some notation other than a plea, verdict, dismissal, *nolle*, etc. was made in the "Remarks" column of the docket book, including continuances, bail set, bench warrants issued, or for which remarks are ambiguous; excludes cases for which no notation was made.

Source: Sangamon County Circuit Court Criminal Docket, 1870–80, University of Illinois at Springfield, Illinois Regional Archives Depository

NOTES

Abbreviations

ACCC   Adams County Circuit Court, Quincy, Illinois
ALPL   Abraham Lincoln Presidential Library, Springfield, Illinois
CHM   Chicago History Museum, Chicago, Illinois
ISA   Illinois State Archives, Springfield, Illinois
SCRC   Special Collections Research Center, University of Chicago
NARA   National Archives and Records Administration, Washington, DC
NARA-GL   National Archives and Records Administration, Great Lakes, Chicago, Illinois
UIS-IRAD   University of Illinois at Springfield, Illinois Regional Archives Depository,
WCC   Will County Coroner's Office
WIU-IRAD   Western Illinois University, Illinois Regional Archives Depository,
WLCL   William L. Clements Library, University of Michigan

Introduction

Epigraph: Cormac McCarthy, *The Crossing* (New York: Alfred A. Knopf, 1994), 411.

1. This account of Gus Reed's death, and the more detailed account that appears in chapter 6, are both based on the Joliet Penitentiary Testimony on Inhuman Treatment of Prisoners, Special Collections Research Center, University of Chicago (hereafter SCRC). For the determination of the coroner's jury, see Will County Coroner's Record for Guss [*sic*] Reed, Will County Coroner's Office (hereafter WCC).

2. The 1870 manuscript federal census also identified Gus Reed as "mulatto" because the census taker apparently copied from the penitentiary register. No specific evidence could be located to identify the race of either of his parents. I refer to him most often as simply "black," which I believe accurately characterizes how he would have been viewed in his own time, while avoiding derogatory, subjective, or otherwise problematic terminology.

3. For discussions of what is sometimes called the "New Biography" see "AHR Roundtable: Historians and Biography," *American Historical Review* 114, no. 3 (June 2009): 573–661; Jo Burr Margadant, ed., *The New Biography: Performing Femininity in Nineteenth-Century France* (Berkeley: University of California Press, 2000); Peter France and William St. Clair, eds., *Mapping Lives: The Uses of Biography* (Oxford: Oxford University Press for the British Academy, 2002). Although not ostensibly biographical, Barton A. Myers, *Executing Daniel Bright: Race, Loyalty, and Guerilla Violence in a Coastal Carolina Community, 1861–1865* (Baton Rouge: Louisiana State

University Press, 2009) provides an excellent example of the value of human-scale microhistory to access significant historical themes. The goals of this methodology are also similar to those expounded in James F. Brooks, Christopher R. N. Decorse, and John Walton, eds., *Small Worlds: Method, Meaning, and Narrative in Microhistory* (Santa Fe, NM: School for Advanced Research Press, 2008) and also those voiced eloquently by Jill Lepore, "Historians Who Love Too Much: Reflections on Microhistory and Biography," *Journal of American History* 88 (June 2001): 129–44; and Richard D. Brown, "Microhistory and the Post-Modern Challenge," *Journal of the Early Republic* 23 (Spring 2003): 1–20.

4. For an examination of the allowances for servitude and slavery in the Northwest Territory, and in Illinois and Indiana specifically, see Paul Finkelman, "Evading the Ordinance: The Persistence of Bondage in Indiana and Illinois," *Journal of the Early Republic* 9 (Spring 1989): 343–70; Finkelman, "Slavery and the Northwest Ordinance: A Study in Ambiguity," *Journal of the Early Republic* 6 (Winter 1986): 343–70; Finkelman, "Slavery, the 'More Perfect Union,' and the Prairie State," *Illinois Historical Journal* 80 (Winter 1987): 248–69. See also Peter S. Onuf, "From Constitution to Higher Law: The Reinterpretation of the Northwest Ordinance," *Ohio History* 94 (Winter/Spring 1985): 5–33. For the persistence of slavery and race issues in antebellum Illinois, see James Simeone, *Democracy and Slavery in Frontier Illinois: The Bottomland Republic* (DeKalb: Northern Illinois University Press, 2000); Robert P. Howard, *Illinois: A History of the Prairie State* (Grand Rapids, MI: William B. Eerdmans, 1972); Clarence Walworth Alvord, *The Illinois Country, 1673–1818* (1920; Urbana: University of Illinois Press, 1987; Theodore Calvin Pease, *The Frontier State, 1818–1848* (1919; Urbana: University of Illinois Press, 1987); and Norman Dwight Harris, *The History of Negro Servitude in Illinois, and the Slavery Agitation in that State, 1719–1864* (Chicago: McClurg, 1904).

5. Abraham Lincoln to Major General Stephen A. Hurlbut, November 14, 1864, in Roy P. Basler, ed., *The Collected Works of Abraham Lincoln*, vol. 8 (New Brunswick, NJ: Rutgers University Press, 1953), 106–7.

6. Leslie A. Schwalm, "'Overrun with Free Negroes': Emancipation and Wartime Migration in the Upper Midwest," *Civil War History* 50 (June 2004): 148.

7. Heather Cox Richardson, *West from Appomattox: The Reconstruction of America after the Civil War* (New Haven: Yale University Press, 2007); Elliott West, *The Last Indian War: The Nez Perce Story* (New York: Oxford University Press, 2009); Eugene H. Berwanger, *The West and Reconstruction* (Urbana: University of Illinois Press, 1981), framed the "western response to Reconstruction" but only hinted at the shape of a uniquely western reconstruction. For the broadening of Reconstruction Era studies, see also Nicole Etcheson, *A Generation at War: The Civil War in a Northern Community* (Lawrence: University Press of Kansas, 2011); Hugh Davis, *"We Will Be Satisfied with Nothing Less": The African American Struggle for Equal Rights in the North during Reconstruction* (Ithaca, NY: Cornell University Press, 2011); Desmond King and Stephen Tuck, "De-centring the South: America's Nationwide White Supremacist Order after Reconstruction," *Past and Present* 194 (February 2007): 213–53; Carol A. Horton, *Race and the Making of American Liberalism* (New York: Oxford University Press, 2005); David Quigley, *Second Founding: New York City, Reconstruction, and the*

Making of American Democracy (New York: Hill and Wang, 2004); Heather Cox Richardson, *The Death of Reconstruction: Race, Labor, and Politics in the Post–Civil War North, 1865–1901* (Cambridge, MA: Harvard University Press, 2001); Sven Beckert, *The Monied Metropolis: New York City and the Consolidation of the American Bourgeoisie, 1850–1896* (Cambridge: Cambridge University Press, 1993); Phyllis F. Field, *The Politics of Race in New York: The Struggle for Black Suffrage in the Civil War Era* (Ithaca, NY: Cornell University Press, 1982); William Gillette, *Retreat from Reconstruction: 1869–1879* (Baton Rouge: Louisiana State University Press, 1979).

8. The African American experience in the Midwest was first explored several decades ago. See David Gerber, *Black Ohio and the Color Line, 1860–1915* (Urbana: University of Illinois Press, 1976); V. Jacque Voegeli, *Free but Not Equal: The Midwest and the Negro during the Civil War* (Chicago: University of Chicago Press, 1967); Emma Lou Thornbrough, *The Negro in Indiana before 1900: A Study of a Minority* (Indianapolis: Indiana Historical Bureau, 1957); Leon Litwack, *North of Slavery: The Negro in the Free States, 1790–1860* (Chicago: University of Chicago Press, 1961); George Hesslink, *Black Neighbors: Negroes in a Northern Rural Community* (Indianapolis: Bobbs-Merrill, 1974); Eugene H. Berwanger, *The Frontier against Slavery: Western Anti-Negro Prejudice and the Slavery Extension Controversy* (Urbana: University of Illinois Press, 1967). Several recent studies have refocused attention on the migrations of Southern blacks into the Midwest and the communities they formed there during and after the Civil War, combining the social history of the black migrants with the response they received in the predominantly white communities in which they arrived, demonstrating that postemancipation black migration was both a demographically and cultural significant phenomenon that reshaped many Midwestern communities. See Jack S. Blocker Jr., *A Little More Freedom: African Americans Enter the Urban Midwest, 1860–1930* (Columbus: Ohio State University Press, 2008); Darrel E. Bigham, *On Jordan's Banks: Emancipation and Its Aftermath in the Ohio River Valley* (Lexington: University Press of Kentucky, 2006); Leslie A. Schwalm, *Emancipation's Diaspora: Race and Reconstruction in the Upper Midwest* (Chapel Hill: University of North Carolina Press, 2009). See also Michael P. Johnson, "Out of Egypt: The Migration of Former Slaves to the Midwest during the 1860s in Comparative Perspective," in *Crossing Boundaries: Comparative History of Black People in Diaspora*, ed. Darlene Hine and Jacqueline McLeod (Bloomington: Indiana University Press, 1999), 223–45; Allan Johnston, "Being Free: Black Migration and the Civil War," *Australasian Journal of American Studies* 6, no. 1 (1987): 3–21; Darrel Bigham, "Work, Residence, and the Emergence of the Black Ghetto in Evansville, Indiana, 1865–1900," *Indiana Magazine of History* 76 (December 1980): 287–318; Jack S. Blocker, Jr., "Black Migration to Muncie, 1860–1930," *Indiana Magazine of History* 92 (December 1996): 297–320; Elizabeth Regosin, *Freedom's Promise: Ex-Slave Families and Citizenship in the Age of Emancipation* (Charlottesville: University Press of Virginia, 2002). For the impact of the Exoduster migration and Great Migration, see Nell Irvin Painter, *Exodusters: Black Migration to Kansas after Reconstruction* (New York: Knopf, 1977); Robert Athearn, *In Search of Canaan: Black Migration to Kansas, 1879–80* (Lawrence: Regents Press of Kansas, 1978); and James Grossman, *Land of Hope: Chicago, Black Southerners, and the Great Migration* (Chicago: University of Chicago Press, 1989).

9. Barbara Fields has argued against a view of racism and white supremacy as fixed or static concepts. Following Fields, this study does not treat these ideologies as unchanging or immutable but seeks to describe the evolving contours of an intellectual tradition of racism to which Democrats and others resistant to black rights appealed. See Barbara Fields, "Ideology and Race in American History," in *Region, Race, and Reconstruction: Essays in Honor of C. Vann Woodward,* ed. J. Morgan Kousser and James M. McPherson (New York: Oxford University Press, 1982), 143–77.

10. For the beginnings of the white resistance, see Schwalm, *Emancipation's Diaspora.* See also Edward Noyes, "White Opposition to Black Migration into Civil War Wisconsin," *Lincoln Herald* 73 (September 1971): 181–93. Mark Neely has suggested that social and cultural factors were at least as important as political rhetoric in determining the pervasiveness of popular racism throughout the era of the Civil War. See especially chapter 4, "Minstrelsy, Race, and the Boundaries of American Political Culture," in Mark E. Neely Jr., *The Boundaries of American Political Culture in the Civil War Era* (Chapel Hill: University of North Carolina Press, 2005). See citations in chapter 2 and chapter 4 of the present volume for works on Democratic partisanship and the retrenchment of white supremacy. For the interplay of politics, cultures of law, and perceptions of criminality, see Steven Wilf, *Law's Imagined Republic: Popular Politics and Criminal Justice in Revolutionary America* (New York: Cambridge University Press, 2010).

Chapter One: Georgia Roots

Epigraph: Robert Falls, quoted in Lawrence W. Levine, *Black Culture and Black Consciousness: Afro-American Folk Thought from Slavery to Freedom* (New York: Oxford University Press, 1977), 122.

1. "Reed," *Chicago Daily Tribune,* May 12, 1878, and "Justifiable," *Chicago Daily Tribune,* May 11, 1878. Joliet Penitentiary Register of Prisoners and Prison Mittimus Files for Gus Reed, Illinois State Archives (hereafter ISA). Will County Coroner's Record for Guss [sic] Reed, Physician's Certificate of Death for Guss [sic] Reed, Will County Death Records, Will County Coroner's Office, University of Illinois, Springfield, Illinois Regional Archives Depository (hereafter UIS-IRAD).

2. The age Gus Reed gave when he was jailed in 1878 would have had him born in 1842, but this is the only instance in which he reported his age this way. On the functioning of the justice system and the punishment of slaves and free blacks in Georgia, see Glenn McNair, *Criminal Injustice: Slaves and Free Blacks in Georgia's Criminal Justice System* (Charlottesville: University of Virginia Press, 2009).

3. In 1850, free blacks numbered 2,931 to the state's total population of 906,185, while slaves numbered 381,682. J. D. B. DeBow, *The Seventh Census of the United States: 1850* (Washington, DC: Robert Armstrong, 1853), 365. Gus Reed gave his occupation in 1874 as a farmer, suggesting that he may have grown up on a farm or plantation. For his claim that he was a farmer, see Joliet Penitentiary Register of Prisoners, ISA. There were several families of free black Reeds/Reids in Savannah, but it is not certain that Gus was one of them, as he was not verifiably recorded in the city's register of free blacks. See Registers of Free Persons of Color, vols.

3–5, City of Savannah, Research Library and Municipal Archives. On slavery in Georgia, see notes below and Diana Ramey Berry, *Swing the Sickle for the Harvest Is Ripe: Gender and Slavery in Antebellum Georgia* (Urbana: University of Illinois Press, 2007); Susan Eva O'Donovan, *Becoming Free in the Cotton South* (Cambridge, MA: Harvard University Press, 2007); Erskine Clarke, *Dwelling Place: A Plantation Epic* (New Haven: Yale University Press, 2005); William Dusinberre, *Them Dark Days: Slavery in the American Rice Swamps* (Athens: University of Georgia, 1999); Whittington B. Johnson, *Black Savannah: 1788–1864* (Fayetteville: University of Arkansas Press, 1996); and Joseph Reidy, *From Slavery to Agrarian Capitalism in the Cotton Plantation South: Central Georgia, 1800–1880* (Chapel Hill: University of North Carolina Press, 1991).

4. Marie Jenkins Schwartz, *Born in Bondage: Growing Up Enslaved in the Antebellum South* (Cambridge, MA: Harvard University Press, 2000), 8–9.

5. On the tightening of laws aimed at both free blacks and slaves in Georgia, see Clarence L. Mohr, *On the Threshold of Freedom: Masters and Slaves in Civil War Georgia* (Athens: University of Georgia Press, 1986); and Julia Floyd Smith, *Slavery and Rice Culture in Low Country Georgia, 1750–1860* (Knoxville: University of Tennessee Press, 1985).

6. Mohr, *On the Threshold of Freedom*, 51.

7. For slaves leaving plantations, see especially Stephen V. Ash, *When the Yankees Came: Conflict and Chaos in the Occupied South, 1861–1865* (Chapel Hill: University of North Carolina Press, 1995), 154–155; and Ash, *The Black Experience in the Civil War South* (Santa Barbara, CA: Praeger/ABC-CLIO, 2010).

8. Timothy James Lockley, *Lines in the Sand: Race and Class in Lowcountry Georgia, 1750–1860* (Athens: University of Georgia Press, 2001), 111, 114.

9. Jeff Forret, *Race Relations at the Margins: Slaves and Poor Whites in the Antebellum Southern Countryside* (Baton Rouge: Louisiana State University Press, 2006), 94.

10. Emily Burke quoted in Betty Wood, *Women's Women, Men's Work: The Informal Slave Economies of Lowcountry Georgia* (Athens: University of Georgia Press, 1995), 97.

11. North Carolina slaveholder William D. Valentine quoted in Eugene D. Genovese, *Roll, Jordan, Roll: The World the Slaves Made* (New York: Vintage, 1976), 601.

12. "Jonathan Freeman's Letters to the Illinois Gazette," *Edwardsville Spectator*, November 1, 1823.

13. James Bolton interview, recorded by Sarah H. Hall in *The American Slave: A Composite Autobiography*, ed. George P. Rawick, vol. 12, pt. 1 (1941; Westport, CT: Greenwood Publishing, 1976), 96.

14. Alec Pope interview, recorded by Sadie B. Hornsby in Rawik, *American Slave*, vol. 13, pt. 3, 175.

15. Thomas Jefferson, *Notes on the State of Virginia* (Richmond: J. W. Randolph, 1853), 154.

16. "General Superintendent of Contrabands in the Department of the Tennessee to the Headquarters of the Department," in Ira Berlin, Thavolia Glymph, Steven F. Miller, Joseph P. Reidy, Leslie S. Rowland, and Julie Saville, eds., *Freedom: A Documentary History of Emancipation, 1861–1867*, series 1, vol. 3 (New York: Cambridge University Press, 1990), 684–98.

17. John Brown, *Slave Life in Georgia: A Narrative of the Life, Sufferings, and Escape of John Brown, a Fugitive Slave*, ed. F. N. Boney (1855; 1972; Savannah, GA: Beehive Press, 1991), 71–72.

18. Frances A. Kemble and Frances A. Butler Leigh, *Principles and Privilege: Two Women's Lives on a Georgia Plantation* (Ann Arbor: University of Michigan Press, 1995), 277.

19. Frederick Douglass, *Life and Times of Frederick Douglass, His Early Life as a Slave, His Escape from Bondage, and His Complete History to the Present Time* (Hartford, CT: Park, 1881), 99.

20. Brown, *Slave Life in Georgia*, 158.

21. Benjamin Johnson interview, recorded by Edwin Driskell in Rawik, *American Slave*, vol. 12, pt. 2, 322.

22. Isaiah Green interview, recorded by Minnie B. Rose and Edwin Driskell in Rawik, *American Slave*, vol. 12, pt. 2, 52, 58.

23. Tom Hawkins interview, recorded by Sadie B. Hornsby in Rawik, *American Slave*, vol. 12, pt. 2, 131. Eugene Genovese has suggested that owner-approved larceny actually strengthened the bonds within particular plantation communities between slaves and "their" white folks (from whom slaves supposedly would not steal), and whites on different plantations. Genovese, *Roll, Jordan, Roll*, 605.

24. Brown, *Slave Life in Georgia*, 48.

25. Shang Harris interview, recorded by Velma Bell in Rawik, *American Slave*, vol. 12, pt. 2, 119.

26. Slave theft has been a subject of disagreement among historians. One camp, exemplified by Lawrence Levine, believes that slave theft and other slave crime was conducted within a "practical set of norms and behavior" created by slaves to implicitly excuse actions known by them to be morally wrong, but allowable in specific circumstances owing to the conditions of slavery. Slaves did not create a morality counter to that of their masters, and instead felt guilty about their actions, which diminished the power of slave crime to damage the hegemony of the master class. Another camp, which includes the work of Herbert Aptheker and Kenneth M. Stampp, believes that slave theft and other crimes were specifically acts of agency and resistance, and that slaves consciously developed a moral code in opposition to that of their masters. Eugene Genovese adds the important nuance that slaves likely viewed their crimes as both morally right and wrong, but that slave theft actually solidified whites' dominance by confirming negative stereotypes and justifying the strict controls placed on slaves and effectively negating theft as resistance and actually strengthening the hegemony of the master class. Edward L. Ayers similarly notes that slaves did not create an alternative moral system per se to excuse their theft, but rather neutralized the existing one by characterizing their theft as born of necessity or as a counterbalance to the crime of slavery. See Levine, *Black Culture and Black Consciousness*, 123; Genovese, "Roast Pig is a Wonderful Delicacy, Especially When Stolen," in *Roll, Jordan, Roll*, 599–612; Edward L. Ayers, *Vengeance and Justice: Crime and Punishment in the 19th-Century American South* (New York: Oxford University Press, 1984), 125–32. See also William Byrne, "Slave Crime in Savannah, Georgia," *Journal of Negro History* 79, no. 4 (1994): 352–62; Alex Lichtenstein, "'That Disposition to Theft, with Which They

Have Been Branded': Moral Economy, Slave Management, and the Law," *Journal of Social History* 21 (Spring 1988): 413–40.

27. Reverend W. B. Allen in Rawik, *American Slave*, vol. 12, pts. 1 and 2, 14–15.

28. Brown, *Slave Life in Georgia*, 71–72.

29. Quoted in Genovese, *Roll, Jordan, Roll*, 602. On stealing versus taking, see Levine, *Black Culture and Black Consciousness*, 131, and Genovese, *Roll, Jordan, Roll*, 602, 607–8.

30. Will Sheets interview, recorded by Sadie B. Hornsby in Rawik, *American Slave*, vol. 13, pt. 3, 243.

31. Samuel Elliot testimony before the Southern Claims Commission, quoted in Berlin, et al., *Freedom*, series 1, vol. 1, 148–49.

32. Nancy Johnson testimony before the Southern Claims Commissions, quoted in Berlin et al., *Freedom*, series 1, vol. 1, 154.

33. Alice Green interview, recorded by Corry Fowler in Rawik, *American Slave*, vol. 12, pt. 2, 34.

34. For contested and ambiguous views about young former slaves, see Mary Niall Mitchell, *Raising Freedom's Child: Black Children and Visions of the Future after Slavery* (New York: New York University Press, 2008).

35. Mohr, *On the Threshold of Freedom*, 95.

36. Mary Livermore, *My Story of the War: A Woman's Narrative of Four Years Personal Experience* (Hartford, CT: A. D. Worthington, 1889), 342, 345, 349, 352. For black migration to the Midwest during the Civil War, see citations in the Introduction.

37. Kate Masur, "'A Rare Phenomenon of Philological Vegetation': The Word 'Contraband' and the Meanings of Emancipation in the United States," *Journal of American History* 93 (March 2007): 1084.

38. Thomas Bahde, ed., *The Story of My Campaign: The Civil War Memoir of Captain Francis T. Moore, Second Illinois Cavalry* (DeKalb: Northern Illinois University Press, 2011), 59.

39. Albert Chipman to Sophronia Chipman, October 2, 1862, excerpted in Daniel E. Sutherland, ed., "'We Must Do the Best We Can': The Civil War Letters of Albert Chipman, 76th Illinois Infantry: pt. 1," *Military History of the West* 28 (Spring 1998): 61.

40. J. M. Smith to Richard Yates, November 10, 1862, Yates Family Papers, Abraham Lincoln Presidential Library (hereafter ALPL).

41. Mrs. J. B. Roberts to Richard Yates, December 5, 1863, Yates Family Papers, ALPL.

42. Richard Oglesby to Brig. Gen. J. W. Sprague, October 16, 1865, Governor's Correspondence, ISA.

Chapter Two: Illinois in Wartime

Epigraph: John M. Palmer, *Personal Recollections of John M. Palmer: The Story of an Earnest Life* (Cincinnati: R. Clarke, 1901), 281.

1. "'Every Body Likes to Shake Hands with Him': Letters of Elbridge Atwood," *Journal of the Illinois State Historical Society* 72 (June 1979): 139–42.

2. "A Call upon the Farmers," *Illinois State Register,* April 25, 1865.

3. Stout did not record his choice for president in 1864. Entries for October 18, 1861, and May 3–4, 1865, Philemon Stout Diaries, ALPL.

4. C. A. Page, a *Tribune* correspondent, quoted in James T. Hickey, "Springfield, May, 1865," *Journal of the Illinois State Historical Society* 58 (March 1965): 21–33.

5. Robert McClaughry quoted in Rufus R. Wilson, *Intimate Memories of Lincoln* (Elmira, NY: Primavera Press, 1945), 57–58.

6. Elliott B. Herndon to William Herndon, n.d. [1865–66] in Douglas L. Wilson and Rodney O. Davis, eds., *Herndon's Informants: Letters, Interviews, and Statements about Abraham Lincoln* (Urbana: University of Illinois Press, 1998), 459. The original letter is in very poor condition, and the text was partially reconstructed for inclusion in the cited volume. For the sake of clarity, I have omitted the brackets that appeared in the reconstructed text. On the "anti-Lincoln tradition" see Don E. Fehrenbacher, *Lincoln in Text and Context: Collected Essays* (Stanford: Stanford University Press, 1987), 197–213.

7. Stephen A. Douglas, *The Spurious Kansas Memorial: Debate in the Senate of the United States on the Memorial of James H. Lane* (Washington, DC: Union Office, 1856), 17.

8. John Hay to Charles E. Hay, January 24, 1860, George L. Huntington Papers, ALPL; and Hay quoted in Tyler Dennett, *John Hay: From Poetry to Politics* (New York: Dodd, Mead, 1933), 32.

9. Kenneth J. Winkle, *The Young Eagle: The Rise of Abraham Lincoln* (Dallas: Taylor, 2001), 264. *National Anti-Slavery Standard* 12 (June 19, 1851), 15. "Illinois in Spring-Time," *Atlantic Monthly* 2 (September 1858), 483. For antebellum antiblack prejudice in the west, see Berwanger, *The Frontier against Slavery.* For race and racism in antebellum and wartime Illinois, see Eric Foner, *The Fiery Trial: Abraham Lincoln and American Slavery* (New York: W. W. Norton, 2010). Mark Neely has observed that Illinois was the only state of the contiguous United States not to pass personal liberty laws before the Civil War. See Mark E. Neely Jr., *The Fate of Liberty: Abraham Lincoln and Civil Liberties* (New York: Oxford University Press, 1991), xvi.

10. "Obituary—Death of an Old Pioneer," *Illinois State Register,* January 3, 1867. For Archer Herndon, see also David Donald's biography of William Herndon, *Lincoln's Herndon* (New York: Knopf, 1948).

11. *History of Sangamon County* (Chicago: Inter-state Publishing, 1881), 519–20.

12. For Elliott Herndon's career, see "The Mortuary Record," *Illinois State Journal,* April 14, 1895. For the political and slavery views of migrants from the Upper South such as the Herndons, see Nicole Etcheson, *The Emerging Midwest: Upland Southerners and the Political Culture of the Old Northwest, 1787–1861* (Bloomington: Indiana University Press, 1996).

13. "Fugitive Slave Case," *Illinois State Journal,* August 1, 1857.

14. William Herndon to Theodore Parker, August 4, 1857, William Herndon Correspondence, ALPL.

15. "Fugitive Slaves," *Illinois State Register,* August 3, 1857. For newspaper coverage of the Clements case, see multiple articles and editorials in the *Illinois State Journal* and *Illinois State Register,* August 1–2, 1857, and the *Chicago Daily Tribune,* August 5, 1857.

16. Stephen L. Hansen, *The Making of the Third Party System: Voters and Parties in Illinois, 1850–1876* (Ann Arbor, MI: UMI Research Press, 1980), refers to the National Democrats in Illinois as Danites, a term that was used derogatorily at the time to signal blind obedience, but which is somewhat misleading because of its primary association with Mormon history. For an insightful analysis of the slavery issue in the disruption of party politics in the 1850s, see Michael A. Morrison, *Slavery and the American West: The Eclipse of Manifest Destiny and the Coming of the Civil War* (Chapel Hill: University of North Carolina Press, 1997). See also Michael F. Holt, *The Political Crisis of the 1850s* (New York: Wiley, 1978).

17. "The Status of the Negro," *Illinois State Democrat*, October 2, 1858. For other examples of the *Democrat*'s coverage of blacks and slavery, see "A Scene for Abolitionists," and "What Anti-Slavery Has Done," *Illinois State Democrat*, July 4, 1860.

For Northern Democrats in the antebellum and Civil War eras, see Jean H. Baker, *Affairs of Party: The Political Culture of Northern Democrats in the Mid-Nineteenth Century* (1983; New York: Fordham University Press, 1998); Etcheson, *Emerging Midwest* and Etcheson, *Generation at War;* Adam I. P. Smith, *No Party Now: Politics in the Civil War North* (New York: Oxford University Press, 2006); Jennifer L. Weber, *Copperheads: The Rise and Fall of Lincoln's Opponents in the North* (New York: Oxford University Press, 2006); Joel H. Silbey, *A Respectable Minority: The Democratic Party in the Civil War Era, 1860–1868* (New York: Norton, 1977); Frank L. Klement, *The Copperheads in the Middle West* (Chicago: University of Chicago Press, 1960); Forrest G. Wood, *Black Scare: The Racist Response to Emancipation and Reconstruction* (Berkeley: University of California Press, 1968); and W. Sherman Jackson, "Emancipation, Negrophobia and Civil War Politics in Ohio, 1863–1865," *Journal of Negro History* 65 (Summer 1980): 250–60. For the Democratic race rhetoric in Illinois, see Bruce Tap, "Race, Rhetoric, and Emancipation: The Election of 1862 in Illinois," *Civil War History* 39 (June 1993): 101–25.

18. Entries for July 25 and October 18, 1860, Philemon Stout Diaries, ALPL.

19. *History of Sangamon County,* 272–77. For an example of National Democratic campaign literature, see *Address to the Democracy and the People of the United States, by the National Democratic Executive Committee* (Washington, DC, 1860).

20. General Record of the US District Court, Southern District of Illinois, vol. 1, National Archives and Records Administration, Great Lakes (hereafter NARA-GL). The federal commissioner's dockets from Springfield have apparently been lost, but a copy of the docket from 1860–61 survives in the Adams-Snyder Family Papers, ALPL.

21. For personal liberty laws, see Thomas Morris, *Free Men All: The Personal Liberty Laws of the North, 1780–1861* (Baltimore: Johns Hopkins University Press, 1974).

22. Neely, *Fate of Liberty,* xvi. Hansen, *Making of the Third Party System,* portrays the factional disputes of the 1850s and the death of Douglas in 1861 as indications that the Democratic Party in Illinois was in complete disarray by the beginning of the war. This interpretation does not take into account the ongoing activity of local Democratic committees and organizations, nor does it account for the sweeping Democratic electoral successes in 1862.

23. Octavia Roberts Corneau, ed., "A Girl in the Sixties: Excerpts from the Journal of Anna Ridgely [Mrs. James L. Hudson]" (Springfield, IL: Journal Printing, 1929), 20.

24. Richard Merrick, like Elliott Herndon, was later alleged to be a member of the Springfield chapter of the treasonous Order of American Knights. Richard T. Merrick, *The Emancipation Proclamation. State Rights. National Convention. Speech of Richard T. Merrick, before the Young Men's Democratic Invincible Club, Chicago, Dec. 11, 1862.* [n.p.].

25. Orlando B. Ficklin to Unknown, December 7, 1862, Orlando B. Ficklin Papers, ALPL.

26. "The Temporary Suspension of the Negro Hegira," *Illinois State Register,* October 21, 1862. "Working Men of Springfield!" *Illinois State Register,* November 1, 1862; "The Negro Invasion of Illinois," *Illinois State Register,* October 7, 1862.

27. "Slavery in Illinois," reprinted from the *Chicago Post* in the *Illinois State Register,* October 8, 1862.

28. "The Copperhead K.G.C. Organ in This City . . . ," *Illinois State Journal,* March 31, 1863. For the Knights of the Golden Circle and treason allegations, see Frank Klement, *Dark Lanterns: Secret Political Societies, Conspiracies, and Treason Trials in the Civil War* (Baton Rouge: Louisiana State University Press, 1984); for Illinois specifically, see Frank Klement, "Copperhead Secret Societies in Illinois during the Civil War," *Journal of the Illinois State Historical Society* 48 (Summer 1955): 152–80; see also Klement, *Copperheads in the Middle West.* Klement convincingly argued that such organizations, although they did exist in some form, were not as threatening as Republicans claimed, and that rumors of their activities were manufactured to serve Republican interests by scaring the electorate and shaming Democrats into switching parties. For recent revisions of Klement's thesis, see Weber, *Copperheads;* Joan E. Cashin, "Deserters, Civilians, and Draft Resistance in the North," in *The War Was You and Me: Civilians in the American Civil War,* ed. Joan E. Cashin (Princeton: Princeton University Press, 2002), 262–85; and Robert Churchill, "Liberty, Conscription, and a Party Divided: The Sons of Liberty Conspiracy of 1863–1864," *Prologue: The Journal of the National Archives* 30 (Winter 1998): 295–303. See also Mark A. Lause, *A Secret Society History of the Civil War* (Urbana: University of Illinois Press, 2011); and David C. Keehn, *Knights of the Golden Circle: Secret Empire, Southern Secession, Civil War* (Baton Rouge: Louisiana State University Press, 2013), which examines the K.G.C. in more detail and takes them more seriously than any other previous study. For resistance to the draft and desertion in Illinois, see Robert E. Sterling, "Civil War Draft Resistance in Illinois," *Journal of the Illinois State Historical Society* 64 (September 1971): 244–66, and Robert E. Sterling, "Discouragement, Weariness, and War Politics: Desertions from Illinois Regiments during the Civil War," *Illinois Historical Journal* 82 (Winter 1989): 239–62.

29. Adam I. P. Smith, *No Party Now,* argues for a strong antiparty sentiment during the war, as both Democratic and Republican partisans mobilized a language of Union and nation. However, the persistence of Democratic critiques of Republican and Union Party war aims and policies suggests more partisan consistency. Especially in Illinois, divisions between Democrats and Republicans clearly persisted, as did a willingness to define those divisions in sharply partisan terms. See, for example, Michael Vorenberg, *Final Freedom: The Civil War, the Abolition of Slavery, and the Thirteenth Amendment* (Cambridge: Cambridge University Press, 2001), for the argument

that Democratic support of the Thirteenth Amendment by 1865 was a calculated party tactic intended to win back disaffected constituents, not an expression of antiparty patriotism. For the wartime exposés of the K.G.C., see *An Authentic Exposition of the "K.G.C.," "Knights of the Golden Circle": or, A History of Secession from 1834 to 1861 by a Member of the Order* (Indianapolis: C. O. Perrine, 1861); I. Winslow Ayer, *The Great North-Western Conspiracy in All Its Startling Details* (Chicago: Rounds & James, 1865); Benn Pitman, ed., *The Trials for Treason at Indianapolis, Disclosing the Plans for Establishing a North-Western Confederacy. Being the Official Record of the Trials before the Military Commission* (Cincinnati: Moore, Wilstach & Baldwin, 1865); United States Army, Office of the Judge Advocate General, *Report of the Judge Advocate General on "The Order of American Knights" alias "The Sons of Liberty": A Western Conspiracy in Aid of the Southern Rebellion* (Washington, DC: Chronicle Print., 1864); United States Army, Office of the Judge Advocate General, *The Great Conspiracy. Vallandigham Commander. Military Organization. Assassination Tolerated. Collusion with Rebels* (Albany, NY: Weed, Parsons, 1864).

30. John M. Palmer, *Personal Recollections of John M. Palmer: The Story of an Earnest Life* (Cincinnati: R. Clarke, 1901), 281.

31. Corneau, "Girl in the Sixties," 23.

32. Currency Van Nattan to Joseph Van Nattan, March 16, 1863, Van Nattan–Renne Family Papers, ALPL.

33. Cyrus Gifford to Governor Richard Yates, February 10, 1863, Governor's Correspondence, ISA.

34. James Brewster to Governor Richard Yates, March 6, 1863, Yates Family Papers, ALPL.

35. John Stucker to Governor Richard Yates, March 12, 1863, Governor's Correspondence, ISA.

36. W. R. Morrison to Governor Richard Yates, March 31, 1863, Governor's Correspondence, ISA.

37. Elizabeth Howell to Governor Richard Yates, April 1, 1863, Yates Family Papers, ALPL.

38. Cyrus Gifford to Governor Richard Yates, February 10, 1863, Governor's Correspondence, ISA. For perceptions of Illinois as a potential war zone and the mobilization of home guards and home front militias, see Thomas Bahde, "'Our Cause Is a Common One': Home Guards, Union Leagues, and Republican Citizenship in Illinois, 1861–1863," *Civil War History* 56 (March 2010): 66–98.

39. Report of Colonel G. M. Mitchell, April 8, 1864, in *The War of the Rebellion: A Compilation of the Official Records of the Union and Confederate Armies*, ser. 1, vol. 32, pt. I (Washington, DC: Government Printing Office, 1902), 633–34.

40. Report of Lieutenant James Oakes, April 18, 1865, in *The War of the Rebellion*, ser. 1, vol. 32, pt. I, 630–33.

41. John T. Stuart to his wife, April 1, 1864, Transcript of Letters, 1855–1866, Portfolio 1, Stuart-Hay Family Papers, ALPL. For the Charleston Riot, see Robert D. Sampson, "'Pretty Damned Warm Times': The 1864 Charleston Riot and the 'Inalienable Right of Revolution,'" *Illinois Historical Journal* 89 (Summer 1996): 99–116; Ken Anderson, "The Role of Abraham Lincoln and Members of His Family in the

Charleston Riot during the Civil War," *Lincoln Herald* 79 (June 1977): 53–60; and Charles Coleman and Paul Spence, "The Charleston Riot, March 28, 1864," *Journal of the Illinois State Historical Society* 33 (March 1940): 7–56.

42. Report of William Taylor to Colonel J. P. Sanderson, July 12, 1864, in *War of the Rebellion*, ser. 2, vol. 7, 745–46.

43. Edward F. Hoffman to Colonel J. P. Sanderson, June 13, 1864, in *War of the Rebellion*, ser. 1, vol. 32, pt. 1, 309–10.

44. Wheeler Wright to Greenberry Wright and Greenberry Wright to Richard Yates, March 24, 1863, Yates Family Papers, ALPL.

45. "What Illinois Demands," *Illinois State Register*, November 10, 1862.

46. Criminal Docket and General Record Book of US District Court for the Southern District of Illinois, vol. 1–2, NARA-GL. Kellee Blake, "Aiding and Abetting: Disloyalty Prosecutions in the Federal Civil Courts of Southern Illinois, 1861–1866," *Illinois Historical Journal* 87 (Summer 1994): 95–108; Kellee Blake, "Ten Firkins of Butter and Other 'Traitorous' Aid," *Prologue: The Journal of the National Archives* 30 (Winter 1998): 289–93; Scott Owen Reed, "Military Arrests of Lawyers in Illinois during the Civil War," *Western Illinois Regional Studies* 6, no. 2 (1983): 5–22. For arrests of civilians generally, see Neely, *Fate of Liberty*, 54–55, including the sensational case of Dr. Israel Blanchard of Jackson County, Illinois, brother-in-law of Democratic politician and Union General John A. Logan. See also Stephen C. Neff, *Justice in Blue and Gray: A Legal History of the Civil War* (Cambridge, MA: Harvard University Press, 2010), 150–66.

47. Criminal Docket and General Record Book of US District Court for the Southern District of Illinois, vol. 1–2, NARA-GL; "United States Circuit and District Courts," *Illinois State Journal*, June 5, 1866.

48. Stephen A. Douglas to Virgil Hickox, May 10, 1861, reprinted as a broadside, "'The Patriot's Duty,' Douglas' Last Admonition to his Countrymen," ALPL.

49. Thomas Gregg, *History of Hancock County, Illinois* (Chicago: Chas. C. Chapman, 1880), 728–30. For migration to western Illinois, and specifically to the township in which the McClaughrys settled, see Susan Sessions Rugh, *Our Common Country: Family Farming, Culture, and Community in the Nineteenth-Century Midwest* (Bloomington: Indiana University Press, 2001).

50. George Safford to his sister Abbie(?), n.d. (probably September/October 1862), Safford Family Papers, ALPL.

51. For the motivations of Northern soldiers and the refiguring of political opinions, see especially Steven J. Ramold, *Across the Divide: Union Soldiers View the Northern Home Front* (New York: New York University Press, 2013); Chandra Manning, *What This Cruel War Was Over: Soldiers, Slavery, and the Civil War* (New York: Alfred A. Knopf, 2007); Joseph Allan Frank, *With Ballot and Bayonet: The Political Socialization of American Civil War Soldiers* (Athens: University of Georgia Press, 1998); James M. McPherson, *For Cause and Comrades: Why Men Fought in the Civil War* (New York: Oxford University Press, 1997).

52. Counties of Adams (179 free blacks), Brown (19 free blacks), Hancock (20 free blacks), Henderson (2 free blacks), McDonough (8 free blacks), Pike (67 free blacks), Schuyler (14 free blacks), and Warren (43 free blacks), from census figures in Carl G.

Hodges and Helene H. Levene, *Illinois Negro History Makers* (Illinois Emancipation Centennial Commission, 1964), 59–61. For the slave and free black populations of Tennessee, Mississippi, Arkansas, and Louisiana, see Joseph C. G. Kennedy, *Population of the United States in 1860* (Washington, DC: Government Printing Office, 1864).

53. Sidney Little to Sarah P. Durant, December 12, 1862, Sidney O. Little Papers, William L. Clements Library, University of Michigan (hereafter WLCL).

54. For soldiers' views on race from a different part of the country, see David A. Cecere, "Carrying the Home Front to War: Soldiers, Race, and New England Culture during the Civil War," in *Union Soldiers and the Northern Home Front: Wartime Experiences, Postwar Adjustments*, ed. Paul A. Cimbala and Randall M. Miller (New York: Fordham University Press, 2002), 293–323; and for a broader discussion of soldiers' experiences with and opinions on emancipation, see Manning, *What This Cruel War Was Over*; Ira Berlin, "Who Freed the Slaves? Emancipation and Its Meaning," in *Union and Emancipation: Essays on Politics and Race in the Civil War Era*, ed. David W. Blight and Brooks D. Simpson (Kent, OH: Kent State University Press, 1997), 105–21.

55. Samuel Gordon to Permilia Gordon, December 21, 1862, Samuel Gordon Papers, ALPL.

56. Samuel Gordon to Permilia Gordon, May 6, 1863, Samuel Gordon Papers, ALPL.

57. Samuel Gordon to Permilia Gordon, November 16, 1863, Samuel Gordon Papers, ALPL.

58. Samuel Gordon to Unknown, January 24, 1863, Samuel Gordon Papers, ALPL.

59. Samuel Gordon to Permilia Gordon, July 10, 1864, Samuel Gordon Papers, ALPL.

60. Samuel Gordon to Permilia Gordon, September 15, 1864, Samuel Gordon Papers, ALPL.

61. Samuel Gordon to Permilia Gordon, June 24, 1863, Samuel Gordon Papers, ALPL.

62. George Safford to Sister, June 2, 1863, Safford Family Papers, ALPL.

63. Sidney Little to Sarah P. Durant, December 19, 1862, and January 11, 1863, Sidney O. Little Papers, WLCL.

64. Civil War Journal of Thomas Mix, Company B, 118th Regiment, Illinois Volunteers, entry for May 4, 1863, deciphered by Ellen M. Earley, 1992, ALPL.

65. Sidney Little to Sarah P. Durant, April 12, 1863, Sidney O. Little Papers, WLCL.

66. Sidney Little to Elvin H. Little, June 15, 1863, Sidney O. Little Papers, WLCL.

67. George Safford to "My Dear Friend," May 22, 1864, Safford Family Papers, ALPL.

68. Smith, *No Party Now*, 93.

69. Sidney Little to Sarah P. Durant, April 12, 1863, Sidney O. Little Papers, WLCL.

70. William Rand to his father, February 14, 1863, Rand Family Papers, ALPL.

71. William Rand to his father, February 25, 1863, Rand Family Papers, ALPL.

72. William Rand to his father, October 7, 1864, Rand Family Papers, ALPL. Rand's copy of the pamphlet "The Spirit of the Chicago Convention" is also in Box 2, Folder 2, of the Rand Family Papers.

73. William Rand to Parents, November 16, 1864, Rand Family Papers, ALPL. Susan Sessions Rugh, notes that McClaughry's Company B closely split its informal vote with 22 for Lincoln and 20 for McClellan ("'Awful Calamities Now upon Us':

The Civil War in Fountain Green, Illinois," *Journal of the Illinois State Historical Society* 93 [March 2000]: 27).

74. William Rand to Brother Lin, February 28, 1863, Rand Family Papers, ALPL.

75. Dale Baum argues that partisan rifts actually deepened during the war despite the Union Party's efforts to attract disaffected Democrats (*The Civil War Party System: The Case of Massachusetts, 1848–1876* [Chapel Hill: University of North Carolina Press, 1984]). Evidence from Illinois seems to support this view. On the complex attitudes of soldiers on the slavery and race questions, as well as home front loyalties, see Ramold, *Across the Divide;* Chandra Manning, "A 'Vexed Question': White Union Soldiers on Slavery and Race," in *The View from the Ground: Experiences of Civil War Soldiers,* ed. Aaron Sheehan-Dean (Lexington: University Press of Kentucky, 2007) and Manning, *What This Cruel War Was Over;* Etcheson, *Generation at War;* Scott Reynolds Nelson and Carol Sheriff, *A People at War: Civilians and Soldiers in American's Civil War, 1854–1877* (New York: Oxford University Press, 2007); Randall C. Jimerson, *The Private Civil War: Popular Thought during the Sectional Conflict* (Baton Rouge: Louisiana State University Press, 1988); and Reid Mitchell, "The Northern Soldier and His Community," in *Toward a Social History of the American Civil War: Exploratory Essays,* ed. Maris A. Vinovskis (Cambridge: Cambridge University Press, 1990), 78–92.

76. George Safford to Sister Mary, September 25, 1864, Safford Family Papers, ALPL.

77. William Rand to Father, March 31, 1863, Rand Family Papers, ALPL.

78. Sidney Little to Sarah P. Durant, April 12, 1863, Sidney O. Little Papers, WLCL.

79. "Democrats Once More to the Breach!" broadside, dated November 4, 1864, ALPL.

80. Rugh, "'Awful Calamities Now upon Us,'" 9, 28. Rugh also describes the extent of Hancock County's commitment to the Democratic Party, including electoral behavior as well as instances of organized draft resistance.

81. Section 1 of the proposed article unequivocally prevented any further black migration into the state. Hancock County voters approved this section with 82 percent of the vote. The second section, preventing blacks from voting or holding public office, was approved with 98 percent, and the third section empowering the legislature to pass any additional laws necessary to the enforcement of the other two sections passed with 96 percent of the vote. For the Hancock County vote, see Gregg, *History of Hancock County,* 455. See Article XVIII of the proposed constitution in *Journal of the Constitutional Convention of the State of Illinois; convened at Springfield, January 7, 1862* (Springfield: C. H. Lanphier, 1862), 1098.

82. "Negro Immigration vs. The Constitution," *Carthage Republican,* October 2, 1862.

83. "Free Negroes in Illinois," *Carthage Republican,* October 30, 1862.

84. Sworn statements of Metgar Couchman and William Hamilton in *People v. Nelson,* Case File #1877, Adams County Circuit Court, Office of the Clerk of the Circuit Court (hereafter ACCC). The Hancock County files for the Nelson case are housed in Adams County, where the case was appealed in 1863. N. H. Purple, *A Compilation of the Statutes of the State of Illinois, of a General Nature,* pt. 2 (Chicago: Keen and Lee, 1856), 781.

85. Gregg, *History of Hancock County,* 390–91.

86. "Keep It Before the People," *Carthage Republican,* August 9, 1860, and "Negro Equality," *Carthage Republican,* February 7, 1861. *Cuffy* was a derogatory term for blacks derived from a common slave name.

87. Purple, *Statutes of the State of Illinois,* 781. Case file for *People v. Nelson,* Adams County Circuit Court, ACCC. For the conditions of sale, see the public notice reprinted in "Barbarism in Illinois," *Chicago Tribune,* March 3, 1863. The transaction for Prise could not be verified, and a later newspaper report noted that Prise had escaped because his purchaser was not used to keeping slaves. See "Owns a Nigger," *Quincy Whig and Republican,* December 31, 1862; and "Correction," *Quincy Whig and Republican,* January 3, 1863. For Annie Long, see Arthur Charles Cole, *The Era of the Civil War, 1848–1870* (1919; Freeport, NY: Books for Libraries Press, 1971), 335. Cole also cites another case of a black man who returned to Illinois with Doctor L. D. Kellogg of the 17th Illinois Infantry, but gives no further details.

88. Case file for *People v. Nelson,* Adams County Circuit Court, ACCC. The *Quincy Whig and Republican* reported on April 7, 1863, that Senator Orville Browning, a Quincy attorney and friend of Abraham Lincoln recently ousted from his US Senate seat, argued in defense of Nelson in the Adams County circuit court. The case file for the Illinois Supreme Court hearing also states that Orville Browning and his longtime legal partner Nehemiah Bushnell prepared the arguments in the Adams County case. Browning, although he was in Quincy at the time, makes no mention of the case in his diary. Theodore Calvin Pease and James Randall, eds., *The Diary of Orville Hickman Browning,* vol. 1, *1850–1864* (Springfield: Illinois State History Library, 1925), 625–27.

89. In 1862, Bates wrote an opinion at the request of Secretary of the Treasury Salmon P. Chase in which he laid out the case for this particular view of black citizenship. See Edward Bates, *Opinion of Attorney General Bates on Citizenship* (Washington, DC: Government Printing Office, 1863). The details of the case are discussed with documents in James P. McClure, Leigh Johnsen, Kathleen Norman, and Michael Vanderlan, "Circumventing the Dred Scott Decision: Edward Bates, Salmon P. Chase, and the Citizenship of African Americans," *Civil War History* 43 (December 1997): 279–309. The attorneys for Nelson are listed as Grimshaw and Williams, which is probably the partnership of Quincy attorneys Jackson Grimshaw and Archibald Williams, although the partnership seems to have dissolved in 1861 when Williams was appointed a federal judge. Williams also died in 1863, making his appearance unlikely. Their arguments before the Illinois Supreme Court appear in the case file for *Nelson v. The People of the State of Illinois,* Supreme Court of Illinois Records, ISA.

90. *Eells v. The People,* 5 Ill. 498 (1843).

91. *Nance, a girl of color v. Howard,* 1 Ill. 242 (1828); *Phoebe, a girl of color v. Jay,* 1 Ill. 268 (1828). As late as 1843, *Phoebe* was cited as precedent for upholding the state indenture laws in *Sarah, alias Sarah Borders, a woman of color v. Andrew Borders,* 5 Ill. 341 (1843). For summaries and commentary on the cases, see Helen T. Catterall, ed., *Judicial Cases concerning American Slavery and the Negro,* vol. 5 (Washington, DC.: Carnegie Institution, 1937). See also Paul Finkelman, "Evading the Ordinance: The Persistence of Bondage in Indiana and Illinois," *Journal of the Early Republic* 9 (Spring 1989): 21–51; Finkelman, "Slavery, the 'More Perfect Union,' and the Prairie

State," *Illinois Historical Journal* 80 (Winter 1987): 248–69; and Newton N. Newborn, "Judicial Decision Making and the End of Slavery in Illinois," *Journal of the Illinois State Historical Society* 98 (March 2005): 7–33.

92. *Matthew Chambers v. The People of the State of Illinois*, 5 Ill. 351 (1843).
93. *Julius A. Willard v. The People of the State of Illinois*, 5 Ill. 461 (1843).
94. Ibid.
95. *Eells v. The People*, 5 Ill. 498 (1843).
96. *Thornton's Case*, 11 Ill. 332 (1849).
97. *Eells v. The People*, 5 Ill. 498 (1843), and *Moore, Executor of Eells v. The People*, 55 US 13 (1853).
98. *Nelson (a mulatto) v. The People of the State of Illinois*, 33 Ill. 390 (1864).

Chapter Three: Black Springfield

Epigraph: *Proceedings of the Illinois State Convention of Colored Men, Assembled at Galesburg, October 16th, 17th, and 18th* (Chicago: Church, Goodman and Donnelley, 1867), 8–9.

1. Palmer, *Personal Recollections*, 327–30. For Palmer's activism in Kentucky, see Bigham, *On Jordan's Banks*, 67–68.

2. On penitentiary intake forms, Gus Reed claimed that both of his parents were alive in Georgia, but he never named them. Joliet Penitentiary Prison Mittimus File for Gus Reed, ISA.

3. For William Florville, see Richard E. Hart, "Springfield's African Americans as a Part of the Lincoln Community," *Journal of the Abraham Lincoln Association* 20 (Winter 1999): 35–54; Richard E. Hart, "Honest Abe and the African Americans," *Illinois Times*, February 12–18, 1998, 6–11; Lloyd Ostendorf, "Faces Lincoln Knew . . . Photographs from the Past: The Story of William Florville; Mr. Lincoln's Barber," *Lincoln Herald* 79 (Spring 1977): 29–32; John E. Washington, *They Knew Lincoln* (New York: E. P. Dutton, 1942), 183–202; and *History of Sangamon County*, 736–37. For blacks in Lincoln's Springfield, see Winkle, *Young Eagle*; and David Donald, *Lincoln* (London: Jonathan Cape, 1995). Older studies virtually ignore blacks in antebellum Springfield, with the occasional exception of William Florville. See Paul M. Angle, *"Here I Have Lived": A History of Lincoln's Springfield* (New Brunswick, NJ: Rutgers University Press, 1935); and Louis O. Renne, *Lincoln and the Land of the Sangamon* (Boston: Chapman and Grimes, 1945).

4. James Oliver Horton and Lois E. Horton, *In Hope of Liberty: Culture, Community, and Protest among Northern Free Blacks, 1700–1860* (New York: Oxford University Press, 1997), xi. See also James Oliver Horton, *Free People of Color: Inside the African American Community* (Washington, DC: Smithsonian Institution Press, 1993).

5. Manuscript Census, 1850 and 1860. The size of the black population is derived from the author's count of the manuscript census. Kennedy, *Population of the United States in 1860*, 99, lists only 203 "free colored" citizens in Springfield. All calculations in this section are based on the author's count.

6. For boarding in antebellum black communities, see Horton and Horton, *In Hope of Liberty*, 96–98.

7. Corneau, "A Girl in the Sixties," 18. "Becky" was Rebecca Wood, a forty-eight-year-old, Maryland-born mulatto, according to the 1860 manuscript federal census. Rebecca Smith and Charlotte Sims also appear in the 1860 manuscript federal census. For free black women in the antebellum period, see Erica Armstrong Dunbar, *A Fragile Freedom: African American Women and Emancipation in the Antebellum City* (New Haven: Yale University Press, 2008).

8. Manuscript Census for 1860, and Kennedy, *Statistics of the United States in 1860*, 299. For the Vance family, see Lloyd Ostendorf and Walter Oleksy, eds., *Lincoln's Unknown Private Life: An Oral History by His Black Housekeeper Mariah Vance*, 1850–1860 (Mamaroneck, NY: Hastings House, 1995), 146–47. Mariah Vance's recollections, as recorded by Adah Sutton between 1900 and 1904, are problematic on the subject of the Lincoln family, but there is no reason to question Vance's brief statements about her own life. For a critique of Vance's published recollections, see James O. Hall, "Review Essay: *Lincoln's Unknown Private Life*," *Journal of the Abraham Lincoln Association* 19 (Winter 1998): 73–95.

9. Quoted in Richard Hart, "The Spirit of Springfield's Early African-Americans," *Program Papers of the Sangamon County Historical Society* (presented May 21, 2002), 12.

10. Ibid., 13–14.

11. Springfield Public Schools Board of Education Minutes, December 4, 1854, UIS-IRAD. Racial distinctions in such laws were common, especially in a Black Laws state like Illinois. That same year, the new ordinance providing for a municipal police force specified that "The Mayor, Marshal, and every member of the police department are hereby severally authorized to call upon any or all white male inhabitants of the city over the age of eighteen years, to arrest in quelling any riotous or disorderly conduct or to aid in arresting or safe keeping any person accused of a crime or breach of law or ordinance." See Springfield City Council Minutes, May 22, 1854, UIS-IRAD. Adding "white" in both cases was part of an accepted legalistic formula and social code that had existed in America since the colonial period. For a discussion of racial distinctions in such laws, see Horton and Horton, *In Hope of Liberty*.

12. Springfield Public Schools Board of Education Minutes, December 21, 1858, UIS-IRAD.

13. Hart, "Spirit of Springfield's Early African-Americans," 12–15. Springfield Public Schools Board of Education Minutes, UIS-IRAD. For the multiple roles of the antebellum black church, see Horton and Horton, *In Hope of Liberty*.

14. J. R. Kerr-Ritchie, *Rites of August First: Emancipation Day in the Black Atlantic World* (Baton Rouge: Louisiana State University Press, 2007), 8–9.

15. "Celebration," *Illinois State Democrat*, August 4, 1858. See also Hart, "Spirit of Springfield's Early African-Americans."

16. J. H. Magee, *The Night of Affliction and Morning of Recovery* (Cincinnati: Author, 1873), 16–42.

17. *Proceedings of the State Convention of Colored Citizens of the State of Illinois, Held in the City of Alton, November 13, 14, and 15th, 1856* (Chicago: Hays and Thompson, 1856).

18. William H. Herndon to Unknown, February 11, 1860, William H. Herndon Collection, ALPL.

19. For the Underground Railroad in Springfield, see Winkle, *Young Eagle,* 263–64; and in Illinois, see Larry Gara, "The Underground Railroad in Illinois," *Journal of the Illinois State Historical Society* 56 (Autumn 1963): 508–28.

20. Roster of the 29th US Colored Infantry from Illinois State Archives online Illinois Civil War Veterans Database, www.cyberdriveillinois.com/GenealogyMWeb/civilwar.html (accessed January 4, 2006). See also *History of Sangamon County,* 415. For the history of the 29th US Colored Infantry, see Edward A. Miller Jr., *The Black Civil War Soldiers of Illinois: The Story of the Twenty-ninth US Colored Infantry* (Columbia: University of South Carolina Press, 1998).

21. *History of Sangamon County,* 736.

22. "The Colored Regiment," *Illinois State Register,* January 6, 1864.

23. Johnson, "Out of Egypt," 229.

24. For migration figures, see Johnson, "Out of Egypt." For the view that postemancipation black migration was relatively insignificant, see William J. Collins, "When the Tide Turned: Immigration and the Delay of the Great Black Migration," *Journal of Economic History* 57 (September 1997): 607–32; Richard K. Vedder, Lowell Galloway, Philip E. Graves, and Robert L. Sexton, "Demonstrating Their Freedom: The Post-Emancipation Migration of Black Americans," *Research in Economic History* 10 (1986): 213–39; Daniel M. Johnson and Rex R. Campbell, *Black Migration in America: A Social Demographic History* (Durham, NC: Duke University Press, 1981); William Cohen, *At Freedom's Edge: Black Mobility and the Southern White Quest for Racial Control* (Baton Rouge: Louisiana State University Press, 1991). For postemancipation exploitation of black workers, see especially Gerald David Jaynes, *Branches without Roots: Genesis of the Black Working Class in the American South, 1862–1882* (New York: Oxford University Press, 1986); Frank McGlynn and Seymour Drescher, eds., *The Meaning of Freedom: Economics, Politics, and Culture after Slavery* (Pittsburgh: University of Pittsburgh Press, 1992); and Eric Foner, *Nothing But Freedom: Emancipation and Its Legacy* (Baton Rouge: Louisiana State University Press, 1983).

25. See Blocker, *Little More Freedom,* for this "age of the village," as Blocker calls it, between rural life in the South and urban life in the North. Blocker states that many migrants did not settle in prewar centers of black population, but rather "avoided existing black clusters and instead selected communities where few or no African American migrants had lived before" (32). Springfield would seem to be an exception, although the broader point that "Gilded Age migrants to the Lower Midwest dispersed themselves across a rapidly growing urban system" (32) is an important observation.

26. For blacks in Evansville and Muncie, Indiana, see Darrel E. Bigham, *We Only Ask a Fair Trial: A History of the Black Community of Evansville, Indiana* (Bloomington: Indiana University Press, 1987); Bigham, "Work, Residence, and the Emergence of the Black Ghetto in Evansville, Indiana"; and Blocker, "Black Migration to Muncie, 1860–1930." See also Thornbrough, *Negro in Indiana.*

27. For Pulaski County, see Shirley Carlson, "Black Migration to Pulaski County, Illinois: 1860–1900," *Illinois Historical Journal* 80 (Spring 1987): 37–46.

28. Schwalm, "'Overrun with Free Negroes,'" 153.

29. Illinois State Census for 1865, microfilm reel #30–2184, ISA. See also "The Results of the Recent Census," *Illinois State Register*, September 11, 1865, which gives the following breakdown of the black population by ward: First Ward: 106 Males, 102 Females; Second Ward: 90 Males, 79 Females; Third Ward: 9 Males, 11 Females; Fourth Ward: 41 Males, 48 Females. Total: 486.

30. The statistical abstract of the 1870 federal census lists 808 colored residents of Springfield, but the author's count of the manuscript census sheets revealed only 757 black and mulatto residents. All calculations in this section are based on the number derived from author's count. See Francis A. Walker, *The Statistics of the Population of the United States* (Washington, DC: Government Printing Office, 1872), 119.

31. See *History of Sangamon County*, 736–44 for all individuals named in this paragraph.

32. Manuscript Census, 1870.

33. Ibid.

34. Ibid.

35. Last Will and Testament of William Florville, dated April 3 and April 18, 1868, William Florville Papers, ALPL.

36. There is some discrepancy about the date of Mahlon Chavious's death. One source places it in 1879; others indicate that Alseen had already remarried by 1863. For the Florville family, see *History of Sangamon County*, 736–37; and John Carroll Power, *History of the Early Settlers of Sangamon County*, Illinois (Springfield, IL: Edwin A. Wilson, 1876), 303. For Clark Duncan, see *History of Sangamon County*, 741–42 and *Centennial City and Township Directory* (Springfield, IL: Illinois Journal, 1876), 235.

37. Palmer, *Personal Recollections*, 327–30.

38. Manuscript Census, 1870 and 1880.

39. For miners and rolling mill operators, see *Centennial City Directory* (1876) for Springfield, and a brief piece titled "Negro Miners," *Illinois State Register*, December 31, 1872. We know less about the wealth of the community in 1870 than we do a decade earlier. Only 4 percent (twenty-eight individuals) of the black residents reported any real or personal wealth to the census taker in 1870. Discounting the highest value (farmer Thomas Wright's combined $11,000 estate) and lowest value (teamster John Oglesby's modest $800), the average family reporting any real or personal wealth fell between $1,000 and $3,000, with the great majority invested in real estate. These numbers may be misleading, however, as so few black Springfielders reported any wealth at all.

40. Springfield Public Schools Board of Education Minutes, December 9, 1862, UIS-IRAD.

41. *Annual Report of the Superintendent of Public Schools of Springfield, Illinois* (Springfield: Johnson and Bradford, 1863), 53.

42. *Annual Report of the Superintendent of Public Schools of Springfield, Illinois* (Springfield: Johnson and Bradford, 1866). Springfield Public Schools Board of Education Minutes, October 27, 1866 and June 29, August 31, 1867, UIS-IRAD.

43. *Annual Report of the Superintendent of Public Schools of Springfield, Illinois* (Springfield: Johnson and Bradford, 1867), 18–19.

44. "Our Public Schools," *Illinois State Register*, June 20, 1870; "The City Schools," *Illinois State Register*, December 31, 1870; "1871. The State Register's Annual Review," *Illinois State Register*, December 30, 1871.

45. Springfield Public Schools Board of Education Minutes, July 1 and August 5, 1872, UIS-IRAD.

46. See Springfield Public Schools Board of Education Minutes, UIS-IRAD, for the day-to-day involvement of the board in the affairs of the Colored School.

47. "Convention of Colored Citizens," *Illinois State Register*, January 14, 1865. Mitch Kachun, *Festivals of Freedom: Memory and Meaning in African American Emancipation Celebrations, 1808–1915* (Amherst: University of Massachusetts Press, 2003). See also William H. Wiggins, Jr., *O Freedom!: Afro-American Emancipation Celebrations* (Knoxville: University of Tennessee Press, 1987); and for American traditions of festive culture and politics, see David Waldstreicher, *In the Midst of Perpetual Fetes: The Making of American Nationalism, 1776–1820* (Chapel Hill: University of North Carolina Press, 1997).

48. "Reception and Dinner to the 29th US Colored Regiment, Speeches, Etc.," *Illinois State Journal*, November 23, 1865.

49. "Fred. Douglass. The Assassination and Its Consequences," *Illinois State Journal*, April 4, 1866. There is no mention in the newspaper accounts of the lectures whether any of Springfield's more distinguished black residents, such as William Florville, attended either lecture.

50. "Reconstruction. A Lecture by Fred. Douglass," *Illinois State Journal*, April 5, 1866.

51. Before the event, the *Illinois State Journal* reported that Douglass would attend and speak, but a later story on the festivities did not mention his attendance or any speech by him. "Emancipation Day," *Illinois State Journal*, September 22 and 23, 1868. Douglass visited again in 1872 to deliver a lecture on Santo Domingo, which the *Journal* described only as "highly interesting." See *Illinois State Journal*, January 19, 1872. For the significance of black bands, see Kerr-Ritchie, *Rites of August First*, 102.

52. "Glad Tidings," *Illinois State Journal*, March 31, 1870.

53. "Meeting of the Colored Citizens," *Illinois State Register*, April 2, 1870, and "Meeting of the Colored Citizens," *Illinois State Journal*, April 4, 1870. Spencer and Cyrus Donnegan, both active leaders in the community, were also both from Kentucky, although we do not know if they were related.

54. For postbellum black political culture, see Julie Saville, "Rites and Power: Reflections on Slavery, Freedom and Political Ritual," *Slavery and Abolition* 20 (April 1999): 81–102, and Julie Saville, *The Work of Reconstruction: From Slave to Wage Laborer in South Carolina, 1860–1870* (Cambridge: Cambridge University Press, 1994). For local festive culture as community and identity-consciousness building, see Kathleen Neils Conzen, "Ethnicity as Festive Culture: Nineteenth-Century German America on Parade," in Werner Sollors, ed. *The Invention of Ethnicity*, ed. Werner Sollors (New York: Oxford University Press, 1989): 44–76.

55. "The Ratification of the Fifteenth Amendment," *Illinois State Register*, April 13, 1870.

56. "The Fifteenth Amendment," *Illinois State Register*, March 30 and 31, 1871; and "Anniversary Day," *Illinois State Journal*, March 31, 1871. For another example of the

liberty wagon, see "The XVth Amendment," *Cairo Bulletin*, April 12, 1870. See also Kachun, *Festivals of Freedom*, 131–32.

57. "The Fifteenth Amendment," *Illinois State Register*, March 31, 1871. See also "The Fifteenth Amendment," *Illinois State Register*, March 30, 1871.

58. Houston could not be located in the federal census or city directories, but was listed among the delegates in the published proceedings of the 1864 convention. See Howard Holman Bell, *Minutes of the Proceedings of the National Negro Conventions, 1830–1864* (New York: Arno Press, 1969).

59. *Proceedings of the Illinois State Convention of Colored Men, Assembled at Galesburg, October 16th, 17th, and 18th* (Chicago: Church, Goodman and Donnelley, 1867).

60. "Colored Convention," *Illinois State Register*, December 3, 1873.

61. Christian G. Samito, *Becoming American under Fire: Irish Americans, African Americans, and the Politics of Citizenship during the Civil War Era* (Ithaca, NY: Cornell University Press, 2009), 220.

62. "The Springfield Niggers . . . ," *Illinois State Register*, August 8, 1870. For the significance of black fraternal organizations especially, see Theda Skocpol, Ariane Liazos, and Marshall Ganz, *What a Mighty Power We Can Be: African American Fraternal Groups and the Struggle for Racial Equality* (Princeton: Princeton University Press, 2008).

63. Saville, *Work of Reconstruction*, 170–77.

64. For postwar militia companies, including black companies, as the foundations of the early Illinois National Guard, and as civic organizations, see Eleanor Hannah, *Manhood, Citizenship, and the National Guard: Illinois, 1870–1917* (Columbus: Ohio State University Press, 2007).

65. "West India, Celebration of Emancipation," *Illinois State Register*, August 1, 1871. In addition to the Hannibal Zouaves, the *Chicago Tribune* reported on July 24, 1869, that the governor had furnished arms and accoutrements to a black company from Chicago commanded by Captain E. C. Freeman, identified as "Company C of the National Guard." Eleanor Hannah misidentifies this company as being from Springfield, but gives much other good information on the early formation of black militias in Illinois in *Manhood, Citizenship, and the National Guard*, 35–36.

66. "It Seems There Are Two Colored Militia Companies . . . ," *Illinois State Register*, September 23, 1871.

67. "Gone to the Front," *Illinois State Register*, October 11, 1871.

68. "Fifteenth Amendment," *Illinois State Journal*, April 2, 1872.

69. "The Second Day," *Illinois State Journal*, October 16, 1874.

70. Blocker, *Little More Freedom*, 30.

71. Andrew R. L. Cayton and Peter S. Onuf, *The Midwest and the Nation: Rethinking the History of an American Region* (Bloomington: Indiana University Press, 1990), 97.

Chapter Four: A White Man's Country

Epigraph: "Democrats of Sangamon County!" *Illinois State Register*, April 3, 1864.

1. *Popular Rally at Springfield, September 11th, 1865. Endorsement of President Johnson's Reconstruction Policy. Speeches of Gen. John A. M'Clernand, Messrs. Geo W. Shutt, and Wm. M. Springer* (Springfield: State Register Caloric Print, 1865), 8–9.

2. Silbey, *Respectable Minority,* 28–29.

3. Lawrence Grossman, *The Democratic Party and the Negro: Northern and National Politics, 1868–92* (Urbana: University of Illinois Press, 1976), 3, 101–2.

4. Using Maryland as an example, Jean Baker has referred to this consistent partisanship from antebellum to postbellum as "the politics of continuity," a term that also aptly describes Illinois politics between the late 1850s and 1870s. Jean Baker, *The Politics of Continuity: Maryland Political Parties from 1858 to 1870* (Baltimore: Johns Hopkins University Press, 1973). For a broader look at partisan continuity through the Civil War era, see Joel Silbey, *The American Political Nation, 1838–1893* (Stanford: Stanford University Press, 1991); and Edward L. Gambill, *Conservative Ordeal: Northern Democrats and Reconstruction, 1865–1869* (Ames: Iowa State University Press, 1981).

5. For the political impact of race in popular culture, see especially Neely, *Boundaries of American Political Culture,* esp. chap. 4, "Minstrelsy, Race, and the Boundaries of American Political Culture."

6. Paul D. Escott has recently noted the strong organization and broad base of the Democratic Party in 1864, and Paul M. Angle observed similarly of Illinois and of Springfield specifically that the majority of the Democratic rank and file remained extraordinarily loyal to the party during the Civil War. See Paul D. Escott, *"What Shall We Do with the Negro?": Lincoln, White Racism, and Civil War America* (Charlottesville: University of Virginia Press, 2009), 122; and Paul M. Angle, *"Here I Have Lived": A History of Lincoln's Springfield,* new ed. (Chicago: Abraham Lincoln Book Shop, 1971), 272–74.

7. Henry Bryant to David E. Head, September 25, 1863, Davidson-Springer Family Papers, ALPL.

8. S. Corning Judd to "Such of the Hancock Democracy as it may concern," September 28, 1863, Davidson-Springer Family Papers, ALPL.

9. Samuel Gordon to Permilia Gordon, January 10 and 13, 1863, Samuel Gordon Papers, ALPL. This letter, although written before Davidson became editor, likely continued to express the opinion of many former Democrats in the 118th Illinois throughout the war. For political divisions in Hancock County, see Rugh, "Awful Calamities Now upon Us."

10. McClaughry, in *Intimate Memories of Lincoln,* 57–58.

11. "Major McClaughry. Abolition Candidate for Circuit Clerk," *Carthage Republican,* November 3, 1864.

12. "Stop That Falsehood!" *Carthage Republican,* September 7, 1865; "Keep It Before the People!" "Will He Answer?" and "A Returned Soldier Catechises Major McClaughry," *Carthage Republican,* October 5, 1865.

13. "The Funeral of Private Thomas E. Mix" and "The 118th Illinois Mounted Infantry," *Carthage Republican,* October 19, 1865.

14. "Major McClaughry on Negro Suffrage," *Carthage Republican,* October 26, 1865.

15. "Reply of 'A Returned Soldier,'" *Carthage Republican,* October 26, 1865.

16. "An Awful Record," *Carthage Republican,* November 2, 1865.

17. "The Result—Causes," *Carthage Republican,* November 16, 1865.

18. For Sangamon County election results, see *History of Sangamon County,* 272–77.

19. "Democratic County Convention," *Illinois State Register,* October 12, 1865.

20. For Elliott Herndon's activities, see "Democratic Club," *Illinois State Register,* January 15, 1864; "Democracy of Springfield," *Illinois State Register,* August 22, 1868. For the activities of groups in the Second Ward and the ward's reputation, see "Loyal Boys in Blue," *Illinois State Journal,* September 23, 1868; "Dastardly Outrage," *Illinois State Journal,* September 24, 1868; "Second Ward," *Illinois State Register,* April 11, 1870.

21. George M. Fredrickson, *The Black Image in the White Mind: The Debate on Afro-American Character and Destiny, 1817–1914* (New York: Harper and Row, 1971), 174. See especially J. H. Van Evrie, *Negroes and Negro "Slavery": The First an Inferior Race: The Latter Its Normal Condition,* 3rd ed. (New York: Van Evrie, Horton, 1863), reissued in 1868 as *White Supremacy and Negro Subordination;* and Josiah Nott and George Gliddon, *Types of Mankind; or, Ethnological Researches,* 7th ed. (Philadelphia: Lippincott, Grambo, 1855). For the long-term impact of this retrenchment of mainstream white supremacist assumptions on attitudes toward race and justice, see Kevin Boyle, *Arc of Justice: A Saga of Race, Civil Rights, and Murder in the Jazz Age* (New York: Henry Holt, 2004).

22. Abraham Lincoln in the fourth debate with Stephen Douglas, Charleston, Illinois, September 18, 1858, quoted in *Collected Works of Abraham Lincoln,* ed. Roy Basler, vol. 3 (New Brunswick, NJ: Rutgers University Press, 1953), 145–46.

23. Sidney George Fisher, *The Laws of Race, as Connected with Slavery* (Philadelphia: Willis P. Hazard, 1860), 10, 11, 14.

24. Reverend J. M. Sturtevant, "The Destiny of the African Race in the United States," *Continental Monthly,* 3 (May 1863): 600–610.

25. "The Fate of Contraband," *Illinois State Register,* January 20, 1864.

26. "A Skirmish," *Illinois State Register,* November 3, 1865.

27. "A Soldier's Idea of the Abolitionists," *Illinois State Register,* November 4, 1865.

28. Text of bill and Lyman Trumbull quoted in Eric Foner, *Reconstruction: America's Unfinished Revolution, 1863–1877* (New York: Harper and Row, 1988), 243. For the Civil Rights Act, see George Rutherglen, *Civil Rights in the Shadow of Slavery: The Constitution, Common Law, and the Civil Rights Act of 1866* (New York: Oxford University Press, 2013).

29. "The Civil Rights Bill," *Illinois State Register,* April 3, 1866.

30. "A Motley Crowd," *Illinois State Register,* July 16, 1866.

31. For visiting minstrel shows, see, for example, the advertisement for "Harry Robinson's Minstrels," *Illinois State Register,* December 27, 1872.

32. Advertisement for Macallister, *Illinois State Register,* February 21, 1871.

33. "The Civil Rights Bill," *Illinois State Register,* February 27, 1871.

34. "Macallister Again," *Illinois State Register,* February 28, 1871.

35. Robert McCaul, *The Black Struggle for Public Schooling in Nineteenth-Century Illinois* (Carbondale: Southern Illinois University Press, 1987), provides an excellent overview of school segregation and desegregation in the state. See also Davison M. Douglas, *Jim Crow Moves North: The Battle over Northern School Segregation, 1865–1954* (New York: Cambridge University Press, 2005), and Davis, *"We Will Be Satisfied With Nothing Less."*

36. *Sixth Biennial Report of the Superintendent of Public Instruction of the State of Illinois, 1865–1866*, ALPL.

37. *Seventh Biennial Report of the Superintendent of Public Instruction of the State of Illinois, 1867–1868*, ALPL.

38. *Eighth Biennial Report of the Superintendent of Public Instruction for the State of Illinois, 1869–1870*, ALPL.

39. *Tenth Biennial Report of the Superintendent of Public Instruction of the State of Illinois, 1873–1874*, ALPL.

40. Springfield Public Schools Board of Education Minutes, October 7, 1873, UIS-IRAD. Gertrude Wright completed a regular four-year course of study and graduated with the class of 1877. See *History of Sangamon County*, 595.

41. "The School Question," *Illinois State Register*, April 21, 1870.

42. "Negro Children in the Ward Schools," *Illinois State Register*, October 11, 1870.

43. "The School Question," *Illinois State Register*, September 7, 1870.

44. "The City Election," *Illinois State Register*, April 3, 1872.

45. "Negroes in the Public Schools," *Illinois State Register*, March 30, 1872.

46. "Our City Schools," *Illinois State Journal*, October 9, 1873.

47. "The School Board Outrage," *Illinois State Register*, October 9, 1873.

48. "A Sensible Colored Man," *Illinois State Register*, October 13, 1873.

49. "Separate Schools for the Colored," *Illinois State Register*, October 14, 1873.

50. "The Register Has Already . . . ," *Illinois State Register*, October 16, 1873.

51. Springfield Public Schools Board of Education Minutes, November 1, 1873, UIS-IRAD.

52. "School Board Outrage!" *Illinois State Register*, November 3, 1873, and "The *Journal* of To-day . . . ," *Illinois State Register*, November 6, 1873. At the November school board meeting, one of the teachers from the Colored School was reassigned to the ward schools, and although it remained open with one teacher, the board voted that the Colored School should be discontinued as soon as practicable and the property rented or otherwise disposed of. Springfield Public Schools Board of Education Minutes, UIS-IRAD.

53. "The Suffrage System," *Illinois State Register*, February 18, 1870.

54. "While Woman Suffrage . . . ," *Illinois State Register*, March 11, 1870.

55. "The African at the Helm of State," *Illinois State Register*, April 16, 1870; "A White Man's Government," *Illinois State Register*, January 6, 1870.

56. "The African at the Helm of State," *Illinois State Register*, April 16, 1870. For debates within the Republican Party regarding the Fifteenth Amendment and the subsequent efforts to enforce it, see Xi Wang, *The Trial of Democracy: Black Suffrage and Northern Republicans, 1860–1910* (Athens: University of Georgia Press, 1997).

57. "Rowdyism," *Illinois State Register*, December 2, 1865.

58. "The Suffrage System," *Illinois State Register*, February 18, 1870. For the development during this era of a broad consensus about popular enforcement of community norms through violence, see Christopher Waldrep, *The Many Faces of Judge Lynch: Extralegal Violence and Punishment in America* (New York: Palgrave Macmillan, 2002), especially chapter 5.

59. "Patriotic Disgust," *Illinois State Register*, April 8, 1870.

60. "The Township Election," *Illinois State Register*, April 6, 1870. The Republican *Illinois State Journal* pointed out that the front doors of the polling place were not opened on time, and that Democratic pollsters were secretly allowing only whites to enter through the back door to cast votes. When the deception was uncovered, the front doors were forced open, and the black voters admitted. See *Illinois State Journal*, April 6, 1870.

61. "The Township Election," *Illinois State Register*, April 6, 1870. Notice of the ratification of the 15th Amendment had actually been received the previous week, a fact well known to the editors of the *Register*.

62. "The Election Yesterday," and "The Great Result of April 12th," *Illinois State Register*, April 13, 1870.

63. "Patriotic Disgust," *Illinois State Register*, April 8, 1870.

64. "Over an Hundred Negroes . . . ," and "A Lot of Scalawags . . . ," *Illinois State Register*, April 10, 1872.

65. "The City Election," *Illinois State Register*, April 10, 1872.

66. "The Baltimore Nomination," *Illinois State Register*, July 11, 1872.

67. "The Negroes and the 'Balance of Power,'" *Illinois State Register*, April 10, 1872.

68. "For Greeley and Brown," *Illinois State Register*, August 2, 1872.

69. "Liberalism, The Meeting Last Night," *Illinois State Register*, August 15, 1872.

70. "The Negroes and the Journal," *Illinois State Register*, August 16, 1872.

71. "The Negro Trouble Again," *Illinois State Register*, August 17, 1872.

72. "Riot at Clinton," *Illinois State Register*, August 16, 1872.

73. "The Conduct of the Negroes," *Illinois State Register*, October 14, 1872.

74. Ibid.

75. "The Wigwam on Saturday Night," *Illinois State Register*, October 14, 1872.

76. "Tanners on the Rampage, the Negroes Take the Town," *Illinois State Register*, October 22, 1872.

77. "The Tanners Again," *Illinois State Register*, October 23, 1872.

78. "The Radical Meeting," *Illinois State Register*, October 28, 1872.

79. "The Negro Tanners of Chicago . . . ," *Illinois State Register*, November 4, 1872.

80. "The Free Ballot," *Illinois State Register*, November 5, 1872.

81. "The Tanners' Festival," *Illinois State Register*, November 11, 1872.

82. In 1876, a white voter in the Second Ward was killed by a blow to the head from a brick supposedly thrown by "a negro ruffian," part of a gang of blacks reportedly trying to take over the polls, but the witnesses' testimony was so confused that no charges were ever brought against the alleged rioters. See *Illinois State Register*, November 8, 10, 15, 27, 1876.

83. "The Election," *Illinois State Register*, April 6, 1870.

84. "About a Harness," *Illinois State Register*, September 18, 1874; "Circuit Court," *Illinois State Register*, October 18, 1876; and "Circuit Court," *Illinois State Register*, October 20, 1876.

85. "Resisted an Officer," *Illinois State Register*, October 23, 1876; and "Isaac Parks, Capt.," *Illinois State Register*, October 25, 1876.

86. "Arrested for Larceny," *Illinois State Register*, October 13, 1876.

Chapter Five: The Underworld

Epigraph: Hinton Rowan Helper, *The Negroes in Negroland; The Negroes in America; and Negroes Generally* (New York: G. W. Carlton, 1868), ix.

1. "Nabbed at Last," *Illinois State Journal,* July 22, 1874.
2. For the dedication of Lincoln's tomb, see the *Illinois State Register* and *Illinois State Journal,* October 15–16, 1874. Gus Reed had been in the county jail since July. He pleaded guilty to larceny on October 16, and was sentenced to Joliet on October 20. Entries for May 3–4, 1865, Philemon Stout Diaries, ALPL.
3. Blocker, *Little More Freedom,* 91.
4. For the first black convict from Sangamon County, see entry for prisoner #2142, W. W. Baugh, alias "Coon Ball," November 16, 1863, Joliet Penitentiary Register of Prisoners, ISA.
5. "Robbery," *Illinois State Register,* September 24, 1874.
6. "The Negro Riot," *Illinois State Register,* March 11, 1872.
7. "Another Descent of the Freedmen," *Illinois State Register,* March 5, 1866.
8. Sangamon County Circuit Court Judge's Docket and Record for 1866, UIS-IRAD; *Illinois State Register,* May 8, May 10, May 11, May 31, September 2, 1866.
9. "Police Courts," *Illinois State Register,* April 23, 1867, and May 18, 1867.
10. Sangamon County Circuit Court Dockets, UIS-IRAD; Joliet Penitentiary Register of Prisoners, ISA; 1870 Manuscript Census.
11. Roger Lane, *Roots of Violence in Black Philadelphia, 1860–1900* (Cambridge, MA: Harvard University Press, 1986), 95. For postemancipation black property offenses and moral economy, see also Gilles Vandal, "Property Offenses, Social Tension and Racial Antagonism in Post–Civil War Rural Louisiana," *Journal of Social History* 31 (Fall 1997): 127–53.
12. "A 'Dark' Transaction," *Illinois State Journal,* April 27, 1869.
13. Sangamon County Circuit Court Condensed Dockets, UIS-IRAD. Joliet Penitentiary Register of Prisoners, ISA.
14. "Circuit Court," *Illinois State Register,* March 6 and 13, 1874; "A Desperado Caught," *Illinois State Register,* July 21, 1874.
15. "A Desperado Caught," *Illinois State Register,* July 21, 1874; "Nabbed at Last," *Illinois State Journal,* July 22, 1874; "The State Capital," *The Inter-Ocean,* July 22, 1874. See also "Arrest of a Noted Desperado," *Jacksonville Journal,* July 23, 1874, which noted that Gus also went by the alias "Jo Boleen," the only such reference.
16. "Circuit Court," *Illinois State Journal,* October 17, 1874; "The Courts," *Illinois State Journal,* October 21, 1874; "Crime and Criminals," *The Inter-Ocean,* June 27, 1877; "A Desperado Arrested," *Illinois State Register,* June 27, 1877. Joliet Penitentiary Register of Prisoners, ISA.
17. Entry for Augustus Reed, June 27, 1877, Christian County Jail Register of Prisoners, UIS-IRAD. No further records from the trial have survived.
18. Justice of the Peace Docket Book for Springfield, 1877–1878, UIS-IRAD; "Police Items," *Illinois State Register,* January 25, 1878.
19. "Burglaries," *Illinois State Register,* November 14, 1877. The story initially misidentified Gus as "Jacob Reed," but this was corrected in later stories.

20. "Criminal Notes," *Illinois State Register*, December 4, 1877.

21. "Burglaries," *Illinois State Register*, November 14, 1877; "Police Points," *Illinois State Register*, November 22, 1877; "Criminal Notes," *Illinois State Register*, December 4, 1877, and "A Search," *Illinois State Register*, December 5, 1877.

22. For the reference to the robbery at Elliott Herndon's house, see "Circuit Court," *Illinois State Register*, March 22, 1878.

23. "The Courts," *Illinois State Register*, February 26, 1878; "Circuit Court," *Illinois State Register*, March 22, 1878; "Circuit Court," *Illinois State Journal*, March 22, 1878; "Circuit Court," *Illinois State Register*, March 24, 1878; "Off for Joliet," *Illinois State Journal*, March 27, 1878; "Nabbed at Last," *Illinois State Register*, July 22, 1874. Sangamon County Circuit Court Dockets and Case Files, UIS-IRAD; Joliet Penitentiary Register of Prisoners, ISA.

24. "Police Business," *Illinois State Registers*, September 9, 1871. For complaints about the police, see "A Great Abuse," *Illinois State Register*, March 16, 1872; "More Evidence of Rottenness," *Illinois State Journal*, September 16, 1874; and "Our Police System," *Illinois State Journal*, September 17, 1874.

25. "Harvest Home: The Criminal Crop Garnered," *Illinois State* Register, March 16, 1874. Gus Reed had recently escaped from the jail when the reporter visited.

26. Sangamon County Circuit Court Criminal Dockets, 1870–1880, UIS-IRAD. For courts and crime in nineteenth-century Illinois, see Stacy Pratt McDermott, *The Jury in Lincoln's America* (Athens: Ohio University Press, 2012); Stephen Daniels, "Continuity and Change in Patterns of Case Handling: A Case Study of Two Rural Counties," *Law and Society Review* 19 (September 1985): 381–420; Beverly A. Smith, "Murder in a Rural Setting: Logan County Homicides, 1865–1900," *Western Illinois Regional Studies* 13, no. 1 (1990): 61–79; and Susan Sessions Rugh, "Civilizing the Countryside: Class, Gender, and Crime in Nineteenth-Century Rural Illinois," *Agricultural History* 76 (Winter 2002): 58–81. For the perception and reality of increasing crime after the Civil War, see also Don Harrison Doyle, *The Social Order of a Frontier Community: Jacksonville, Illinois, 1825–70* (Urbana: University of Illinois Press, 1978).

27. "The Police Court," *Illinois State Register*, February 25, 1865.

28. Justice of the Peace Dockets for Springfield, 1877–78, UIS-IRAD.

29. For the period of this study, only the dockets from 1877–80 survive. Justice of the Peace Dockets for Springfield, UIS-IRAD. For Edward Wilson and Annie Smith, see entries #74 and #75 on August 16, 1877.

30. Justice of the Peace Dockets for Springfield, April 27, 1878, UIS-IRAD.

31. Entries for May 26, May 28, September 9, September 10, and October 13, 1877, and March 16, 1878, Justice of the Peace Dockets for Springfield, UIS-IRAD.

32. Entries for December 10 and 22, 1877, Justice of the Peace Dockets for Springfield, UIS-IRAD.

33. "The Police Court," *Illinois State Register*, February 25, 1865.

34. "Negro Testimony," *Illinois State Register*, February 28, 1865.

35. "The Beginning of Negro Equality," *Illinois State Register*, November 1, 1865. For alleged O.A.K. members in Springfield, see *War of the Rebellion*, series 2, vol. 7, 298, 746.

36. "A Black Jury," *Illinois State Register*, August 23, 1866.

37. "Fourteenth Amendment," *Illinois State Register*, July 12, 1870.

38. "Colored Juror," *Illinois State Register,* March 18, 1873.

39. Looking only at first appearances for each term of the circuit court between 1870 and 1880 provides a general idea of the most common types of crime in Springfield. Since many cases were continued beyond one or two terms of the court, using only appearances for each term prevents counting continued cases more than once. Even if the case was ultimately dismissed or the suspect was found not guilty, these cases help construct a crime profile for the city during this decade, indicating not only the crimes committed, but those alleged as well. The data here includes all of Sangamon County, not only Springfield. Even taking the county as a whole and including both charges and convictions, the data in this section probably still underestimates the prevalence of crime in Springfield and Sangamon County. Sangamon County Circuit Court Criminal Dockets, 1870–80, UIS-IRAD.

40. Corneau, "Girl in the Sixties," 10.

41. "Going for 'Em," *Illinois State Register,* August 29, 1873.

42. "Burglaries," *Illinois State Register,* August 27, 1873.

43. "Thieves," *Illinois State Journal,* March 26, 1869.

44. "Sentenced," *Illinois State Register,* October 10, 1873; and Case No. 57, October Term 1873, Sangamon County Circuit Court Docket Book, UIS-IRAD.

45. "Circuit Court Items," *Illinois State Register,* October 17, 1873; and Case 73, October Term 1873, Sangamon County Circuit Court Docket Book, UIS-IRAD.

46. Lockley, *Lines in the Sand,* 99. The harshness of property crime sentences, especially compared to violent crime, has also been noted by Vandal, "Property Offenses, Social Tension and Racial Antagonism," 139.

47. Sangamon County Circuit Court Criminal Dockets, 1870–80, UIS-IRAD.

48. "A Motley Crowd," *Illinois State Register,* October 3, 1874.

49. Sangamon County Circuit Court Criminal Dockets, 1870–80, UIS-IRAD.

50. All of the cases mentioned above are described in *History of Sangamon County,* 528–29.

51. "Circuit Court Items," *Illinois State Register,* October 15 and 16, 1873. Only a few cases of "assault with intent to kill" were fully prosecuted by the circuit court between 1870 and 1880, so it is difficult to determine a typical sentence for this crime. Gilmore's sentence for larceny was consistent with general patterns of sentencing for property crimes. The use of the courts by black Springfielders, and their treatment there, suggests support for Roger Lane's observation of late nineteenth-century Philadelphia that "despite the general climate of discrimination, the city's courts typically lived up to the ideal of blind justice when dealing with people of different colors" (*Roots of Violence,* 83). For black access to local-level courts, see also Laura F. Edwards, "Status without Rights: African Americans and the Tangled History of Law and Governance in the Nineteenth-Century US South," *American Historical Review* 112 (April 2007): 365–93; and Christopher Waldrep and Donald G. Nieman, eds., *Local Matters: Race, Crime, and Justice in the Nineteenth-Century South* (Athens: University of Georgia Press, 2001).

52. In 1870, Edward Walker, a black sixteen-year-old farmhand, was found guilty of assaulting a white woman with intent to commit rape, and received only one year in the state penitentiary. See coverage in "Attempted Rape," *Illinois State Register,*

August 17, 1870; see also "The Rape Case," August 17, 1870; "Committed," August 18, 1870; and "Circuit Court," October 4, 1870. See also Sangamon County Circuit Court Condensed Docket, UIS-IRAD for Edward Walter [sic], charged with "assault to commit rape" and found guilty by jury; and entry for Edward Walker, received at the penitentiary October 14, 1870, Joliet Penitentiary Register of Prisoners, ISA. A brief item titled "Disorderly" in the *Register* from November 15, 1870, indicates that "negro convicts" from the city jail were put to work cleaning the streets, and advised the keeper of the jail to "keep order among his hands" because of complaints about their use of profane language while they worked. It was common for all prisoners in the city jail to perform street work, and this is the only reference that could be located to a crew composed of only black prisoners.

53. "Murderous Assault," *Illinois State Register*, September 15, 1873; and "Sentenced," *Illinois State Register*, November 6, 1873.

54. "Going for 'Em," *Illinois State Register*, August 29, 1873.

55. "Robbery," *Illinois State Register*, September 24, 1874.

56. "Dull," *Illinois State Register*, November 14, 1873. For the role of the press in stoking fears about crime, and for promoting extralegal citizen violence as a legitimate response, see Waldrep, *Many Faces of Judge Lynch*, esp. chap. 5.

57. "A Springfield Darkey . . . ," *Illinois State Register*, December 6, 1872.

58. "Couldn't Go Ba'Foot," *Illinois State Register*, November 30, 1872.

59. "Let Me Out ob Heah . . . ," *Illinois State Register*, April 4, 1863.

60. William L. Van Deburg, *Hoodlums: Black Villains and Social Bandits in American Life* (Chicago: University of Chicago Press, 2004), 34.

61. "Another Descent of the Freedmen," *Illinois State Register*, March 5, 1866.

62. "Respect for the Rights of Negroes," *Illinois State Register*, January 8, 1868.

63. Roger Lane observes the same tendency to emphasize the race of black offenders in crime reporting in nineteenth-century Philadelphia (*Roots of Violence*, 146). See also Jon-Christian Suggs, *Whispered Consolation: Law and Narrative in African American Life* (Ann Arbor: University of Michigan Press, 2000), 147–49.

64. "Discharged," *Illinois State Register*, June 2, 1871; "A Dark Deed, Indeed," *Illinois State Register*, December 27, 1871; "A 'Dark' Transaction," *Illinois State Journal*, April 27, 1869.

65. "Harvest Home: The Criminal Crop Garnered," *Illinois State Register*, March 16, 1874; and "Again in Trouble," *Illinois State Register*, May 14, 1873; "A Speck of War," *Illinois State Register*, June 8, 1873; "At Last," *Illinois State Register*, November 20, 1873.

66. "Offending Darkeys," *Illinois State Register*, December 17, 1873; "A Drunken Negress," *Illinois State Register*, May 8, 1873; and "Disturbances," *Illinois State Journal*, October 13, 1873.

67. "Arrest of Burglars," *Illinois State Register*, March 14, 1870.

68. "Cutting Affray," *Illinois State Register*, January 18, 1873.

69. "Brutal Assault," *Illinois State Register*, December 20, 1872.

70. "Fugitive African," *Illinois State Register*, April 24, 1871.

71. "Petty Larceny," *Illinois State Register*, April 14, 1876.

72. Sangamon County Circuit Court Criminal Dockets, 1870–80, UIS-IRAD.

73. "Assaulted by a Negro," *Illinois State Register*, November 20, 1873.

74. "Assaulted by a Negro," *Illinois State Register*, June 25, 1873.
75. "Attempted Rape," *Illinois State Register*, October 31, 1873.
76. "Indecent Assault," *Illinois State Register*, November 1, 1876.
77. "Wanted," *Illinois State Register*, June 5, 1873.
78. "A Reform Demanded," *Illinois State Register*, June 4, 1873.
79. Total population of Springfield in 1860: 9,320; 1870: 17,364; 1880: 19,743. Walker, *Statistics of the . . . United States* (1870), 119, and *Statistics of the Population of the United States at the Tenth Census* (Washington, DC: Government Printing Office, 1882), 142.
80. "House Thieves and Burglars About," *Illinois State Register*, January 7, 1864.
81. "Disgraceful Conduct," *Illinois State Register*, January 26, 1864.
82. "Robberies," *Illinois State Register*, July 1, 1865, and "Worthy of Attention," *Illinois State Register*, October 18, 1865.
83. "An Important Call—Second Ward Meeting," *Illinois State Register*, August 16, 1865; "Second Ward Meeting Last Evening," *Illinois State Register*, August 29, 1865; and "Worthy of Attention," *Illinois State Register*, October 18, 1865.
84. "Sangamon County Circuit Court," *Illinois State Register*, October 18, 1865.
85. "A Vigilance Committee," *Illinois State Register*, January 24, 1866.
86. "A Clearing Out Needed," *Illinois State Register*, May 16, 1871.
87. "Crime," *Illinois State Register*, July 6, 1871.
88. Lane, *Roots of Violence*, 28.
89. "That Rollicking Vagabond . . . ," *Illinois State Register*, November 1, 1876; and "A Motley Crowd," *Illinois State Register*, October 3, 1874.
90. "Police Matters," *Illinois State Register*, August 14, 1866.
91. "A Hard Lot," *Illinois State Register*, October 29, 1870.
92. "A Delectable Locality," *Illinois State Register*, June 6, 1871.
93. "Terrible Fight," *Illinois State Register*, March 6, 1872; and "The Row in the First Ward," *Illinois State Register*, March 9, 1872; "The Negro Riot," *Illinois State Register*, March 11, 1872. A similar fight occurred in 1871 when "a lot of colored individuals" fought with "as hard a set of miserable women as ever collected together in any locality"; see "A Lively Skirmish," *Illinois State Register*, November 20, 1871.
94. "Burglaries," *Illinois State Register*, November 14, 1877.
95. "Arrest of Burglar—Recovery of Stolen Goods," *Illinois State Register*, March 14, 1870, and "Preliminary Examination," *Illinois State Register*, March 15, 1870.
96. "Shooting," *Illinois State Register*, July 12, 1872.
97. "A Little Darkey . . . ," *Illinois State Register*, November 29, 1873.
98. "A Desperado Caught," *Illinois State Register*, July 21, 1874.

Chapter Six: The Penitentiary

Epigraph: Edgar Lee Masters, *Spoon River Anthology: An Annotated Edition*, ed. John E. Hallwas (Urbana: University of Illinois Press, 1992), 269.
1. All quotes above from Aaron Benedict Mead to his mother, June 24, 1877, Aaron Benedict Mead Papers, ALPL.

2. Prisoner Mittimus Files for Augustus Reed (#5314), John Fisher (#5315), Scott Burton (#5316), Illinois State Penitentiary, ISA.

3. Entry for Augustus Reed (#5314), Register of Prisoners, Illinois State Penitentiary, ISA.

4. "A Desperado Caught," *Illinois State Register,* July 22, 1864.

5. For Gus Reed's second incarceration in 1874, see Prisoner Mittimus File for Augustus Reed (#8654) and entry for Augustus Reed (#8654), Register of Prisoners, Illinois State Penitentiary, ISA.

6. Aaron Benedict Mead to his mother, June 24, 1877, Aaron Benedict Mead Papers, ALPL.

7. Joliet Penitentiary Testimony on Inhuman Treatment of Prisoners, SCRC.

8. All quotes and details regarding the death of Gus Reed in this and the following paragraphs are from Joliet Penitentiary Testimony on Inhuman Treatment of Prisoners, SCRC, unless otherwise noted.

9. Roberts Bartholow, *A Treatise on the Practice of Medicine for the Use of Students and Practitioners* (New York: D. Appleton, 1881), 373–76.

10. Will County Coroner's Record for Guss [sic] Reed, Will County Coroner's Office, WCC. See also "Gus Reed," *Joliet Republican,* May 15, 1878.

11. "The Fatal Gag," *Joliet Republican,* May 11, 1878.

12. "A Convict Was Done to Death . . . ," *Chicago Daily News,* May 17, 1878; "Torture," *Chicago Tribune,* May 17, 1878; and "The Rack," May 18, 1878.

13. "Small Talk," *Courier-Journal,* May 22, 1878; "Brutal Treatment," *Washington Post,* May 24, 1878.

14. Joliet Penitentiary Testimony on Inhuman Treatment of Prisoners, SCRC.

15. "Jug Handle Justice," *Joliet Republican,* May 29, 1878 and "Died under the Gag," *Illinois State Register,* May 14, 1878.

16. "An Investigation," *Joliet Republican,* May 15, 1878.

17. "Secret 'Investigation,'" *Chicago Daily Tribune,* May 16, 1878; "The Penitentiary Commissioners . . . ," *Chicago Daily Tribune,* May 16, 1878.

18. Rebecca M. McLennan argues persuasively for a moment of crisis in penitentiary management during this period, and indeed for a series of rolling crises in penitentiary management as states sought not only to legitimate the forced labor of convicts but also to make it both financially profitable and socially valuable. McLennan responds in part to Michel Foucault, *Discipline and Punish: The Birth of the Prison,* trans. Alan Sheridan (New York: Pantheon, 1977), who claimed that the larger aim of the industrial production system of penitentiary management was to create docile worker-subjects for the carceral state. McLennan's focus on the prisoner as a productive body is compatible with Foucault's notion of penal industrial discipline, but adds the significant consideration of continuing public and political involvement in the creation, establishment, and critique of this system of convict control. Rebecca M. McLennan, *The Crisis of Imprisonment: Protest, Politics, and the Making of the American Penal State, 1776–1941* (Cambridge: Cambridge University Press, 2008).

19. Gustave de Beaumont and Alexis de Tocqueville, *On the Penitentiary System in the United States* (Philadelphia: Carey, Lea, and Blanchard, 1833), 30–31.

20. "The Joliet Murder," *Illinois State Register,* January 3, 1874. For the development of prisons in the nineteenth century, see Mark Colvin, *Penitentiaries, Reformatories, and Chain Gangs: Social Theory and the History of Punishment in Nineteenth-Century America* (New York: St. Martin's Press, 1997); and Blake McKelvey, *American Prisons: A History of Good Intentions* (Montclair, NJ: Patterson Smith, 1977).

21. See, for example, *Harper's Weekly,* July 4, 1863, 429. See also Margaret Abruzzo, *Polemical Pain: Slavery, Cruelty, and the Rise of Humanitarianism* (Baltimore: Johns Hopkins University Press, 2011).

22. John McElroy, *Andersonville: A Story of Rebel Military Prisons* (Toledo: D. R. Locke, 1879), x.

23. See especially Myra C. Glenn, *Campaigns against Corporal Punishment: Prisoners, Sailors, Women, and Children in Antebellum America* (Albany: State University of New York Press, 1984); and Elizabeth B. Clark, "'The Sacred Rights of the Weak': Pain, Sympathy, and the Culture of Individual Rights in Antebellum America," *Journal of American History* 82 (September 1995): 463–93. See also Timothy J. Gilfoyle, *A Pickpocket's Tale: The Underworld of Nineteenth-Century New York* (New York: W. W. Norton, 2006), 42–58. On Civil War prisons and their impact on American culture, see Benjamin G. Cloyd, *Haunted by Atrocity: Civil War Prisons in American Memory* (Baton Rouge: Louisiana State University Press, 2010); and Reid Mitchell, *Civil War Soldiers* (New York: Viking, 1988), 44–55.

24. These descriptions conform to a general formula in reporting on prisoner abuse, violent crime, flogging, and so on in play since the eighteenth century, described by Karen Halttunen as the "pornography of pain." See Karen Halttunen, "Humanitarianism and the Pornography of Pain in Anglo-American Culture," *American Historical Review* 100, no. 2 (1995): 303–34. See also Abruzzo, *Polemical Pain.*

25. "Justifiable," *Chicago Daily Tribune,* May 11, 1878.

26. "Gus Reed," *Joliet Republican,* May 15, 1878.

27. "Secret 'Investigation,'" *Chicago Daily Tribune,* May 16, 1878.

28. "Prison Punishment," *Illinois State Journal,* May 16, 1878.

29. "The Joliet Prison Investigation," *Illinois State Journal,* May 17, 1878.

30. "The Penitentiary," *Chicago Daily Tribune,* August 25, 1874.

31. On the nuances of the private-public shift in penitentiary management, see McLennan, *Crisis of Imprisonment.*

32. Andrew Shuman to Governor John Palmer, June 23, 1869, Governor's Correspondence, ISA. See also *Report of the Joint Committee of Investigation into the Affairs of the Illinois State Penitentiary* (Springfield, IL: Journal Printing Office, 1872), 59.

33. Andrew Shuman to Governor John Palmer, November 12, 1869, Governor's Correspondence, ISA.

34. Telegrams from J. W. Wham to Governor John Beveridge, February 18, 20, 23, 24, 1874, Governor's Correspondence, ISA.

35. "The Joliet Murder," *Illinois State Register,* January 3, 1874; "The Prison Bath," *Chicago Daily Tribune,* December 31, 1873.

36. "The Penitentiary Investigation," *Chicago Daily Tribune,* January 19, 1874.

37. "Logan, Beveridge, and the Penitentiary Bath," *Chicago Daily Tribune,* January 25, 1874; "The Penitentiary," *Joliet Republican,* August 8, 1874.

38. McClaughry was listed as Hancock County clerk in 1869 in *Journal of the Constitutional Convention of the State of Illinois* (Springfield, IL: State Journal Printing Office, 1870), 31.

39. It is quite likely that McClaughry's experience in stone quarrying contributed to his selection for the position at the Joliet penitentiary, which ran a large quarry in addition to its other industrial production facilities. For McClaughry's career between 1865 and 1874, see Gregg, *History of Hancock County, Illinois*, 728–30; Newton Bateman, Paul Selby, J. Seymour Currey, and Charles J. Scofield, eds., *Historical Encyclopedia of Illinois and History of Hancock County* (Chicago: Munsell, 1921), 359; *Kansas: A Cyclopedia of State History*, vol. 3, pt. 2 (Chicago: Standard, 1912), 810–12; and "Robert Wilson McClaughry," *Monmouth College Oracle* 15, no. 34 (1911): 31–32. Frank Morn's problematic biography of Robert McClaughry gives some slightly different information, but since Morn does not consistently cite sources, it is difficult to verify some of his details and claims. The work should be consulted with caution, but is currently the only biography of Robert McClaughry. See Frank Morn, *Forgotten Reformer: Robert McClaughry and Criminal Justice Reform in Nineteenth-Century America* (Lanham, MD: University Press of America, 2010).

40. David A. Wallace to Governor John Beveridge, August 10, 1874, Governor's Correspondence, ISA.

41. "Convict Labor," *Chicago Daily Tribune*, March 6, 1875.

42. "Convict Labor to Let," *Illinois State Journal*, October 15, 1874.

43. Convict Labor," *Chicago Daily Tribune*, March 6, 1875.

44. "The Penitentiary," *Chicago Daily Tribune*, April 3, 1875; and "The Penitentiary," *Chicago Daily Tribune*, March 20, 1875.

45. "The Penitentiary," *Chicago Daily Tribune*, January 8, 1876.

46. "Our Police—Shall the City Be Protected?" *Illinois State Register*, July 20, 1865.

47. Christopher Tiedeman, *A Treatise on the Limitations of Police Power in the United States* (St. Louis: F. H. Thomas Law Book Co., 1886), 116–17. Eric Monkkonen has described the late nineteenth-century "dangerous class" as composed of five different groups: rural criminals, urban criminals, rural paupers, urban paupers, and tramps, but there were many variations on these categories, and his statistical analysis downplays the middle-class apprehensions that branded these groups dangerous. See Eric Monkkonen, *The Dangerous Class: Crime and Poverty in Columbus, Ohio, 1860–1885* (Cambridge, MA: Harvard University Press, 1975).

48. Edward Morse, "Natural Selection and Crime," *Popular Science Monthly*, August 1892, 439.

49. For tramps and vagabonds, see Eric Monkkonen, ed., *Walking to Work: Tramps in America, 1790–1935* (Lincoln: University of Nebraska Press, 1984); Kenneth Kusmer, *Down and Out, on the Road: The Homeless in American History* (Oxford: Oxford University Press, 2002). For the role of "outsider" definitions in lynching, see Waldrep, *Many Faces of Judge Lynch*.

50. Eric Monkkonen has argued through a statistical analysis of police departments and arrest trends that the rise of the urban police was not necessarily tied to a rise in industrialism, unemployment, and urban disorder. Monkkonen's thesis disregards contemporary perceptions of the crime problem and calls for reform of the

criminal justice system. See Monkkonen, *Police in Urban America, 1860–1920* (Cambridge: Cambridge University Press, 1981); on the rise of the professional police, see also Roger Lane, *Policing the City: Boston, 1822–1885* (Cambridge: Harvard University Press, 1967); Samuel Walker, *A Critical History of Police Reform: The Emergence of Professionalism* (Lexington, MA: Lexington Books, 1977); David R. Johnson, *Policing the Urban Underworld: The Impact of Crime on the Development of the American Police, 1800–1887* (Philadelphia: Temple University Press, 1979); Sidney L. Harring, *Policing a Class Society: The Experience of American Cities, 1865–1915* (New Brunswick, NJ: Rutgers University Press, 1983); Samuel Walker, *Popular Justice: A History of American Criminal Justice* (New York: Oxford University Press, 1998); and Allen Steinberg, *The Transformation of Criminal Justice: Philadelphia, 1800–1880* (Chapel Hill: University of North Carolina Press, 1989).

51. Robert W. McClaughry, "Warden's Report," in *Report of the Commissioners of the Illinois State Penitentiary at Joliet for the Two Years Ending September 30, 1880* (Springfield: H. W. Rokker, 1880), 17.

52. McClaughry's first American publication of the Bertillon system is *Alphonse Bertillon's New Method for Identification of Criminals by Anthropometric Descriptions: A Discourse Delivered by Himself at the International Prison Congress at Rome, November 22, 1885,* Trans. Gallus Muller, Clerk of the Illinois State Penitentiary, presented for consideration of the "Warden's Association for the Registration of Criminals" by R. W. McClaughry, Warden of the Illinois State Penitentiary, and Secretary of the Association (Joliet, IL: Joliet Printing, 1887).

53. "To Identify Criminals," *Chicago Daily Tribune,* February 14, 1891.

54. Ibid., and "Plans of the Police," *Chicago Daily Tribune,* March 11, 1891.

55. "Crooks and 'Con' Men to Be Cared For," *Chicago Daily Tribune,* October 12, 1891, and "To Identify Criminals," *Chicago Daily Tribune,* February 14, 1891.

56. "For the Identification of Criminals," *Chicago Daily Tribune,* February 22, 1893. Before the exposition was even half over, McClaughry resigned, citing "personal and business interests," but sources close to McClaughry reported that he had clashed with Mayor Carter Harrison over the city's toleration of illegal gambling and the erosion of the police commissioner's authority. McClaughry's son Matthew continued as the head of the department's Bureau of Identification after his father's departure. For McClaughry's resignation, see *Chicago Daily Tribune,* July 25 and 28, and August 25 and 26, 1893.

57. W. A. McCorn, "Degeneration in Criminals as Shown by the Bertillon System of Measurement and Photographs," *American Journal of Insanity* 53 (July 1896): 48.

58. Ibid., 47.

59. For the rise of criminal anthropology, see especially Simon A. Cole, *Suspect Identities: A History of Fingerprinting and Criminal Identification* (Cambridge, MA: Harvard University Press, 2001).

60. Henry M. Boies, *The Science of Penology: The Defense of Society against Crime* (New York: G. P. Putnam's Sons, 1901), 20, 60.

61. The problem of the habitual criminal was exacerbated by the rise in street crime in the 1870s and 1880s, but it was not a new one for students of crime. Scientists, both amateur and professional, had been trying to read personality or psychology on the

body since the eighteenth century. Biological theories of human behavior and race difference circulated through both Europe and the Americas, and by the 1820s these theories had gained popular attention with the writings of Charles Caldwell and the American edition of British scientist George Combe's *Elements of Phrenology* (1834), which expanded on both the practice and theory of anthropometric measurements of the brain and cranium. Both noted that careful physical observation could determine what feelings and intellectual faculties a person possessed, including traits that bore on criminality: combativeness, destructiveness, judgment, and temperament. Caldwell and Combe also joined such scientists and theologians as Samuel Morton, Louis Agassiz, and John Bachman in debating whether the perceived differences between human races constituted evidence of separate or common origins. The concerns that motivated early scientific examinations into the physiology of race difference were rooted in an intellectual climate that assumed a direct and positive linkage between physiological traits and behavioral manifestations; attempts to create a physical taxonomy of human behavioral types continued to structure scientific inquiry for decades. Charles Caldwell, *Elements of Phrenology* (Lexington, KY: A. G. Meriwether, 1824) and a second, expanded edition under the same title in 1827; George Combe, *Elements of Phrenology*, 4th ed. (Boston: Marsh, Capen, and Lyon, 1834). Samuel Morton, *Crania Americana; or, A Comparative View of the Skulls of Various Aboriginal Nations of North and South America* (Philadelphia: J. Dobson, 1839). This was the scientific milieu into which Charles Darwin's *On the Origin of Species by Means of Natural Selection, or The Preservation of Favoured Races in the Struggle for Life* (London: John Murray, 1859) first appeared. For the development of biological theories of race, see William Stanton, *The Leopard's Spots: Scientific Attitudes Toward Race in America, 1815–59* (Chicago: University of Chicago Press, 1960); Thomas F. Gossett, *Race: The History of an Idea in America* (Dallas: Southern Methodist University Press, 1963); John S. Haller Jr., *Outcasts from Evolution: Scientific Attitudes of Racial Inferiority, 1859–1900* (Urbana: University of Illinois Press, 1971); Stephen Jay Gould, *The Mismeasure of Man* (New York: W. W. Norton, 1981); Ann Fabian, *The Skull Collectors: Race, Science, and America's Unburied Dead* (Chicago: University of Chicago Press, 2010); and Sarah E. Chinn, *Technology and the Logic of American Racism: A Cultural History of the Body as Evidence* (London: Continuum, 2000). For biological theories of race and crime specifically, see Arthur E. Fink, *Causes of Crime: Biological Theories in the United States, 1800–1915* (Philadelphia: University of Pennsylvania Press, 1938); Nicole Hahn Rafter, *Creating Born Criminals* (Urbana: University of Illinois Press, 1997); Cole, *Suspect Identities;* and Gould, *Mismeasure of Man*. See also Mark H. Haller, *Eugenics: Hereditarian Attitudes in American Thought* (New Brunswick, NJ: Rutgers University Press, 1963); William H. Tucker, *The Science and Politics of Racial Research* (Urbana: University of Illinois Press, 1994). For an overview of the varieties of proslavery thought, including racial pseudoscience, see Paul Finkelman, "The Significance and Persistence of Proslavery Thought," in *The Problem of Evil: Slavery, Freedom, and the Ambiguities of American Reform*, ed. Steven Mintz and John Stauffer (Amherst: University of Massachusetts Press, 2007), 95–114. For the intellectual milieu in which antebellum racial theorists worked, see Louis Menand, *The Metaphysical Club: A Story of Ideas in America* (New York: Farrar, Straus and Giroux, 2001), and Tucker, *Science and Politics of Racial Research*, 9–28.

62. Nott and Gliddon, *Types of Mankind,* 83, 260.
63. Van Evrie, *Negroes and Negro "Slavery,"* 310.
64. Ibid., 312–13.
65. Ibid.
66. *Moore, Executor of Eells v. The People,* 55 US 13 (1853).
67. Dr. Samuel Cartwright, "Negro Freedom: An Impossibility under Nature's Laws," *De Bow's Review* 5 (May–June 1861): 651. Ariela J. Gross, *Double Character: Slavery and Mastery in the Antebellum Southern Courtroom* (Princeton: Princeton University Press, 2000), has compellingly argued that the courtroom use of experts in race science during the antebellum era helped establish the legal presumption of biological difference between whites and blacks. For antebellum attitudes toward blacks and crime, see also Leonard P. Curry, *The Free Black in Urban America, 1800–1850: The Shadow of the Dream* (Chicago: University of Chicago Press, 1981), esp. chap. 7, "An Indolent, Disorderly, and Corrupt Population: Black Crime and Vice in the City."
68. On Lombroso, see especially Mary Gibson, *Born to Crime: Cesare Lombroso and the Origins of Biological Criminology* (Westport, CT: Praeger, 2002).
69. William Noyes, "The Criminal Type," *Journal of Social Science* 24 (April 1888): 32. For the individualistic approach in Progressive criminology and penology, see David Rothman, *Conscience and Convenience: The Asylum and its Alternatives in Progressive America* (Boston: Little, Brown, 1980).
70. Noyes, "Criminal Type," 36–38.
71. Ibid., 43. For the idea of criminal preemption, see also W. Duncan McKim, *Heredity and Human Progress* (New York: G. P. Putnam's Sons, 1900), who stated that heredity produced a tendency to crime and advocated executing criminals wholesale so their faulty heritage could not be passed on.
72. On the link between environment and behavior in midcentury thought, especially in cities, see Joan Burbick, *Healing the Republic: The Language of Health and the Culture of Nationalism in Nineteenth-Century America* (Cambridge: Cambridge University Press, 1994); David Schuyler, *The New Urban Landscape: The Redefinition of City Form in Nineteenth-Century America* (Baltimore: Johns Hopkins University Press, 1986); Paul Boyer, *Urban Masses and Moral Order in America, 1820–1920* (Cambridge, MA: Harvard University Press, 1978); Priscilla Clement, *Welfare and the Poor in the Nineteenth-Century City: Philadelphia, 1800–1854* (Rutherford, NJ: Fairleigh Dickinson University Press, 1985).
73. Havelock Ellis, *The Criminal* (New York: Charles Scribner's Sons, 1890), 309.
74. Hamilton D. Wey, "Criminal Anthropology," *Proceedings of the National Prison Association* (Pittsburgh: Shaw Brothers, 1891), 285.
75. Ibid., 287.
76. Robert W. McClaughry, "Crimes and Criminals," address before the Illinois State Bar Association, January 10 and 11, 1888, [n.p.], ALPL. McClaughry did, however, believe strongly in separating prisoners into grades or classes to keep "criminals by nature" separate from those able to be rehabilitated. He promoted the Bertillon system in part to facilitate this categorization. See McClaughry, "Warden's Report," 17; see also "The Pennsylvania Industrial Reformatory at Huntingdon," and "Letter

from R. W. McClaughry, General Superintendent," *Journal of Prison Discipline and Philanthropy* (January 1891): 37–46.

77. The question of heredity or environment in producing criminals was part of a broader scientific conversation at the turn of the century on the relative weight of each in all areas of human development. On children and Progressive Era reform, see especially Anthony Platt, *The Child Savers: The Invention of Delinquency* (Chicago: University of Chicago Press, 1969); Susan Tiffin, *In Whose Best Interest?: Child Welfare Reform in the Progressive Era* (Westport, CT: Greenwood Press, 1982); Elizabeth J. Clapp, *Mothers of All Children: Women Reformers and the Rise of Juvenile Courts in Progressive Era America* (University Park: Pennsylvania State University Press, 1998). For the role of race specifically in juvenile justice reforms, see Geoff K. Ward, *The Black Child-Savers: Racial Democracy and Juvenile Justice* (Chicago: University of Chicago, 2012); and Miroslava Chavez-Garcia, *States of Delinquency: Race and Science in the Making of California's Juvenile Justice System* (Berkeley: University of California Press, 2012).

78. Frederick H. Wines, *Punishment and Reformation* (New York: Thomas Y. Crowell, 1895), 275.

79. Ibid., 296–97.

80. George E. Dawson, "A Study in Youthful Degeneracy," *Pedagogical Seminary* 4 (December 1896): 256.

81. Eugene S. Talbot, *Degeneracy: Its Causes, Signs, and Results* (London: Walter Scott; and New York: Charles Scribner's Sons, 1899), 347. Robert McClaughry served as the superintendent of the Illinois State Reformatory at Pontiac from 1893 to 1897, and also served as superintendent of the Industrial Reformatory at Huntingdon, Pennsylvania from 1888 to 1891. For his time at Huntingdon, see "The Pennsylvania Industrial Reformatory at Huntingdon," and "Letter from R. W. McClaughry, General Superintendent," *Journal of Prison Discipline and Philanthropy* (January 1891): 37–46; and for his time at Pontiac, see Alexander W. Pisciotta, "A House Divided: Penal Reform at the Illinois State Reformatory, 1891–1915," *Crime and Delinquency* 37 (April 1991): 165–85.

82. Talbot, *Degeneracy*, 18. See also Talbot, "A Study of the Stigmata of Degeneracy among the American Criminal Youth," *Journal of the American Medical Association* 30 (April 9, 1898): 849–956. Arthur MacDonald also published extensively on the "stigmata of degeneration" and the value of juvenile reformatories to correct hereditary criminality. See MacDonald, *Criminology* (New York: Funk and Wagnalls, 1892) and MacDonald, *Juvenile Crime and Degeneration: Including Stigmata of Degeneration* (Washington, DC: Government Printing Office, 1908). See also August Drähms, *The Criminal: His Personnel and Environment, A Scientific Study* (New York: Macmillan, 1900), who advocated juvenile reformatories as the only true remedy to crime. For an application of the heredity/environment theory in adult criminals, see Arthur Sweeney, "Crime and Insanity," *Northwestern Lancet* 17 (May 15, 1897): 203–11.

83. Frances Kellor, *Experimental Sociology: Descriptive and Analytical* (New York: Macmillan, 1901), 12. A series of articles by Kellor titled "The Criminal Negro," also appeared in the liberal progressive journal *The Arena* in 1901.

84. Talbot, *Degeneracy*, 99.

85. Ibid., 100–101.

86. The historian Khalil Gibran Muhammad, *The Condemnation of Blackness: Race, Crime, and the Making of Modern Urban America* (Cambridge, MA: Harvard University Press, 2010), has referred to this shift in emphasis from biological to environmental racial determinism as incriminating both the biology and the culture of back communities. For a contemporary discussion of black crime, see W. E. B. DuBois, *Some Notes on Negro Crime, Particularly in Georgia* (Atlanta: Atlanta University Press, 1904).

87. Frederick L. Hoffman, *Race Traits and Tendencies of the American Negro* (New York: Published for the American Economic Association by Macmillan, 1896), 217–28. For an extensive look at Hoffman and his work, see Muhammad, *Condemnation of Blackness*.

88. J. Sanderson Christison, *Crime and Criminals*, 2nd ed. (Chicago: Published by the author, 1899), 4, 55.

89. Kellor, *Experimental Sociology*, 156.

90. Jefferson, *Notes on the State of Virginia*, 154.

91. Kellor, *Experimental Sociology*, 31.

92. Walter Willcox, "Negro Criminality," reprinted in Alfred H. Stone, *Studies in the American Race Problem* (New York: Doubleday, Page, 1908), 444–45.

93. Ibid., 448–49.

94. George T. Winston, "The Relation of the Whites to the Negroes," in *America's Race Problem: Addresses at the Annual Meeting of the American Academy of Political and Social Science, Philadelphia, April Twelfth and Thirteenth, MCMI* (New York: McClure, Phillips, 1901), 109.

95. Ibid., 115.

96. Charles McCord, *The American Negro as a Dependent, Defective, and Delinquent* (Nashville, TN: Benson, 1914), 13–14.

97. Ibid., 317.

98. As Vernon J. Williams Jr. points out in *Rethinking Race: Franz Boas and His Contemporaries* (Lexington: University Press of Kentucky, 1996), Boas and his students in the 1890s were already part of a significant countermovement to delegitimize the notion of fundamental race difference, and especially physiological manifestations of such difference. However, as Williams also notes, even Boas still harbored suspicions that certain characteristics were perhaps racially contingent.

Epilogue: Springfield, 1908

Epigraph: R. W. Shufeldt, *The Negro: A Menace to American Civilization* (Boston: Richard G. Badger/Gorham Press, 1907), 176–77.

1. This account of the 1908 Springfield race riot is based on Roberta Senechal's masterly *The Sociogenesis of a Race Riot: Springfield, Illinois, in 1908* (Urbana: University of Illinois Press, 1990), esp. chap. 1, "Riot, Ruin and Rebellion . . . ," 15–54. Senechal gives Burton's age as fifty-six at the time of the riot, but based on his age (twenty-three) recorded in the 1870 census, he would have been sixty-one in 1908.

2. *Springfield Record*, August 18, 1908, quoted in Senechal, *Sociogenesis of a Race Riot*, 47.

3. Henry M. Boies, *Prisoners and Paupers: A Study of the Abnormal Increase of Criminals and the Public Burden of Pauperism in the United States; The Causes and Remedies* (New York: G. P. Putnam's Sons, 1893), 266.

4. *East Saint Louis Daily Journal*, quoted in Harper Barnes, *Never Been a Time: The 1917 Race Riot That Sparked the Civil Rights Movement* (New York: Walker, 2008), 104.

5. For other regional race riots of this era, see Charles L. Lumpkins, *American Pogrom: The East St. Louis Race Riot and Black Politics* (Athens: Ohio University Press, 2008); Barnes, *Never Been a Time*; Brian Butler, *An Undergrowth of Folly: Public Order, Race Anxiety, and the 1903 Evansville, Indiana Riot* (New York: Garland, 2000); William Tuttle, *Race Riot: Chicago in the Red Summer of 1919* (1970; Urbana: University of Illinois Press, 1996); Elliott M. Rudwick, *Race Riot at East St. Louis, July 2, 1917* (Carbondale: Southern Illinois University Press, 1964).

6. Blocker, *Little More Freedom*, 125. Waldrep, *Many Faces of Judge Lynch*, argues alternatively that racially motivated violence required a stable sense of racial hierarchy, a base of community support, and a general agreement that such violence was necessary. Similarly, see Lisa Arellano, *Vigilantes and Lynch Mobs: Narratives of Community and Nation* (Philadelphia: Temple University Press, 2012), for perceptions among vigilantes and their publics of an "ideal vigilantism" that responded to community norms and legitimately corrected transgressions against them.

7. "Rowdyism," *Illinois State Register*, December 2, 1865. For extralegal racial violence as a class-based response to a perceived crisis in criminal justice, see Michael J. Pfeifer, *Rough Justice: Lynching and American Society, 1847–1947* (Urbana: University of Illinois Press, 2004). See also Waldrep, *Many Faces of Judge Lynch*.

8. James Ford Rhodes, *History of the United States from the Compromise of 1850 to the Final Restoration of Home Rule at the South in 1877*, vol. 6, 1866–1872 (1906; New York: Macmillan, 1912), 38–39.

9. S. W. Wetmore, *Behind the Bars at Joliet: A Famous Prison, Its Celebrated Inmates, and Its Mysteries* (Joliet, IL: J. O. Gorman, 1892), 182–83.

10. On legal cultures in relation to criminal justice, see Christopher Waldrep, *Roots of Disorder: Race and Criminal Justice in the American South, 1817–80* (Urbana: University of Illinois Press, 1998).

SELECTED BIBLIOGRAPHY

Published Primary Sources

Address of the National Democratic State Central Committee of Illinois. n.p., 1858.
Address to the Democracy and the People of the United States, by the National Democratic Executive Committee. Washington, DC, 1860.
America's Race Problem: Addresses at the Annual Meeting of the American Academy of Political and Social Science, Philadelphia, April Twelfth and Thirteenth, MCMI. New York: McClure, Phillips, 1901.
An Authentic Exposition of the "K.G.C.," "Knights of the Golden Circle": or, A History of Secession from 1834 to 1861 by a Member of the Order. Indianapolis: C. O. Perrine, 1861.
Annual Report of the Superintendent of Public Schools of Springfield, Illinois. Springfield: Johnson and Bradford, 1867.
Ayer, I. Winslow. The Great North-Western Conspiracy in All Its Startling Details. Chicago: Rounds & James, 1865.
———. The Great Treason Plot in the North during the War. Chicago : U.S. Publishing Co., 1895.
Basler, Roy P., ed., The Collected Works of Abraham Lincoln. New Brunswick, NJ: Rutgers University Press, 1953.
Bateman, Newton, Paul Selby, J. Seymour Currey, and Charles J. Scofield, eds. Historical Encyclopedia of Illinois and History of Hancock County. Chicago: Munsell, 1921.
Bateman, Newton, and Paul Selby, eds. Historical Encyclopedia of Illinois and History of Sangamon County. Chicago: Munsell, 1912.
Bates, Edward. Opinion of Attorney General Bates on Citizenship. Washington, DC: Government Printing Office, 1863.
Beaumont, Gustave de, and Alexis de Tocqueville. On the Penitentiary System in the United States. Philadelphia: Carey, Lea, and Blanchard, 1833.
Bell, Howard Holman, ed. Minutes of the Proceedings of the National Negro Conventions, 1830–1864. New York: Arno Press, 1969.
Biennial Report of the Superintendent of Public Instruction of the State of Illinois. Springfield, IL: Baker and Bailhache, 1865–66, 1867–68, 1869–70, 1873–74.
Boies, Henry M. Prisoners and Paupers: A Study of the Abnormal Increase of Criminals and the Public Burden of Pauperism in the United States; The Causes and Remedies. New York: G. P. Putnam's Sons, 1893.
———. The Science of Penology: The Defense of Society Against Crime. New York: G. P. Putnam's Sons, 1901.
Brown, John. Slave Life in Georgia: A Narrative of the Life, Sufferings, and Escape of John Brown, a Fugitive Slave. Edited by F.N. Boney. 1855; 1972. Savannah, GA: Beehive Press, 1991.

Caldwell, Charles. *Elements of Phrenology*. 2nd ed.. Lexington, KY: A. G. Meriwether, 1827.
Cartwright, Samuel. "Negro Freedom: An Impossibility under Nature's Laws." *De Bow's Review* 5 (May–June 1861): 648–60.
Christison, J. Sanderson. *Crime and Criminals*. 2nd ed. Chicago: Published by the Author, 1899.
Combe, George. *Elements of Phrenology*. 4th ed. Boston: Marsh, Capen, and Lyon, 1834.
Corneau, Octavia Roberts, ed. "A Girl in the Sixties: Excerpts from the Journal of Anna Ridgely [Mrs. James L. Hudson]." Springfield, IL: Journal Printing, 1929.
Davidson, Alexander, and Bernard Stuvé. *A Complete History of Illinois from 1673 to 1873*. Springfield: D. L. Phillips, 1877.
Dawson, George E. "A Study in Youthful Degeneracy." *Pedagogical Seminary* 4 (December 1896): 221–58.
Drähms, August. *The Criminal: His Personnel and Environment, A Scientific Study*. New York: Macmillan, 1900.
DuBois, W. E. B. *Some Notes on Negro Crime, Particularly in Georgia*. Atlanta: Atlanta University Press, 1904.
Dugdale, Richard Louis, *"The Jukes": A Study in Crime, Pauperism, Disease and Heredity*. New York: G. P. Putnam's Sons, 1877.
Ellis, Havelock. *The Criminal*. New York: Charles Scribner's Sons, 1890.
First Annual Report of the Board of Managers of the Prison Discipline Society. 5th ed. Boston: T. R. Marvin, 1827.
Fisher, Sidney George. *The Laws of Race, as Connected with Slavery*. Philadelphia: Willis P. Hazard, 1860.
Gregg, Thomas. *History of Hancock County*. Chicago: Chapman, 1880.
Halstead, M. *Caucuses of 1860. A History of the National Political Conventions of the Current Presidential Campaign*. Columbus, OH: Follett, Foster, 1860.
Henderson, Charles. *The Cause and Cure of Crime*. Chicago: A. C. McClurg, 1914.
History of Sangamon County, Illinois. Chicago: Inter-state Publishing, 1881.
Hoffman, Frederick L. *Race Traits and Tendencies of the American Negro*. New York: Published for the American Economic Association by Macmillan, 1896.
Illustrated Historical Atlas of Hancock County, Illinois. Chicago: A. T. Andreas, 1874.
Journal of the Constitutional Convention of the State of Illinois; convened at Springfield, January 7, 1862. Springfield: C. H. Lanphier, 1862.
Kellor, Frances. *Experimental Sociology: Descriptive and Analytical*. New York: Macmillan, 1901.
Kemble, Frances A., and Frances A. Butler Leigh. *Principles and Privilege: Two Women's Lives on a Georgia Plantation*. Ann Arbor: University of Michigan Press, 1995.
Lathrop, Rev. S. G. *Crime and Its Punishment and Life in the Penitentiary*. Joliet, IL: Published by the Author, 1866.
Livermore, Mary. *My Story of the War: A Woman's Narrative of Four Years Personal Experience*. Hartford, CT: A. D. Worthington, 1889.
Lydston, George, and Eugene Talbot. "Studies of Criminals. Degeneracy of Cranial and Maxillary Development in the Criminal Class, with a Series of Criminal

Skulls and Histories Typical of the Physical Degeneracy of the Criminal." *Alienist and Neurologist* 12 (October 1891): 556–612.

McClaughry, Robert W. "Crimes and Criminals." Address before the Illinois State Bar Association, January 10 and 11, 1888. n.p.

McCord, Charles. *The American Negro as a Dependent, Defective, and Delinquent*. Nashville, TN: Benson, 1914.

McCorn, W. A. "Degeneration in Criminals as Shown by the Bertillon System of Measurement and Photographs." *American Journal of Insanity* 53 (July 1896): 47–56.

McKim, W. Duncan. *Heredity and Human Progress*. New York: G. P. Putnam's Sons, 1900.

MacDonald, Arthur. *Juvenile Crime and Degeneration: Including Stigmata of Degeneration*. Washington, DC: Government Printing Office, 1908.

Magee, J. H. *The Night of Affliction and Morning of Recovery. An Autobiography*. Cincinnati: Published by the Author, 1873.

Merrick, Richard T. *The Emancipation Proclamation. State Rights. National Convention. Speech of Richard T. Merrick, before the Young Men's Democratic Invincible Club, Chicago, Dec. 11, 1862*. n.p.

Morse, Edward. "Natural Selection and Crime." *Popular Science Monthly* (August 1892): 433–46.

Morton, Samuel. *Crania Americana; or, A Comparative View of the Skulls of Various Aboriginal Nations of North and South America*. Philadelphia: J. Dobson, 1839.

Nott, Josiah, and George Gliddon. *Types of Mankind; or, Ethnological Researches*. 7th ed. Philadelphia: Lippincott, Grambo, 1855.

Noyes, William. "The Criminal Type." *Journal of Social Science* 24 (April 1888): 31–42.

Ostendorf, Lloyd, and Walter Oleksy, eds. *Lincoln's Unknown Private Life: An Oral History by His Black Housekeeper Mariah Vance, 1850–1860*. Mamaroneck, NY: Hastings House, 1995.

Palmer, John M. *Personal Recollections of John M. Palmer: The Story of an Earnest Life*. Cincinnati: R. Clarke, 1901.

Parsons, Philip A. *Responsibility for Crime*. Published by the Author, 1909.

Pitman, Benn, ed. *The Trials for Treason at Indianapolis, Disclosing the Plans for Establishing a North-Western Confederacy. Being the Official record of the Trials before the Military Commission*. Cincinnati: Moore, Wilstach & Baldwin, 1865.

Popular Rally at Springfield, September 11th, 1865. Endorsement of President Johnson's Reconstruction Policy. Speeches of Gen. John A. M'Clernand, Messrs. Geo W. Shutt, and Wm. M. Springer. Springfield: State Register Caloric Print, 1865.

Power, John Carroll. *History of Springfield, Illinois, Its Attractions as a Home and Advantages for Business, Manufacturing, Etc*. Springfield: Illinois State Journal, 1871.

———. *History of the Early Settlers of Sangamon County, Illinois*. Springfield: Wilson, 1876.

Proceedings of the Annual Congress of the National Prison Association of the United States held in Toronto, September 10–15, 1887. Chicago: Knight and Leonard, 1889.

Proceedings of the Illinois State Convention of Colored Men, Assembled at Galesburg, October 16th, 17th, and 18th. Chicago: Church, Goodman and Donnelley, 1867.

Proceedings of the State Convention of Colored Citizens of the State of Illinois, Held in the City of Alton, November 13, 14, and 15th, 1856. Chicago: Hays and Thompson, 1856.

Purple, N. H. *A Compilation of the Statutes of the State of Illinois, of a General Nature.* Part II. Chicago: Keen and Lee, 1856.

Rawick, George P. ed. *The American Slave: A Composite Autobiography.* Multiple volumes. 1941. Westport, CT: Greenwood, 1976.

Report of the Adjutant General of the State of Illinois. Vol. 6. Revised by Brig. Gen. J. N. Reece. Springfield: Journal Co., 1900.

Report of the Commissioners of The Illinois State Penitentiary for the Two Years Ending September 30, 1878. Springfield, IL: Weber, Magie, 1878.

Report of the Commissioners of the Illinois State Penitentiary at Joliet for the Two Years Ending September 30, 1880. Springfield: H. W. Rokker, 1880.

Report of the General Superintendent of Police of the City of Chicago to the City Council for the Year Ending December 31, 1891. Chicago: Cameron, Amberg, 1892.

Report of the Joint Committee of Investigation into the Affairs of the Illinois State Penitentiary. Springfield, IL: Illinois Journal Printing Office, 1872.

"Robert Wilson McClaughry." *Monmouth College Oracle* 15, no. 34 (1911): 31–32.

Rummel, Edward. *Rummel's Illinois Hand-Book, and Legislative Manual for 1871.* Springfield, IL: Illinois State Register Printing Office, 1871.

Scofield, Charles. *Historical Encyclopedia of Illinois and History of Hancock County.* Chicago: Munsell Publishing, 1921.

Stidger, Felix G. *Treason history of the Order of Sons of Liberty, formerly Circle of Honor, succeeded by Knights of the Golden Circle, afterward Order of American Knights.* Chicago: The Author, 1903.

Stone, Alfred H. *Studies in the American Race Problem.* New York: Doubleday, Page, 1908.

Sturtevant, Reverend J. M. "The Destiny of the African Race in the United States." *Continental Monthly* 3 (May 1863): 600–610.

Sweeney, Arthur. "Crime and Insanity." *Northwestern Lancet* 17 (May 15, 1897): 203–11.

Talbot, Eugene S. *Degeneracy: Its Causes, Signs, and Results.* London: Walter Scott; and New York: Charles Scribner's Sons, 1899.

———. "A Study of the Stigmata of Degeneracy among the American Criminal Youth." *Journal of the American Medical Association* 30 (April 9, 1898): 849–956.

The War of the Rebellion: A Compilation of the Official Records of the Union and Confederate Armies. Washington, DC: Government Printing Office, 1902.

United States Army, Office of the Judge Advocate General. *Report of the Judge Advocate General on "The Order of American Knights" alias "The Sons of Liberty": A Western Conspiracy in Aid of the Southern Rebellion.* Washington, DC: Chronicle Print., 1864.

United States Army, Office of the Judge Advocate General. *The Great Conspiracy. Vallandigham Commander. Military Organization. Assassination Tolerated. Collusion with Rebels.* Albany, NY: Weed, Parsons, 1864.

Van Evrie, John H. *Negroes and Negro "Slavery": The First an Inferior Race: The Latter Its Normal Condition.* 3rd ed. New York: Van Evrie, Horton, 1863.

———. *White Supremacy and Negro Subordination; or, Negroes a Subordinate Race and (so-called) Slavery Its Normal Condition*. New York: Van Evrie, Horton, 1868.
Wetmore, S. W. *Behind the Bars at Joliet: A Famous Prison, Its Celebrated Inmates, and Its Mysteries*. Joliet, IL: J. O. Gorman, 1892.
Wey, Hamilton D. "Criminal Anthropology." *Proceedings of the National Prison Association* (Pittsburgh: Shaw Brothers, 1891): 274–91.
Weir, James, Jr. "Criminal Anthropology." *Medical Record* 45 (January 13, 1894): 42–45.
———. "Criminal Psychology." *Medical Record* 46 (September 8, 1894): 296–d99.
Wilson, Douglas L., and Rodney O. Davis, eds. *Herndon's Informants: Letters, Interviews, and Statements about Abraham Lincoln*. Urbana: University of Illinois Press, 1998.
Wilson, Rufus R. *Intimate Memories of Lincoln*. Elmira, NY: Primavera Press, 1945.
Wines, E. C., and Theodore Dwight. *Report on the Prisons and Reformatories of the United States and Canada*. Albany, NY: Van Benthuysen and Sons, 1867.
Wines, Frederick H. *Punishment and Reformation*. New York: Thomas Y. Crowell, 1895.

Secondary Sources

Anderson, Ken. "The Role of Abraham Lincoln and Members of His Family in the Charleston Riot during the Civil War." *Lincoln Herald* 79 (June 1977): 53–60.
Angle, Paul M. *"Here I Have Lived": A History of Lincoln's Springfield*, new ed. Chicago: Abraham Lincoln Book Shop, 1971.
Arellano, Lisa. *Vigilantes and Lynch Mobs: Narratives of Community and Nation*. Philadelphia: Temple University Press, 2012.
Ash, Stephen V. *The Black Experience in the Civil War South*. Santa Barbara, CA: Praeger/ABC-CLIO, 2010.
———. *When the Yankees Came: Conflict and Chaos in the Occupied South, 1861–1865*. Chapel Hill: University of North Carolina Press, 1995.
Ayers, Edward L. *Vengeance and Justice: Crime and Punishment in the 19th-Century American South*. New York: Oxford University Press, 1984.
Bahde, Thomas. "'Our Cause Is a Common One': Home Guards, Union Leagues, and Republican Citizenship in Illinois, 1861–1863." *Civil War History* 56 (March 2010): 66–98.
Baker, Jean H. *Affairs of Party: The Political Culture of Northern Democrats in the Mid-Nineteenth Century*. New York: Fordham University Press, 1998.
———. *The Politics of Continuity: Maryland Political Parties from 1858 to 1870*. Baltimore: Johns Hopkins University Press, 1973.
Barnes, Harper. *Never Been a Time: The 1917 Race Riot That Sparked the Civil Rights Movement*. New York: Walker, 2008.
Berry, Daina Ramey. *Swing the Sickle for the Harvest Is Ripe: Gender and Slavery in Antebellum Georgia*. Urbana: University of Illinois Press, 2007.
Berwanger, Eugene H. *The Frontier against Slavery: Western Anti-Negro Prejudice and the Slavery Extension Controversy*. Urbana: University of Illinois Press, 1967.
———. *The West and Reconstruction*. Urbana: University of Illinois Press, 1981.
Bigham, Darrel E. *On Jordan's Banks: Emancipation and Its Aftermath in the Ohio River Valley*. Lexington: University Press of Kentucky, 2006.

———. *We Only Ask a Fair Trial: A History of the Black Community of Evansville, Indiana*. Bloomington: Indiana University Press, 1987.

———. "Work, Residence, and the Emergence of the Black Ghetto in Evansville, Indiana, 1865–1900." *Indiana Magazine of History* 76 (December 1980): 287–318.

Blake, Kellee. "'Aiding and Abetting': Disloyalty Prosecutions in the Federal Civil Courts of Southern Illinois, 1861–1866." *Illinois Historical Journal* 87 (Summer 1994): 95–108.

———. "Ten Firkins of Butter and Other 'Traitorous' Aid: Disloyalty Prosecutions in the Federal Civil Courts, 1861–1866." *Prologue: The Journal of the National Archives* 30 (Winter 1998): 289–93.

Blight, David. *Race and Reunion: The Civil War in American Memory*. Cambridge, MA: Belknap Press of Harvard University Press, 2001.

Blight, David W., and Brooks D. Simpson, eds. *Union and Emancipation: Essays on Politics and Race in the Civil War Era*. Kent, OH: Kent State University Press, 1997.

Blocker, Jack S., Jr. "Black Migration to Muncie, 1860–1930." *Indiana Magazine of History* 92 (December 1996): 297–320.

———. *A Little More Freedom: African Americans Enter the Urban Midwest, 1860–1930*. Columbus: Ohio State University Press, 2008.

Boyer, Paul. *Urban Masses and Moral Order in America, 1820–1920*. Cambridge, MA: Harvard University Press, 1978.

Boyle, Kevin. *Arc of Justice: A Saga of Race, Civil Rights, and Murder in the Jazz Age*. New York: Henry Holt, 2004.

Bridges, Roger D. "Equality Deferred: Civil Rights for Illinois Blacks, 1865–1885." *Journal of the Illinois State Historical Society* 74 (Summer 1981): 83–108.

Butler, Brian. *An Undergrowth of Folly: Public Order, Race Anxiety, and the 1903 Evansville, Indiana Riot*. New York: Garland, 2000.

Byrne, William. "Slave Crime in Savannah, Georgia." *Journal of Negro History* 79, no. 4 (1994): 352–62.

Carlson, Shirley. "Black Migration to Pulaski County, Illinois: 1860–1900." *Illinois Historical Journal* 80 (Spring 1987): 37–46.

Cashin, Joan E., ed. *The War Was You and Me: Civilians in the American Civil War*. Princeton: Princeton University Press, 2002.

Cayton, Andrew R. L., and Peter S. Onuf. *The Midwest and the Nation: Rethinking the History of an American Region*. Bloomington: Indiana University Press, 1990.

Chinn, Sarah E. *Technology and the Logic of American Racism: A Cultural History of the Body as Evidence*. London: Continuum, 2000.

Churchill, Robert. "Liberty, Conscription, and a Party Divided: The Sons of Liberty Conspiracy of 1863–1864." *Prologue: The Journal of the National Archives* 30 (Winter 1998): 295–303.

Cimbala, Paul A., and Randall M. Miller. *Union Soldiers and the Northern Home Front: Wartime Experiences, Postwar Adjustments*. New York: Fordham University Press, 2002.

Clark, Elizabeth B. "'The Sacred Rights of the Weak': Pain, Sympathy, and the Culture of Individual Rights in Antebellum America." *Journal of American History* 82 (September 1995): 463–93.

Cloyd, Benjamin G. *Haunted by Atrocity: Civil War Prisons in American Memory.* Baton Rouge: Louisiana State University Press, 2010.

Cohen, William. *At Freedom's Edge: Black Mobility and the Southern White Quest for Racial Control.* Baton Rouge: Louisiana State University Press, 1991.

Cole, Arthur Charles. *The Era of the Civil War, 1848–1870.* 1919. Freeport, NY: Books for Libraries Press, 1971.

Cole, Simon A. *Suspect Identities: A History of Fingerprinting and Criminal Identification.* Cambridge, MA: Harvard University Press, 2001.

Coleman, Charles H., and Paul H. Spence. "The Charleston Riot, March 28, 1864." *Journal of the Illinois State Historical Society* 33 (March 1940): 7–56.

Collins, William J. "When the Tide Turned: Immigration and the Delay of the Great Black Migration." *Journal of Economic History* 57 (September 1997): 607–32.

Colvin, Mark. *Penitentiaries, Reformatories, and Chain Gangs: Social Theory and the History of Punishment in Nineteenth-Century America.* New York: St. Martin's Press, 1997.

Curry, Leonard P. *The Free Black in Urban America, 1800–1850: The Shadow of the Dream.* Chicago: University of Chicago Press, 1981.

Daniels, Stephen. "Continuity and Change in Patterns of Case Handling: A Case Study of Two Rural Counties." *Law and Society Review* 19 (September 1985): 381–420.

Davis, Hugh. *"We Will Be Satisfied with Nothing Less": The African American Struggle for Equal Rights in the North during Reconstruction.* Ithaca, NY: Cornell University Press, 2011.

Donald, David Herbert. *Lincoln's Herndon.* New York: Alfred A. Knopf, 1948.

———. *"We Are Lincoln Men": Abraham Lincoln and His Friends.* New York: Simon and Schuster, 2003.

Douglas, Davison M. *Jim Crow Moves North: The Battle over Northern School Segregation, 1865–1954.* New York: Cambridge University Press, 2005.

Doyle, Don Harrison. *The Social Order of a Frontier Community: Jacksonville, Illinois, 1825–70.* Urbana: University of Illinois Press, 1978.

Dumm, Thomas. *Democracy and Punishment: Disciplinary Origins of the United States.* Madison: University of Wisconsin Press, 1987.

Dunbar, Erica Armstrong. *A Fragile Freedom: African American Women and Emancipation in the Antebellum City.* New Haven: Yale University Press, 2008.

Edwards, Laura F. "Status without Rights: African Americans and the Tangled History of Law and Governance in the Nineteenth-Century US South." *American Historical Review* 112 (April 2007): 365–93.

Erickson, Gary Lee. "The Last Years of William Henry Herndon." *Journal of the Illinois State Historical Society* 67 (1974): 101–19.

Escott, Paul D. *"What Shall We Do with the Negro?": Lincoln, White Racism, and Civil War America.* Charlottesville: University of Virginia Press, 2009.

Etcheson, Nicole. *The Emerging Midwest: Upland Southerners and the Political Culture of the Old Northwest, 1787–1861.* Bloomington: Indiana University Press, 1996.

———. *A Generation at War: The Civil War Era in a Northern Community.* Lawrence: University Press of Kansas, 2011.

Fabian, Ann. *The Skull Collectors: Race, Science, and America's Unburied Dead.* Chicago: University of Chicago Press, 2010.
Fehrenbacher, Don E. *Lincoln in Text and Context: Collected Essays.* Stanford: Stanford University Press, 1987.
Fink, Arthur E. *Causes of Crime: Biological Theories in the United States, 1800–1915.* Philadelphia: University of Pennsylvania Press, 1938.
Finkelman, Paul. "Evading the Ordinance: The Persistence of Bondage in Indiana and Illinois." *Journal of the Early Republic* 9 (Spring 1989): 21–51.
———. "Slavery, the 'More Perfect Union,' and the Prairie State." *Illinois Historical Journal* 80 (Winter 1987): 248–69.
———. "Slavery and the Northwest Ordinance: A Study in Ambiguity," *Journal of the Early Republic* 6 (Winter 1986), 343–70.
Flanders, Ralph. *Plantation Slavery in Georgia.* Chapel Hill: University of North Carolina Press, 1933.
Foner, Eric. *The Fiery Trial: Abraham Lincoln and American Slavery.* New York: W. W. Norton, 2010.
———. *Nothing But Freedom: Emancipation and Its Legacy.* Baton Rouge: Louisiana State University Press, 1983.
———. *Reconstruction: America's Unfinished Revolution, 1863–1867.* New York: Harper and Row, 1988.
Forret, Jeff. *Race Relations at the Margins: Slaves and Poor Whites in the Antebellum Southern Countryside.* Baton Rouge: Louisiana State University Press, 2006.
Foucault, Michel. *Discipline and Punish: The Birth of the Prison.* Translated by Alan Sheridan. New York: Pantheon, 1977.
Frank, Joseph Allan. *With Ballot and Bayonet: The Political Socialization of American Civil War Soldiers.* Athens: University of Georgia Press, 1998.
Fredrickson, George M. *The Black Image in the White Mind: The Debate on Afro-American Character and Destiny, 1817–1914.* New York: Harper and Row, 1971.
Friedman, Lawrence, and Robert Percival. *The Roots of Justice: Crime and Punishment in Alameda County, California, 1870–1910.* Chapel Hill: University of North Carolina Press, 1981
Gambill, Edward L. *Conservative Ordeal: Northern Democrats and Reconstruction, 1865–1869.* Ames: Iowa State University Press, 1981.
Gara, Larry. "The Underground Railroad in Illinois." *Journal of the Illinois State Historical Society* 56 (Autumn 1963): 508–28.
Genovese, Eugene D. *Roll, Jordan, Roll: The World the Slaves Made.* New York: Vintage, 1976.
Gerber, David. *Black Ohio and the Color Line, 1860–1915.* Urbana: University of Illinois Press, 1976.
Gibson, Mary. *Born to Crime: Cesare Lombroso and the Origins of Biological Criminology.* Westport, CT: Praeger, 2002.
Glenn, Myra. *Campaigns against Corporal Punishment: Prisoners, Sailors, Women, and Children in Antebellum America.* Albany: State University of New York Press, 1984.
Gossett, Thomas F. *Race: The History of an Idea in America.* Dallas: Southern Methodist University Press, 1963.

Gould, Stephen Jay. *The Mismeasure of Man*. New York: W. W. Norton, 1981.
Grossman, James. *Land of Hope: Chicago, Black Southerners, and the Great Migration*. Chicago: University of Chicago Press, 1989.
Grossman, Lawrence. *The Democratic Party and the Negro: Northern and National Politics 1868–92*. Urbana: University of Illinois Press, 1976.
Hahn, Stephen. *A Nation under Our Feet: Black Political Struggles in the Rural South from Slavery to the Great Migration*. Cambridge, MA: Harvard University Press, 2003.
Haller, John S., Jr. *Outcasts from Evolution: Scientific Attitudes of Racial Inferiority, 1859–1900*. Urbana: University of Illinois Press, 1971.
Haller, Mark H. *Eugenics: Hereditarian Attitudes in American Thought*. New Brunswick, NJ: Rutgers University Press, 1963.
———. "Urban Crime and Criminal Justice: The Chicago Case." *Journal of American History* 57 (1970): 619–35.
Halttunen, Karen. "Humanitarianism and the Pornography of Pain in Anglo-American Culture." *American Historical Review* 100, no. 2 (1995): 303–34.
Hannah, Eleanor. *Manhood, Citizenship, and the National Guard: Illinois, 1870–1917*. Columbus: Ohio State University Press, 2007.
Hansen, Stephen L. *The Making of the Third Party System: Voters and Parties in Illinois, 1850–1876*. Ann Arbor, MI: UMI Research Press, 1980.
Harring, Sidney L. *Policing a Class Society: The Experience of American Cities, 1865–1915*. New Brunswick, NJ: Rutgers University Press, 1983.
Hart, Richard E. "The Spirit of Springfield's Early African-Americans, 1818–1859." *Program Papers of the Sangamon County Historical Society*, May 21, 2002.
———. "Springfield's African Americans as a Part of the Lincoln Community." *Journal of the Abraham Lincoln Association* 20 (Winter 1999): 35–54.
Hawes, Joseph, ed. *Law and Order in American History*. Port Washington, NY: Kennikat Press, 1979.
Hawkins, Homer. "Trends in Black Migration from 1863 to 1960." *Phylon* 34, no. 2 (1973): 140–152.
Hess, Earl J. *Liberty, Virtue, and Progress: Northerners and Their War for the Union*. New York: New York University Press, 1988.
Hesslink, George. *Black Neighbors: Negroes in a Northern Rural Community*. Indianapolis: Bobbs-Merrill, 1974.
Hickey, James T. "Springfield, May, 1865." *Journal of the Illinois State Historical Society* 58 (March 1965): 21–33.
Hindus, Michael Stephen. "The Contours of Crime and Justice in Massachusetts and South Carolina, 1767–1878." *American Journal of Legal History* 21 (July 1977): 212–37.
Hindus, Michael S. *Prison and Plantation: Crime, Justice, and Authority in Massachusetts and South Carolina, 1767–1878*. Chapel Hill: University of North Carolina Press, 1980.
Hine, Darlene, and Jacqueline McLeod, eds. *Crossing Boundaries: Comparative History of Black People in Diaspora*. Bloomington: Indiana University Press, 1999.
Hirsch, Adam Jay. *The Rise of the Penitentiary: Prisons and Punishment in Early America*. New Haven: Yale University Press, 1992.

Holt, Michael F. *The Political Crisis of the 1850s*. New York: Wiley, 1978.
Horton, Carol A. *Race and the Making of American Liberalism*. New York: Oxford University Press, 2005.
Horton, James Oliver. *Free People of Color: Inside the African American Community*. Washington, DC: Smithsonian Institution Press, 1993.
Horton, James Oliver, and Lois E. Horton. *In Hope of Liberty: Culture, Community, and Protest among Northern Free Blacks, 1700–1860*. New York: Oxford University Press, 1997.
Ignatieff, Michael. *A Just Measure of Pain: The Penitentiary in the Industrial Revolution, 1750–1850*. New York: Pantheon, 1978.
Jackson, W. Sherman. "Emancipation, Negrophobia and Civil War Politics in Ohio, 1863–1865." *Journal of Negro History* 65 (Summer 1980): 250–60.
Jimerson, Randall C. *The Private Civil War: Popular Thought during the Sectional Conflict*. Baton Rouge: Louisiana State University Press, 1988.
Johnson, Daniel M., and Rex R. Campbell. *Black Migration in America: A Social Demographic History*. Durham, NC: Duke University Press, 1981.
Johnson, David R. *Policing the Urban Underworld: The Impact of Crime on the Development of the American Police, 1800–1887*. Philadelphia: Temple University Press, 1979.
Johnson, Walter. *Soul by Soul: Life Inside the Antebellum Slave Market*. Cambridge, MA: Harvard University Press, 1999.
Johnson, Whittington B. *Black Savannah: 1788–1864*. Fayetteville: University of Arkansas Press, 1996.
Johnston, Allan. "Being Free: Black Migration and the Civil War." *Australasian Journal of American Studies* 6, no. 1 (1987): 3–21.
Kachun, Mitch. *Festivals of Freedom: Memory and Meaning in African American Emancipation Celebrations, 1808–1915*. Amherst: University of Massachusetts Press, 2003.
Keehn, David C. *Knights of the Golden Circle: Secret Empire, Southern Secession, Civil War*. Baton Rouge: Louisiana State University Press, 2013.
Kerr-Ritchie, J. R. *Rites of August First: Emancipation Day in the Black Atlantic World*. Baton Rouge: Louisiana State University Press, 2007.
King, Desmond, and Stephen Tuck. "De-centring the South: America's Nationwide White Supremacist Order after Reconstruction." *Past and Present* 194 (February 2007): 213–53.
Klement, Frank. "Copperhead Secret Societies in Illinois during the Civil War." *Journal of the Illinois State Historical Society* 48 (Summer 1955): 152–80.
———. *The Copperheads in the Middle West*. Chicago: University of Chicago Press, 1960.
———. *Dark Lanterns: Secret Political Societies, Conspiracies, and Treason Trials in the Civil War*. Baton Rouge: Louisiana State University Press, 1984.
Kousser, J. Morgan, and James M. McPherson, eds. *Region, Race, and Reconstruction: Essays in Honor of C. Vann Woodward*. New York: Oxford University Press, 1982.
Kusmer, Kenneth. *Down and Out, on the Road: The Homeless in American History*. Oxford: Oxford University Press, 2002.

Lane, Roger. *Policing the City: Boston, 1822–1885.* Cambridge, MA: Harvard University Press, 1967.
———. *Roots of Violence in Black Philadelphia, 1860–1900.* Cambridge, MA: Harvard University Press, 1986.
Lause, Mark A. *A Secret Society History of the Civil War.* Urbana: University of Illinois Press, 2011.
Levine, Lawrence W. *Black Culture and Black Consciousness: Afro-American Folk Thought from Slavery to Freedom.* New York: Oxford University Press, 1977.
Lichtenstein, Alex. "That Disposition to Theft, with Which They Have Been Branded: Moral Economy, Slave Management, and the Law." *Journal of Social History* 21 (Spring 1988): 413–40.
Litwack, Leon. *Been in the Storm So Long: The Aftermath of Slavery.* New York: Knopf, 1979.
———. *North of Slavery: The Negro in the Free States, 1790–1860.* Chicago: University of Chicago Press, 1961.
Lockley, Timothy James. *Lines in the Sand: Race and Class in Lowcountry Georgia, 1750–1860.* Athens: University of Georgia Press, 2001.
Lumpkins, Charles L. *American Pogrom: The East St. Louis Race Riot and Black Politics.* Athens: Ohio University Press, 2008.
McCaul, Robert L. *The Black Struggle for Public Schooling in Nineteenth-Century Illinois.* Carbondale: Southern Illinois University Press, 1987.
McDermott, Stacy Pratt. *The Jury in Lincoln's America.* Athens: Ohio University Press, 2012.
McDonough, Daniel, and Kenneth W. Noe, eds. *Politics and Culture of the Civil War Era: Essays in Honor of Robert W. Johannsen.* Selinsgrove, PA: Susquehana University Press, 2006.
McGlynn, Frank, and Seymour Drescher, eds. *The Meaning of Freedom: Economics, Politics, and Culture after Slavery.* Pittsburgh: University of Pittsburgh Press, 1992.
McLennan, Rebecca M. *The Crisis of Imprisonment: Protest, Politics, and the Making of the American Penal State, 1776–1941.* Cambridge: Cambridge University Press, 2008.
McNair, Glenn. *Criminal Injustice: Slaves and Free Blacks in Georgia's Criminal Justice System.* Charlottesville: University of Virginia Press, 2009.
McPherson, James M. *For Cause and Comrades: Why Men Fought in the Civil War.* New York: Oxford University Press, 1997.
Manning, Chandra. *What This Cruel War Was Over: Soldiers, Slavery, and the Civil War.* New York: Alfred A. Knopf, 2007.
Masur, Kate. "'A Rare Phenomenon of Philological Vegetation': The Word 'Contraband' and the Meanings of Emancipation in the United States." *Journal of American History* 93 (March 2007): 1050–84.
Masur, Louis. *Rites of Execution: Capital Punishment and the Transformation of American Culture, 1776–1865.* New York: Oxford University Press, 1989.
Melossi, Dario, and Massimo Pavarini. *The Prison and the Factory: Origins of the Penitentiary System.* Totowa, NJ: Barnes and Noble, 1981.

Menand, Louis. *The Metaphysical Club: A Story of Ideas in America.* New York: Farrar, Straus and Giroux, 2001.

Meranze, Michael. *Laboratories of Virtue: Punishment, Revolution, and Authority in Philadelphia, 1760–1835.* Chapel Hill: University of North Carolina Press, 1996.

Miller, Edward A., Jr. *The Black Civil War Soldiers of Illinois: The Story of the Twenty-ninth US Colored Infantry.* Columbia: University of South Carolina Press, 1998.

Mintz, Steven, and John Stauffer, eds., *The Problem of Evil: Slavery, Freedom, and the Ambiguities of American Reform.* Amherst: University of Massachusetts Press, 2007.

Mitchell, Reid. *Civil War Soldiers.* New York: Viking, 1988.

Mohr, Clarence L. *On the Threshold of Freedom: Masters and Slaves in Civil War Georgia.* Athens: University of Georgia Press, 1986.

Monkkonen, Eric. *Crime, Justice, History.* Columbus: Ohio State University Press, 2002.

———. *The Dangerous Class: Crime and Poverty in Columbus, Ohio, 1860–1885.* Cambridge, MA: Harvard University Press, 1975.

———. *Murder in New York City.* Berkeley: University of California Press, 2001.

———. *Police in Urban America, 1860–1920.* Cambridge: Cambridge University Press, 1981.

———. "A Disorderly People?: Urban Order in the Nineteenth and Twentieth Centuries." *Journal of American History* 68 (1981): 539–59.

Morrison, Michael A. *Slavery and the American West: The Eclipse of Manifest Destiny and the Coming of the Civil War.* Chapel Hill: University of North Carolina Press, 1997.

Muhammad, Khalil Gibran. *The Condemnation of Blackness: Race, Crime, and the Making of Modern Urban America.* Cambridge, MA: Harvard University Press, 2010.

Neely, Mark E., Jr. *The Boundaries of American Political Culture in the Civil War Era.* Chapel Hill: University of North Carolina Press, 2005.

———. *The Fate of Liberty: Abraham Lincoln and Civil Liberties.* New York: Oxford University Press, 1991.

Nelson, Scott Reynolds, and Carol Sheriff. *A People at War: Civilians and Soldiers in America's Civil War, 1854–1877.* New York: Oxford University Press, 2007.

Newborn, Newton N. "Judicial Decision Making and the End of Slavery in Illinois." *Journal of the Illinois State Historical Society* 98 (March 2005): 7–33.

Newby, I. A. *Jim Crow's Defense: Anti-Negro Thought in America, 1900–1930.* Baton Rouge: Louisiana State University Press, 1965.

Noyes, Edward. "White Opposition to Black Migration into Civil War Wisconsin." *Lincoln Herald* 73 (September 1971): 181–93.

O'Donovan, Susan Eva. *Becoming Free in the Cotton South.* Cambridge, MA: Harvard University Press, 2007.

Onuf, Peter S. "From Constitution to Higher Law: The Reinterpretation of the Northwest Ordinance." *Ohio History* 94 (Winter/Spring 1985): 5–33.

Ostendorf, Lloyd. "Faces Lincoln Knew . . . Photographs from the Past: The Story of William Florville; Mr. Lincoln's Barber." *Lincoln Herald* 79 (Spring 1977): 29–32.

Peterson, William. "A History of Camp Butler, 1861–1866." *Illinois Historical Journal* 82 (Summer 1989): 74–92.

Pfeifer, Michael J. *Rough Justice: Lynching and American Society, 1847–1947*. Urbana: University of Illinois Press, 2004.

Pickens, Donald K. *Eugenics and the Progressives*. Nashville, TN: Vanderbilt University Press, 1968.

Pisciotta, Alexander. "A House Divided: Penal Reform at the Illinois State Reformatory, 1891–1915." *Crime and Delinquency* 37 (April 1991): 165–85.

Platt, Anthony. *The Child Savers: The Invention of Delinquency*. Chicago: University of Chicago Press, 1977.

Quinn, Camilla A. Corlas. "Forgotten Soldiers: The Confederate Prisoners at Camp Butler, 1862–1863." *Illinois Historical Journal* 81 (Spring 1988): 35–44.

———. "Soldiers on Our Streets: The Effects of a Civil War Military Camp on the Springfield Community." *Illinois Historical Journal* 86 (Winter 1993): 245–56.

Rafter, Nicole Hahn. *Creating Born Criminals*. Urbana: University of Illinois Press, 1997.

Ramold, Steven J. *Across the Divide: Union Soldiers View the Northern Home Front*. New York: New York University Press, 2013.

Reed, Scott Owen. "Military Arrests of Lawyers in Illinois during the Civil War." *Western Illinois Regional Studies* 6, no. 2 (1983): 5–22.

Regosin, Elizabeth. *Freedom's Promise: Ex-Slave Families and Citizenship in the Age of Emancipation*. Charlottesville: University Press of Virginia, 2002.

Reidy, Joseph. *From Slavery to Agrarian Capitalism in the Cotton Plantation South: Central Georgia, 1800–1880*. Chapel Hill: University of North Carolina Press, 1991.

Renne, Louis O. *Lincoln and the Land of the Sangamon*. Boston: Chapman and Grimes, 1945.

Richardson, Heather Cox. *The Death of Reconstruction: Race, Labor, and Politics in the Post–Civil War North, 1865–1901*. Cambridge, MA: Harvard University Press, 2001.

———. *West from Appomattox: The Reconstruction of America after the Civil War*. New Haven: Yale University Press, 2007.

Rothman, David J. *Conscience and Convenience: The Asylum and Its Alternatives in Progressive America*. Boston: Little, Brown, 1980.

———. *The Discovery of the Asylum: Social Order and Disorder in the Early Republic*. Boston: Little, Brown, 1971.

Rudwick, Elliott M. *Race Riot at East St. Louis, July 2, 1917*. Carbondale: Southern Illinois University Press, 1964.

Rugh, Susan Sessions. "'Awful Calamities Now upon Us': The Civil War in Fountain Green, Illinois." *Journal of the Illinois State Historical Society* 93 (March 2000): 9–42.

———. "Civilizing the Countryside: Class, Gender, and Crime in Nineteenth-Century Rural Illinois." *Agricultural History* 76 (Winter 2002): 58–81.

———. *Our Common Country: Family Farming, Culture, and Community in the Nineteenth-Century Midwest*. Bloomington: Indiana University Press, 2001.

Samito, Christian G. *Becoming American under Fire: Irish Americans, African Americans, and the Politics of Citizenship during the Civil War Era*. Ithaca, NY: Cornell University Press, 2009.

Sampson, Robert D. "'Pretty Damned Warm Times': The 1864 Charleston Riot and the 'Inalienable Right of Revolution.'" *Illinois Historical Journal* 89 (Summer 1996): 99–116.

Saville, Julie. "Rites and Power: Reflections on Slavery, Freedom and Political Ritual." *Slavery and Abolition* 20 (April 1999): 81–102.

———. *The Work of Reconstruction: From Slave to Wage Laborer in South Carolina, 1860–1870*. Cambridge: Cambridge University Press, 1994.

Schwalm, Leslie A. *Emancipation's Diaspora: Race and Reconstruction in the Upper Midwest*. Chapel Hill: University of North Carolina Press, 2009.

———. "'Overrun with Free Negroes': Emancipation and Wartime Migration in the Upper Midwest." *Civil War History* 50 (June 2004): 145–74.

Schwartz, Marie Jenkins. *Born in Bondage: Growing Up Enslaved in the Antebellum South*. Cambridge, MA: Harvard University Press, 2000.

Senechal, Roberta. *The Sociogenesis of a Race Riot: Springfield, Illinois, in 1908*. Urbana: University of Illinois Press, 1990.

Sheehan-Dean, Aaron, ed. *The View from the Ground: Experiences of Civil War Soldiers*. Lexington: University Press of Kentucky, 2007.

Silbey, Joel. *The American Political Nation, 1838–1893*. Stanford: Stanford University Press, 1991.

———. *A Respectable Minority: The Democratic Party in the Civil War Era, 1860–1868*. New York: Norton, 1977.

Smith, Adam I. P. *No Party Now: Politics in the Civil War North*. New York: Oxford University Press, 2006.

Smith, Beverly A. "Murder in a Rural Setting: Logan County Homicides, 1865–1900." *Western Illinois Regional Studies* 13, no. 1 (1990): 61–79.

Stanton, William. *The Leopard's Spots: Scientific Attitudes toward Race in America, 1815–59*. Chicago: University of Chicago Press, 1960.

Steinberg, Allen. *The Transformation of Criminal Justice: Philadelphia, 1800–1880*. Chapel Hill: University of North Carolina Press, 1989.

Sterling, Robert E. "Civil War Draft Resistance in Illinois." *Journal of the Illinois State Historical Society* 64 (September 1971): 244–66.

———. "Discouragement, Weariness, and War Politics: Desertions from Illinois Regiments during the Civil War." *Illinois Historical Journal* 82 (Winter 1989): 239–62.

Suggs, Jon-Christian. *Whispered Consolation: Law and Narrative in African American Life*. Ann Arbor: University of Michigan Press, 2000.

Summers, Mark Wahlgren. *A Dangerous Stir: Fear, Paranoia, and the Making of Reconstruction*. Chapel Hill: University of North Carolina Press, 2009.

Tap, Bruce. "Race, Rhetoric, and Emancipation: The Election of 1862 in Illinois." *Civil War History* 39 (June 1993): 101–25.

Thornbrough, Emma Lou. *The Negro in Indiana before 1900: A Study of a Minority*. Indianapolis: Indiana Historical Bureau, 1957.

Tucker, William H. *The Science and Politics of Racial Research*. Urbana: University of Illinois Press, 1994.

Tuttle, William. *Race Riot: Chicago in the Red Summer of 1919*. 1970. Urbana: University of Illinois Press, 1996.

Vandal, Gilles. "Property Offenses, Social Tension and Racial Antagonism in Post–Civil War Rural Louisiana." *Journal of Social History* 31 (Fall 1997): 127–53.

Van Deburg, William L. *Hoodlums: Black Villains and Social Bandits in American Life.* Chicago: University of Chicago Press, 2004.

Vedder, Richard K., Lowell Galloway, Philip E. Graves, and Robert L. Sexton. "Demonstrating Their Freedom: The Post-Emancipation Migration of Black Americans." *Research in Economic History* 10 (1986): 213–39.

Vincent, Stephen. *Southern Seed, Northern Soil: African-American Farm Communities in the Midwest, 1765–1900.* Bloomington: Indiana University Press, 1999.

Vinovskis, Maris A., ed. *Toward a Social History of the American Civil War: Exploratory Essays.* Cambridge: Cambridge University Press, 1990.

Voegeli, V. Jacque. *Free but Not Equal: The Midwest and the Negro during the Civil War.* Chicago: University of Chicago Press, 1967.

Vorenberg, Michael. *Final Freedom: The Civil War, the Abolition of Slavery, and the Thirteenth Amendment.* Cambridge: Cambridge University Press, 2001.

Waldrep, Christopher. *The Many Faces of Judge Lynch: Extralegal Violence and Punishment in America.* New York: Palgrave Macmillan, 2002.

———. *Roots of Disorder: Race and Criminal Justice in the American South, 1817–80.* Urbana: University of Illinois Press, 1998.

Waldrep, Christopher, and Donald G. Nieman, eds. *Local Matters: Race, Crime, and Justice in the Nineteenth-Century South.* Athens: University of Georgia Press, 2001.

Waldstreicher, David. *In the Midst of Perpetual Fetes: The Making of American Nationalism, 1776–1820.* Chapel Hill: University of North Carolina Press.

Walker, Samuel. *A Critical History of Police Reform: The Emergence of Professionalism.* Lexington, MA: Lexington Books, 1977.

———. *Popular Justice: A History of American Criminal Justice.* 2nd ed. New York: Oxford University Press, 1998.

Wallenstein, Peter. *From Slave South to New South: Public Policy in Nineteenth-Century Georgia.* Chapel Hill: University of North Carolina Press, 1987.

Wang, Xi *The Trial of Democracy: Black Suffrage and Northern Republicans, 1860–1910.* Athens: University of Georgia Press, 1997.

Weber, Jennifer. *Copperheads: The Rise and Fall of Lincoln's Opponents in the North.* New York: Oxford University Press, 2006.

West, Elliott. *The Last Indian War: The Nez Perce Story.* New York: Oxford University Press, 2009.

Wiggins, William H. *O Freedom!: Afro-American Emancipation Celebrations.* Knoxville: University of Tennessee Press, 1987.

Winkle, Kenneth J. *The Young Eagle: The Rise of Abraham Lincoln.* Dallas: Taylor, 2001.

Wood, Betty. *Women's Women, Men's Work: The Informal Slave Economies of Lowcountry Georgia.* Athens: University of Georgia Press, 1995.

Wood, Forrest G. *Black Scare: The Racist Response to Emancipation and Reconstruction.* Berkeley: University of California Press, 1968.

INDEX

Page numbers in bold refer to images.

African Americans, 3, 5, 6, 52, 150, 169n8; conventions of, 46, 50–51, 63–65; criminality and, 3, 7, 42, 95, 98, 110–14, 119–21, 142, 146, 151–53, 156–59; migration of, 5–6, 20, 24, 30, 37–40, 43, 46–47, 52–57, 70, 146, 169n8, 180n81, 184n5; as soldiers, 33, 34, 51–52, 60–61; stereotypes of, 32, 71, 93, 111–13, 117, 121, 158, 159, 172n26; suffrage and, 3, 6, 22, 45, 46, 60, 67, 68, 70–76, 78, 87, 88, 90, 93,113, 158. *See also* contrabands; fugitive slaves

Agassiz, Louis, 158, 201n61

anthropometry, 3, 143, 150

Bateman, Newton, 81, 82, 83
Bates, Edward, 40, 181 n89
Beaumont, Gustave de, 134
Bertillon, Alphonse, 3, 143; measurement system of, 3, 143–45, 150
Beveridge, John, 138, 139
Black Laws (Illinois), 15–17, 35, 37–39, 43, 44, 45, 50, 51, 60, 65, 67, 69, 70, 81, 88, 112, 155, 156, 183n11; repeal of, 4, 5, 17, 20, 38, 70, 72, 76, 107, 113
Boies, Henry, 144, 145, 156
Brent, Rev. George, 61, 62, 64, 65
Brown, John (former slave), 12, 13
Buchanan, James, 21, 23
Burton, Scott, 99, 100, 101, 125, 154, 155, 159, 161, 204n1

Camp Butler (Illinois), 28, 30, 51, 54, 60
Canter, Edward (fugitive slave), 51
Carthage Republican, 30, 33, 36, 38, 71
Cartwright, Samuel, 146
Chambers v. The People, 40
Charleston Riot (Illinois), 27
Chicago Inter-Ocean, 101
Chicago Tribune, 8, 35, 131, 133, 136–39, 141, 151
Child, George M., 38, 39
Christison, J. Sanderson, 151
Civil Rights Act (1866), 78
Civil Rights Act (1870), 79, 80

Clements, Frederick (fugitive slave), 21, 22, 83
Coleman, Landon, 61–64
Colored School (Springfield, IL), 49–50, 57–60, 79, 80–87, 190n52
Confederate States of America, 6, 10, 25, 79
contrabands, 12, 15, 16, 24
convicts, 42, 104–5, 124, 126, 130, 135, 138, 141, 146, 152, 164, 195n52, 197n18. *See also* prisoners
Copperheads, 25–27, 29–31, 34–36, 61, 72, 73, 76. *See also* Democratic Party
crime, 3, 7, 74, 78, 95–96, 98, 100–114, 117–18, 121, 137, 141, 142, 147, 153, 156–59, 172n26, 194n39, 199n50, 200n61, 203n82; environment and, 145, 147–53, 156, 203n77, 204n86; heredity and, 145, 147–50, 153, 156, 202n71, 203n77; petty, 9, 102, 104, 107, 109, 117; property, 108–9, 111, 165; race and, 7, 88–96, 98, 100–101, 106, 108, 111–21, 145–47, 150–53, 156, 157, 204n86; vice, 109–10, 165; violent, 109, 110–11, 116, 165, 198n24. *See also* theft
criminals, 3, 42, 68, 90, 98, 101, 112, 115–20, 126, 130, 134, 137, 142–53, 155, 156, 199n47, 202n71, 202n76, 203n77
criminology, 3, 7, 121, 144, 146, 147, 148, 153, 158, 159

Davidson, James M., 71, 72, 73
Dawson, George, 149, 150
Democratic Party, 3, 6, 19–25, 29–31, 33–36, 38, 46, 61–62, 66, 69–71, 74–78, 81, 84, 85, 87–90, 95, 96, 107–8, 113, 139, 155, 157, 170n9, 175n17, 175n22, 176nn28–29, 180n75, 188n6; military service and, 29, 30, 31, 33, 34–36, 71, 74; National Democrats, 22–23, 175n16; opposition to emancipation, 24, 25, 30, 33, 34, 36, 70, 71, 77, 113, 157; racial rhetoric of, 6, 20, 22, 24, 33, 34, 36, 38, 65, 68–71, 74–78, 81, 84, 85, 87–90, 95, 96, 112–13, 114–15, 155, 157, 170n9. *See also* Copperheads

223

desegregation, 78–80; in courts, 107–8; in public schools, 63, 80, 81, 83–87
Donnegan, Cyrus, 62, 66, 79, 91
Donnegan, Spencer, 47, 60, 62, 186n52
Donnegan, William, 155, 159
Douglas, Stephen, 19, 20, 22, 23, 29, 30, 175n22
Douglass, Frederick, 12, 61, 64, 186n50
Dripps, C. T., 130, 131
Duncan, Clark, 56
Dunning, William Archibald, 158

East Saint Louis (Illinois), 156
Eells v. The People, 40, 42
elections, 23, 35, 36, 50, 62, 66, 67, 72, 75, 92, 191n60; violence during, 88–95, 191n82
Ellis, Havelock, 147, 148
emancipation, 2–6, 15, 19, 25, 30–32, 37, 46, 52, 53, 68, 70–72, 74, 97, 113, 119, 157–59; Democratic opposition to, 24, 25, 30, 33, 34, 36, 70, 71, 77, 113, 157; Union soldiers' views on, 30–34, 36
Emancipation Day (West Indian), 50, 66, 91
Emancipation Proclamation, 24, 26, 30, 33, 37, 38, 45, 60, 61, 71, 98, 113
Evansville, IN, 52–53

federal courts, 21–22, 23, 28–29, 80, 104, 112
Ficklin, Orlando, 23, 24
Fifteenth Amendment, 45, 60, 62, 66, 82, 87–88, 89, 95, 112
Fisher, Emma, 102, 106, 120
Fisher, John, 99–103, 106, 120, 125, 161
Fisher, Sidney George, 76
Florville, William, 19, 46–47, 49, 56, 61, 182n3
Fourteenth Amendment, 42, 46, 60, 65, 82, 87, 112
Fugitive Slave Act, 20, 21, 23, 24, 39, 43
fugitive slaves, 20, 21–22, 23, 24, 35, 37–44, 47, 50, 51, 83, 146

Georgia, 1, 2, 4, 9–15, 53, 100, 163; impact of Civil War on, 80; Savannah, 10, 15, 170–71n3; slavery in, 9–13
Gilmore, James, 111, 194 n51
Gliddon, George, 145
Gordon, Samuel, 31–33, 71
Grant, Ulysses S., 62, 90–95
Greeley, Horace, 90–92, 95

Hawley, Orestes, 35, 37–39
Hay, John, 20
Heise, Adolph, 126, 128, 130–33

Herndon, Archer, 21
Herndon, Elliott B., 2, 3, 19, 21–23, 28, 29, 34, 74–76, 94, 103, 107, 118
Herndon, William H., 2, 19, 21–23, 51, 60–62, 83, 118
Hicklin, Hezekiah, 64, 65
Hoffman, Frederick, 151
homicide, 110–11

Illinois, 1–6, 9, 11, 18–44, 45–68, 69–96, 97–121, 122–44, 146, 148, 149, 155, 158, 161, 163, 164, 168n4, 174n9, 175n16, 175n22, 176n28; Adams County, 31, 38, 39, 178n52, 181n88; Alton, 51; black migration to, 5–6, 15–17, 20, 24–25, 37–44, 46–47, 52–57, 67, 146, 169n8, 180n81; Cairo, 15–17, 24, 54; Carthage, 29, 30, 33, 35, 38, 71, 72, 74; Charleston, 27; Chicago, 3, 15, 22–24, 28, 35, 46, 50, 54, 60, 65, 66, 88, 94, 122, 131, 143, 144, 150, 151, 156, 187n64; Coles County, 27; constitution of, 4, 24, 40, 43, 46, 75, 82, 83, 87, 88; Copperhead Constitution, 25, 36, 37; Decatur, 63, 93; East Saint Louis, 156; Fayette County, 28; Fountain Green, 29, 36, 74; Galesburg, 64; Hancock County, 3, 5, 29–31, 34–39, 44, 71–74, 139, 178n52, 180n81; Jacksonville, 63, 66, 77, 98, 101, 120, 125, 162; Joliet, 8, 46, 97, 100, 103, 104, 111, 113, 116, 121, 122, 124–26, 131, 133, 134, 137–39, 141–43, 158, 161, 162; Macon County, 26; Macoupin County, 51; Madison County, 51; McDonough County, 36, 178n52; Monroe County, 26; Montgomery County, 26; public schools, 46, 51, 81–83; Pulaski County, 53; Quincy, 16, 17, 51, 181n88, 181n89; Saline County, 26; Taylorville, 98, 102. *See also* Sangamon County, IL; Springfield, IL
Illinois State Democrat, 22–23
Illinois State Journal, 18, 61, 62, 67, 85, 101, 112, 114, 136–37
Illinois State Penitentiary, 1–3, 8, 9, 43, 46, 95, 97, 98, 103, 104, 107, 109, 111, 113, 121, 122–43, 158, 161, 162, 164; administration of, 133, 137, 138, 139, 141; board of commissioners, 1, 131–33, 135–39, 141; discipline at, 124, 125, 128, 130, 132–35, 138, 139, 141; investigations of, 1, 126, 131–34, 136, 138–39; punishment at, 124, 126, 128, 133, 134, 136, 141; quarry, 46, 125, 137–38, 199n39; reform of, 139–41; solitary confinement, 1, **123**, 124, 126, **127**, 128–33;

treatment of prisoners, 1, 126, 131–36, 138, 141; use of gag, 1, 8–9, 128–33, 136
Illinois State Reformatory, 149, 203n81
Illinois State Register, 18, 21, 22, 24, 25, 28, 52, 63, 65, 66, 69, 75, 78–80, 84–95, 99, 101–5, 107–20, 133, 134, 138, 141
Illinois Supreme Court, 20, 39, 40, 181nn88–89
Indiana, 47, 50, 52–53, 163

Jefferson, Thomas, 12, 151
Johnson, Andrew, 61, 69, 75, 78, 79
Joliet Republican, 131, 133, 136
Jones, John, 60, 65
justice courts. *See* police courts

Kellor, Frances, 150–53
Kentucky, 21, 25, 41, 45, 47, 53–56, 61, 100, 163
Killion, Thomas, 60, 61, 91
Knights of the Golden Circle, 25, 27, 176n28

Leasure, Park, 129–30, 131–33
Lecompton Constitution, 22
Liberal Party, 75, 90–92
Lincoln, Abraham, 2, 4, 23, 29, 30, 31, 36, 46, 63, 76, 181n88; assassination of, 18, 61; criticism of, 19, 24–25, 36, 71, 72; election of, 23, 24; funeral of, 18–20, 61, 69, 71, 97; home of, 61, 62; in Springfield, 5, 49, 183n8; tomb of, 67, 97
Little, Sidney, 31, 33–36, 74
Livermore, Mary, 15
Lombroso, Cesare, 146–48

Magee, Rev. J. H., 51
Mayhew, Benjamin, 126, 130–33
McClaughry, Matthew, 200n56
McClaughry, Robert W., 5, 19, 29, 31, 35, 36, 38, 139, **140**, 148, 179n73, 199n39, 200n56, 202n76, 203n81; Civil War service of, 3, 19, 29–31, 34, 71, 73, 74; political activities of, 3, 19, 29, 30, 34–36, 71–74, 139; as Chicago police chief, 143–44; as proponent of; Bertillon system, 3, 143–44; as warden of Illinois State Penitentiary, 3, 122, 124, 126, 130, 133, 137, 139, 141–43
McClernand, John, 48, 69
McCord, Charles, 152–53
McCorn, W. A., 144–45
Mead, Aaron Benedict, 122–24, 126
militia organizations, 65–67, 75, 97, 177n38, 187nn63–64

Minnesota, 53
Mississippi, 12, 31, 32, 53, 54, 163
Mississippi River, 15, 16, 37
Missouri, 16, 25–27, 36, 41, 43, 47, 51, 53–55, 139, 163
Mix, Thomas, 33, 72
Moore, Executor of Eells v. The People, 42
moral economy, 13–14, 100, 115–16
Morse, Edward, 142
Muncie, IN, 53

Nance v. Howard, 40
National Prison Association, 148
Nelson (fugitive slave), 37–39, 43, 44
Nelson v. The People, 39–40, 42–43, 70, 181nn88–89
Nott, Josiah, 145
Noyes, William, 146–47

Oak Ridge Cemetery, 18, 67, 71, 97
Oglesby, Richard, 16, 26, 60, 139
Ohio, 47, 52, 163
118th Illinois Infantry, 3, 30–34, 72–73
Order of American Knights, 27, 29, 107, 176n24

Palmer, John M., 26, 45–46, 57, 63, 83–84, 85, 92, 139
Parker, Theodore, 22
penitentiaries, 3, 126, 134, 136–43, 146, 157, 159. *See also* Illinois State Penitentiary
Phoebe v. Jay, 40, 181n91
police, 58, 80, 88, 90–92, 94–95, 102–4, 107, 109, 112, 118, 120, 142–44, 157, 183n11
police courts, 2, 102, 104–8, 111, 112, 119
Prigg v. Pennsylvania, 42
prisoners, 124, 126, 128, 131, 132, 135, 137, 142; of war, 135. *See also* convicts
prostitution, 99, 104–6, 107, 110, 118–20, 155, 156, 165

race, 2, 4–7, 17, 66, 70, 71, 90, 98, 111, 121, 145–47, 150, 152, 153, 155–59, 201n61, 202n67, 204n98; science and, 76–77, 145–46, 150–53, 156–57
race mixing, 77, 83, 84, 86, 99, 110, 119
race riots, 154–56, 158, 159
racism, 3, 5–6, 20, 34, 36, 51, 64, 67, 68, 70, 71, 74, 76, 77, 79, 81–83, 85, 87, 93, 95, 108, 150, 153, 156, 157, 170n9; humor and, 95, 112–13, 114, 115. *See also* white supremacy
Rand, William, 35, 36, 74

Reconstruction, 2–6, 19, 60, 64, 65, 69, 70, 75, 76, 97, 157, 158, 160
Reed, Augustus "Gus," 1–7, 8–11, 14, 15, 17, 20, 44, 46, 68, 97–104, 109, 111, 113, 114, 120–22, 124–37, 138, 141–43, 154, 157–60; crimes of, 2, 98–103; death of, 1, 7, 130–37; early life of, 8–11; family of, 5, 9, 20, 46, 98; incarceration of, 2, 3, 8, 46, 101, 103, 121, 125–30; migration to Illinois, 1, 4, 5, 15, 17, 44, 46
Reed, Stephen, 128–133, 159
Republican Party, 6, 22, 24, 30, 31, 35, 37, 38, 46, 60, 61, 66, 70, 72, 74–78, 84–85, 86, 89, 90, 92, 94–96, 107, 114, 117, 139, 176nn28–29, 190n56; Black Laws and, 38, 43, 72; civil liberties and, 20, 24; Democratic converts to, 3, 19, 45, 63, 72, 74; wartime partisanship of, 25
Rhodes, James Ford, 158
Ridgely, Anna, 24, 26, 48, 109
Rosette, John, 54, 83, 85

Safford, George, 33–36, 74
Saint Louis, MO, 23, 29, 37, 48, 54
Sangamon County, IL, 5, 18, 19, 21, 23, 28, 42, 47, 49, 51–53, 74–75, 80, 97, 98, 103, 107, 108, 110, 164, 165, 194n39; circuit court of, 80, 104–5, 106, 107, 108, 110, 112, 118, 136, 165. *See also* Springfield
73rd Illinois Infantry, 26
Sherman, William Tecumseh, 4, 10, 11, 15, 54
slavery, 3, 9–12, 20, 22, 25, 31, 37, 39–41, 43, 48, 50, 57, 61, 62, 64, 70, 76–78, 113, 115–16, 135, 145, 152, 172n26; children and, 9–10; theft and, 11–15, 115–16, 151, 172n26
Springfield, IL, 2, 3, 5, 6, 17–25, 27, 28, 30, 34, 44, 45–68, 69, 71, 74, 78–80, 83–94, 97–121, 125, 136, 139, 141, 154–59, 161–63, 182n5, 183n11, 185n30, 185n38, 188n6, 194n39; black boarding, 48; black celebrations, 50, 60–63, 65, 66; black churches, 49, 50, 54, 56, 60–62, 64; black community, 5, 45–68, 97–98, 106, 185n38; black schools, 49–50, 57–60, 79–87, 190n52; black organizations, 61–63, 65–68; crime, 97–121, 165, 166; economy of, 68, 74, 95,

98, 100; Greasy Row, 98, 110, 119, 120, 155; newspapers, 5, 22, 98, 100, 108, 111, 112, 114, 118, 121, 155, 156; police, 80, 88, 90–91, 92, 94–95, 102–4, 107, 109, 112, 118, 120, 183n11; public schools, 49–50, 58–60, 63, 67, 68, 75, 84, 86, 190n52; race riot, 154–56, 158, 159; Second Ward, 75, 90, 94, 118, 185n29, 189n20, 191n82
Stout, Philemon, 19, 23, 97
Sturtevant, Rev. J. M., 77–78
suffrage, 3, 6, 22, 45, 46, 60, 67, 68, 70–76, 78, 87, 88, 90, 93, 113, 158
Supreme Court of the United States, 42, 146

Talbot, Eugene, 149, 150
Tanners, 92, 94
theft, 95, 98–103, 108, 109, 112–15, 151, 159; by slaves, 11–15, 115–16, 151, 172n26; by Union soldiers, 11, 14
Thirteenth Amendment, 60, 70, 72, 76, 78, 125, 177n29
Thornton's Case, 42
Tocqueville, Alexis de, 134
29th U.S. Colored Infantry, 60, 184n20

Union Party, 34, 35, 72, 74, 176 n29, 180n75

vagabonds, 41, 90, 104, 109, 117–20, 142
Van Evrie, John H., 145–146
vigilantism, 84, 88, 94, 118, 157–58, 205n6

Wey, Hamilton, 147–48
white supremacy, 5, 70–71, 74, 76–77, 145, 156, 170n9, 170n10, 189n21. *See also* racism
Willard v. The People, 41
Willcox, Walter, 152, 153
Williams, Isaac "Ike," 104, 114–15
Wines, Enoch, 148
Wines, Frederick, 148–50
Winston, George, 152–53
Wisconsin, 52, 53
World's Columbian Exposition, 3, 143
Wright, Gertrude, 83–85, 190n40

Yates, Richard, 16, 23, 25, 26, 28, 38

www.ingramcontent.com/pod-product-compliance
Lightning Source LLC
Chambersburg PA
CBHW020647300426
44112CB00007B/279